gage

Canadian School
THESAURUS

gage EDUCATIONAL PUBLISHING COMPANY
A DIVISION OF CANADA PUBLISHING CORPORATION
Vancouver · Calgary · Toronto · London · Halifax

General Editor   T. K. Pratt
                      Professor, Department of English
                      University of Prince Edward Island

Editorial Team   Joe Banel, Caroline Cobham,
                      Christine Dandurand, Ron Edwards,
                      John Grisewood, Susan Hughes,
                      Carolyn Leaver, George Marshall,
                      Sharon Siamon, Darleen Rotozinski,
                      Debbie Sawczak, Carol Waldock

Illustrations   David Ashby, Julian Baker,
                      Julie Banyard, Graham Bardell
                      Ian Howatson, Mark Iley,
                      Josephine Martin, John Marshall,
                      Clive Spong

Cover Design   Campbell Sheffield Design Inc.

Page Design   First Image, Ruth Dwight

Gage would like to thank the following educato

Halina Bartley, Language Arts Consultant
Peterborough County Board of Education
Ontario

Michael Budd, Languages Program Consultant
Essex County Board of Education
Ontario

Andrea Cook
Avalon Consolidated School Board
Newfoundland

Robert Dawe, Language Arts Consultant
Avalon Consolidated School Board
Newfoundland

Wanda Gibbons
Westwind Regional School Division
Alberta

Yvonne Jackson
Peel Board of Education
Ontario

Pauline McCabe, former Language Arts Co-ordinato
London and Middlesex County R.C. School Board
Ontario

Linda Nosbush, Language Arts Consultant
Prince Albert Public Schools
Saskatchewan

Mary Ellen Perley-Waugh
Edmonton Public School Board
Alberta

Wendy Phillips
Richmond School District
British Columbia

Denise Vandriel
Durham Board of Education
Ontario

Canadian Cataloguing in Publication Data

Main entry under title:
Gage Canadian school Thesaurus

ISBN 0-7715-1984-2
1. English language - Synonyms and antonyms - Juvenile
literature.
PE1591.G33 1997   j423'.1   C97-930981-6

ISBN 0-7715-**1984-2**

1 2 3 4 5 FP 01 00 99 98 97

Printed and Bound in Canada

Introduction

This book is called a *thesaurus*, a Greek word meaning *a treasury of information*. Look at this book and you will see that it is a treasury of words. It is a kind of dictionary, but instead of explaining the *meaning* of the word, a thesaurus lists other words that have a *similar* meaning. Suppose you began a letter to a friend with the sentence, *I hope you have a nice time on your holiday*. The word *nice* sounds dull, but when you look it up, you will find a list of interesting words that you could use instead: *pleasant, agreeable, amiable, charming, delightful, kind, acceptable*. Such words are known as **synonyms**. To get back to your letter, you could now write, *I hope you have a **pleasant** time on your holiday*.

As you can see, the thesaurus helps you to find just the right word. Sometimes it gives you the opposite of a word. For example, in the case of *nice*, you will find the opposite word *nasty*. These opposite words are called **antonyms**.

Besides synonyms and antonyms, this thesaurus also gives you **homonyms**. These are words that are easily confused, because although they sound exactly the same (like *right* and *write*), homonyms are spelled differently and have different meanings.

In many entries, there are references to other words in the book that have similar meanings. These are called **cross-references**. For example, if you look up the word *new* you find ▷**novel**. This means that if you look under *novel*, you will find another list of synonyms.

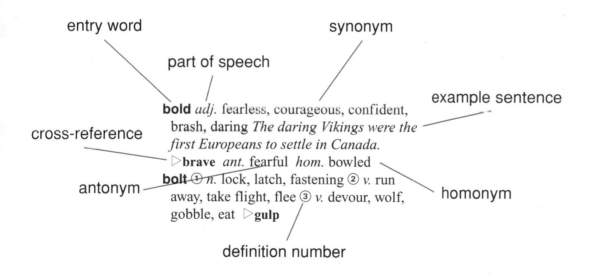

entry word

synonym

part of speech

example sentence

bold *adj.* fearless, courageous, confident, brash, daring *The daring Vikings were the first Europeans to settle in Canada.*
▷**brave** *ant.* fearful *hom.* bowled
bolt ① *n.* lock, latch, fastening ② *v.* run away, take flight, flee ③ *v.* devour, wolf, gobble, eat ▷**gulp**

cross-reference

antonym

homonym

definition number

Word Activities Here's a chance to get to know your thesaurus.

Try some of these word games and activities. (Look in the thesaurus for help.)

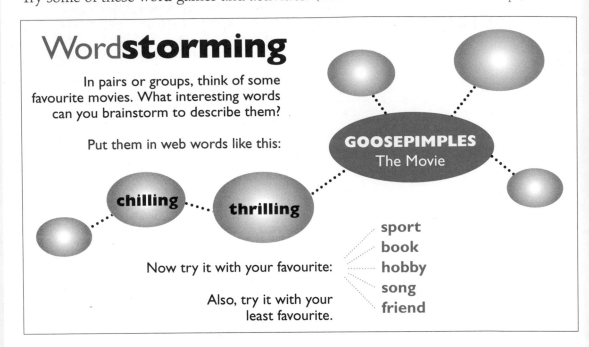

Word**storming**

In pairs or groups, think of some favourite movies. What interesting words can you brainstorm to describe them?

Put them in web words like this:

GOOSEPIMPLES
The Movie

chilling · · · · **thrilling**

Now try it with your favourite:
- sport
- book
- hobby
- song
- friend

Also, try it with your least favourite.

Adjective **Triangles** Increase your word power!

Draw a triangle and think of three synonyms for the word inside.

enormous · massive · **BIG** · collossal

Try it with some of these words:

small   tasty   dull   red
ugly   pretty   loud   rough

Now think of three antonyms for the word in the triangle.

Go ahead,
exaggerate!!!

It's fun to exaggerate. Use the words from the triangle you created to complete these sentences.

❶ That hat isn't big, it's _____.

❷ That band isn't just loud, it's _____.

❸ Those _____ aren't ugly, they're _____.

❹ That _____ isn't just _____, it's _____.

MYSTERY MESSAGES

Create mystery messages like the one below, to share with a partner. Fill in the blanks with unusual words.

"I feel _____ today.

Maybe I'll try _____.

Meet me at ____."

Word **Builder**

Start a list of fun words. Put your words into categories.

This could be a personal list, or a class project.

Verbs with Energy

Nouns about Feelings

Lively Adverbs

Sharp Adjectives

She Said/**He** Said

Imagine how boring it would be to read a novel with dialogue that always ended with *he said*, or *she asked*.

"Shall we dine tonight?" she asked.

"Sounds like a charming idea," he said.

"Well then, let us go," she said.

Think of some fresh words and use them in a dialogue of your own.

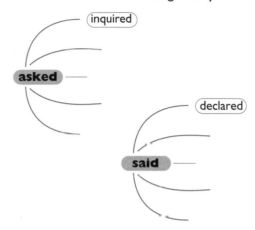

Overused Word Hunt

Go on a hunt for dull, overworked words.

Start with words such as: **nice big good**.

Display the lists in the classroom.

Anyone using one of these words may have to pay a penny fine!

Power Verbs

More exact verbs give your reader a clearer picture.

Blah: The tiny creature ran toward him.
Power: The tiny creature darted toward him.

Put some POWER in these verbs:
go, eat, touch.

Use each POWER verb in a sentence.

dash

jog

run

rush

sprint

A a

abandon *v.* give up, drop, leave, desert, withdraw, surrender, sacrifice, forsake ▷**leave** *ant.* recover, support

abate *v.* lessen, reduce, dwindle, fade

abbey *n.* convent, monastery, seminary, church

abbreviate *v.* shorten, cut, condense *If I don't condense my cartoon strip, it won't fit on the page!* reduce ▷**abridge** *ant.* expand

abdicate *v.* resign, retire, give up ▷**quit**

ability *n.* ① skill, talent, gift, flair, knack, aptitude *ant.* weakness ② means, capacity

able *adj.* skilful, competent, talented, capable, qualified ▷**clever** *ant.* weak

abnormal *adj.* odd, strange, uncommon, unnatural, unusual *ant.* normal

abolish *v.* destroy, cancel, do away with, eliminate, put an end to *ant.* restore

abominable *adj.* disgusting, foul, hateful, horrible, obnoxious, repulsive, atrocious ▷**awful** *ant.* desirable

about *prep.* ① concerning, regarding ② almost, nearly, around *ant.* exactly

above *prep.* over, beyond, exceeding *ant.* below

abridge *v.* condense, compact ▷**abbreviate**

abroad *adv.* overseas, far away, internationally *ant.* home

abrupt *adj.* ① sudden, curt, blunt, brusque, rude, sharp, gruff *ant.* tactful ② steep

absent *adj.* missing, away, gone, elsewhere, lacking *ant.* present

absent-minded *adj.* distracted, forgetful, scatterbrained *ant.* attentive

absolute *adj.* perfect, complete, certain, positive ▷**utter** *ant.* imperfect

absorb *v.* ① soak up, understand, devour, consume, sponge, swallow, digest *ant.* emit ② cushion

absorbed *adj.* fascinated, intent, involved, obsessed *ant.* bored

abstain *adj.* refuse, refrain, give up, keep from, avoid *ant.* indulge

abstract *adj.* complex, deep, theoretical, intangible

absurd *adj.* foolish, ridiculous, illogical, humorous ▷**silly** *ant.* sensible

abundant *adj.* full, rich, plentiful, overflowing *ant.* scarce

abuse ① *v.* (a-*byooz*) hurt, injure, mistreat, violate, bully, damage *ant.* protect ② *n.* (a-*byoos*) mistreatment, violation, injury, insult, misuse

accelerate *v.* speed up, quicken, urge ▷**hurry** *ant.* delay

accent *n.* ① stress, beat, rhythm, emphasis *Put the emphasis on "Oom" when you are playing "Oom-pah-pah."* ② brogue, drawl, pronunciation, twang

accept *v.* ① take, receive, welcome, adopt, embrace *ant.* refuse ② believe, trust, admit, approve *ant.* mistrust ③ stand, endure

Confusable Words

accept means *receive*

except means *other than*

accident *n.* casualty, disaster, crash, misfortune, mishap, chance

acclaim *v.* applaud, praise, approve, honour *The ceremony to honour the firefighters is held at City Hall.* declare, elect *ant.* criticize

accommodate *v.* ① help, oblige *ant.* refuse ② house, lodge ③ adapt, harmonize

accompany *v.* be with, go with, escort, chaperone, follow *ant.* abandon

accomplice *n.* ally, accessory, confederate, helper, partner, conspirator, henchman

accomplish *v.* perform, fulfil, finish, complete ▷**achieve** *ant.* fail

accord ① *v.* agree, consent, harmonize, give, allow *ant.* differ ② *n.* agreement, harmony

account *n.* ① bill, invoice, record, score ② tale, story, narrative *She gave an exciting narrative about meeting a bear in the woods.* history

n. = noun
v. = verb
adj. = adjective
adv. = adverb
conj. = conjunction
prep. = preposition
ant. = antonym
hom. = homonym
▷ = cross-reference

accumulate *v.* collect, grow, gather, hoard, store, increase *ant.* scatter

accurate *adj.* exact, perfect, precise, careful ▷**correct** *ant.* inaccurate

accuse *v.* charge, incriminate, blame, denounce *ant.* defend

accustom *v.* familiarize, adapt, adjust

ache *n. & v.* ① pain, throb ② desire

achieve *v.* fulfil, accomplish, reach, succeed, complete ▷**attain** *ant.* fail

achievement *n.* accomplishment, attainment, completion, performance, deed ▷**feat**

acid *adj.* sharp, acrid, sour, tart, bitter, sarcastic *ant.* sweet, mellow

acknowledge *v.* admit, recognize, thank, accept, reply *ant.* disclaim

acquaint *v.* inform, tell, teach, notify, advise *ant.* conceal

acquaintance *n.* ① friend, pal, associate *"This is my business associate, Martin Chen," said the entrepreneur.* ② knowledge, understanding, experience

acquainted *adj.* aware, familiar, informed

acquire *v.* gain, earn, obtain, get, buy, come by *ant.* lose, forfeit

acquit *v.* discharge, release, clear, dismiss, excuse, free *ant.* convict

acrid *adj.* bitter, harsh, sour, ill-tempered, sarcastic ▷**acid** *ant.* mellow

act ① *n.* action, deed, feat, accomplishment ② *n.* show, performance, presentation ③ *v.* behave, work, function, pretend, perform

action *n.* ① feat, performance, events, deed, operation, movement ② combat ③ lawsuit

active *adj.* busy, mobile, energetic, vigorous, lively *ant.* inert

actual *adj.* ① real, concrete, factual, correct, certain, current *ant.* imaginary ② true, genuine *ant.* fake

acute *adj.* sharp, pointed, keen *With its keen eyesight, the soaring hawk could easily see the tiny mouse below.* penetrating, severe, urgent *ant.* dull

adapt *v.* fit, adjust, accommodate, suit, conform, shape

adaptable *adj.* flexible, usable, adjustable

add *v.* ① total, combine, count, sum up *ant.* subtract ② extend, increase, join, enlarge, attach, include, connect *ant.* detach, remove

address ① *n.* residence, place, home, location ② *n.* speech ③ *v.* lecture, talk to, speak to, call ④ *v.* apply, concentrate on, take care of

adept *adj.* expert, handy, skilful ▷**clever** *ant.* clumsy

adequate *adj.* ① enough, sufficient *The boat was small, but there was sufficient room for two sailors.* plenty, ample *ant.* inadequate ② equal, able, qualified

adjacent *adj.* near, beside, close, next, bordering, touching *ant.* remote

adjoin *v.* border, touch, verge

adjust *v.* ① fix, change, correct, amend, revise *Mei-Ling revised her story to include the new information.* ② adapt, get used to

administer *v.* ① execute, perform *They performed tests that showed the fossil was 65 million years old!* carry out, conduct, direct, manage, govern ② give, dole out

admirable *adj.* praiseworthy, commendable, excellent, wonderful *ant.* despicable

admiration *n.* adoration, affection, approval, delight, respect, esteem *ant.* contempt

Adequate

The boat was small, but there was sufficient room for two sailors.

admire *v.* approve, esteem, appreciate, praise ▷**respect** *ant.* despise

admit *v.* ① let pass, permit, grant, accept, allow, let in ② confess, own up, acknowledge *ant.* deny

adopt *v.* accept, select, choose, employ, take over

adore *v.* worship, idolize, admire, revere, love, venerate *ant.* despise

adorn *v.* beautify, decorate, trim, deck, garnish *ant.* deface

adrift *adv.* loose, afloat, lost, insecure, aimless, distracted

adroit *adj.* handy, skilful, dexterous *With dexterous hands, the surgeon performed the delicate operation.* expert ▷**adept** *ant.* awkward

adult *adj.* grown-up, mature, full-grown *ant.* immature

advance *v.* ① progress, increase, improve ② approach, go, proceed *ant.* retreat ③ lend, loan

advanced *adj.* progressive, ahead, modern

advantage *n.* benefit, upper hand *The Canadiens scored another goal and gained the upper hand in the game.* opportunity, assistance, edge, asset, profit *ant.* hindrance

adventure *n.* experience, venture, exploit, undertaking, risk

adversary *n.* foe, opponent, competitor, rival ▷**enemy** *ant.* ally

adverse *adj.* unfavourable, unfriendly, negative, disapproving, hostile, opposing ▷**unlucky** *ant.* agreeable

advice *n.* counsel, suggestion, guidance, opinion, tip, pointer

advise *v.* counsel, urge, suggest, prompt, inform, recommend

affair *n.* ① matter, business, concern, event ② romance

affect *v.* ① influence, change, act, impress, sway *Carter has made up his mind, and nothing you can say will sway him.* ② assume, adopt, pretend, put on airs

affection *n.* desire, fondness, feeling, kindness, liking ▷**love**

affectionate *adj.* warm-hearted, fond, loving ▷**tender** *ant.* cold

affirm *v.* assert, state, declare, support, maintain *ant.* deny

affix *v.* attach, fasten, unite, connect, add *ant.* detach

afflict *v.* trouble, ail, distress, upset, hurt

afford *v.* produce, provide *The Canadian Prairies provide much of the world's wheat.* yield, bear *ant.* deny

afraid *adj.* scared, frightened, alarmed, terrified ▷**fearful** *ant.* fearless

after *prep.* behind, following, *ant.* before

again *adv.* ① repeatedly, anew, afresh ② furthermore, moreover

against *prep.* ① opposite, over, opposing, resisting ② next to

age ① *n.* period, date, time, era ② *n.* old age, senility *ant.* youth ③ *v.* grow old, mature

aged *adj.* elderly, ancient, antiquated ▷**old** *ant.* youthful

agent *n.* doer, actor, performer, operator, worker, representative, go-between

aggravate *v.* ① intensify, exaggerate, increase, worsen, exacerbate *ant.* mitigate ② irritate, annoy, exasperate *ant.* soothe

aggressive *adj.* offensive, warlike, pushy, assertive, bold, hostile *ant.* peaceful

aghast *adj.* astonished, shocked, horrified, bewildered *ant.* calm

agile *adj.* lithe, nimble, active, fleet, quick moving, alert, sprightly *ant.* clumsy

agitate *v.* disturb, trouble, excite, stir, fluster *ant.* calm

agony *n.* suffering, torment, distress, pangs, anguish, woe ▷**pain** *ant.* comfort

agree *v.* accord, fit, harmonize, concur *"I concur with your opinion of the damage," said the mechanic, nodding.* correspond, coincide, suit *ant.* differ

agreeable *adj.* obliging, welcome, enjoyable ▷**pleasant**

agreement *n.* understanding, harmony, concord *ant.* dispute

ahead *adv.* ① forward, onward ② before, in advance *ant.* behind

Aircraft

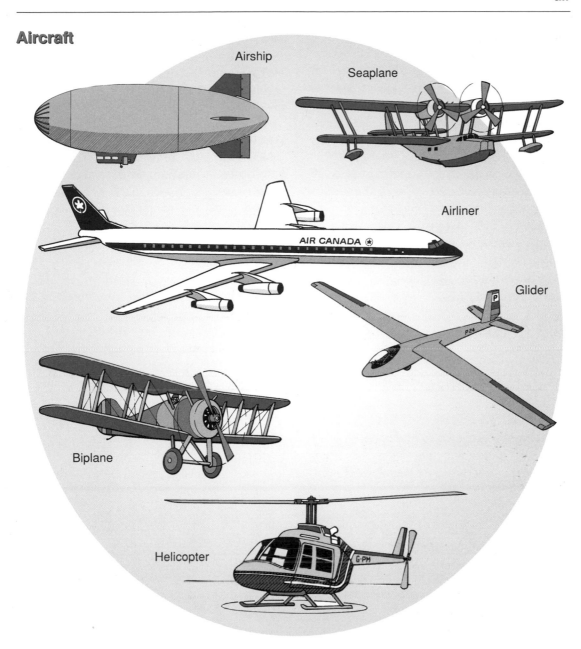

Airship

Seaplane

Airliner

AIR CANADA

Glider

Biplane

Helicopter

aid ① *v.* assist, support, relieve, back
② *n.* benefit, assistance, relief ▷**help**

aim ① *n.* object, goal, purpose, end,
intention, motive, reason ② *v.* point, direct
③ *v.* mean, intend, aspire

aisle *n.* path, corridor, passageway
hom. isle

akin *adj.* related, similar, allied, like
ant. dissimilar

alarm ① *v.* frighten, terrify, startle, panic
▷**scare** *ant.* comfort ② *n.* warning, alert

alert ① *adj.* active, ready, wakeful,
watchful, wary, attentive ② *v.* warn,
notify, signal

alien ① *adj.* foreign, strange, remote
ant. akin ② *n.* foreigner, stranger,
extra-terrestrial

alike *adj.* similar, resembling, like, identical,
same, matching *ant.* different

alive *adj.* living, breathing, warm, alert,
animated, operative *ant.* dead

all *adj.* whole, entire, complete, total

A a A a A a A

allot *v.* give, divide, distribute, dispense, grant, assign *ant.* retain

allow *v.* grant, permit, concede, let, consent *My parents consent to four hours a week on the Internet for each of us.* approve, entitle *ant.* forbid

ally *n.* friend, companion, supporter, accomplice, colleague *ant.* foe

almost *adv.* nearly, about, approximately, around, roughly

alone *adj.* solitary, apart, lone, lonely, lonesome, forlorn *ant.* together

aloud *adv.* loudly, noisily, audibly *hom.* allowed

already *adv.* at this time, now, just now, previously

Confusable Words

already means *by this time*
all ready means *completely ready*

altogether means *completely*
all together means *co-operatively*

---

alter *v.* modify, vary, convert, transform ▷**change** *ant.* retain *hom.* altar

always *adv.* ever, forever, eternally, repeatedly, perpetually *ant.* never

amass *v.* collect, accumulate, heap, gather *ant.* scatter

amaze *v.* astound, surprise, stun, shock, startle, thrill ▷**astonish**

ambition *n.* aspiration, desire, longing, aim ▷**goal**

amend *v.* revise, correct, repair, fix, change, improve, remedy ▷**alter**

amiable *adj.* likable, affable, kindly, pleasant, amicable ▷**agreeable** *ant.* unfriendly

amount *n.* figure, volume, sum, number, total, quantity, capacity

ample *adj.* bountiful, liberal, sufficient, plentiful, enough, substantial ▷**abundant** *ant.* insufficient

amplify *v.* increase, raise, enlarge, elevate, elaborate *My friend had a great idea for a party, so we helped him elaborate his plans.* make louder *ant.* reduce

Alphabets

Arabic

Hebrew

Cyrillic (Russian)

Thai

Egyptian hieroglyphs

Latin — A B C D E F

Sanskrit

Japanese

Greek — A B Γ Δ E Z

Runes (ancient Germanic)

n. = noun
v. = verb
adj. = adjective
adv. = adverb
conj. = conjunction
prep. = preposition
ant. = antonym
hom. = homonym
▷ = cross-reference

amuse v. entertain, charm, please, delight, cheer up *ant.* bore

ancestor n. forebear, parent, forefather, antecedent, predecessor *ant.* child

ancient *adj.* aged, antique, primeval, obsolete, old-fashioned ▷**old** *ant.* modern

anger ① n. wrath, ire, resentment, fury, indignation ▷**rage** ② v. annoy, irritate

angle ① n. corner, bend, point, branch ② aspect, perspective, point of view

angry *adj.* wrathful, irate, resentful, furious, infuriated, indignant, cross, mad, upset *ant.* calm, pleased

anguish n. torment, pain, distress, suffering, misery ▷**agony** *ant.* ease

announce v. broadcast, declare, report, reveal ▷**proclaim** *ant.* conceal

annoy v. tease, irritate, disturb, harass, aggravate, bother, hassle, pester ▷**upset** *ant.* soothe

answer ① n. reply, response, solution *It was a difficult puzzle, but Emma came up with the solution.* ② v. explain, respond, reply, react *ant.* question

anticipate v. expect, prepare, hope for, foresee, predict, await

anxious *adj.* fearful, afraid, apprehensive, worried, concerned, nervous *ant.* confident

apologize v. express regret, excuse, explain, plead, atone *ant.* insult

apparel n. clothes, dress, robes, attire

apparent *adj.* plain, conspicuous, unmistakable, clear, distinct, evident ▷**obvious** *ant.* hidden

appeal v. address, request, urge, invite, ask, plead, beg, implore ▷**attract**

appear v. seem, look, come, arrive, emerge, loom, materialize *ant.* disappear

appearance n. look, shape, form, impression, likeness, image, guise, aspect

appease v. pacify, moderate, satisfy, soften *ant.* provoke

appetite n. hunger, craving, longing, thirst, liking, desire

applaud v. clap, cheer, praise, approve, encourage *ant.* disapprove

apply v. ① use, utilize, employ ② devote *Tom Thomson devoted his life to painting.* direct, dedicate

appoint v. name, assign, nominate

appreciate v. ① value, prize, esteem ② understand, acknowledge, recognize

appropriate *adj.* fitting, suitable, proper, timely, relevant

approve v. acclaim, admire, praise, applaud, commend, appreciate, favour, agree *ant.* disapprove

approximate *adj.* near, close, rough

ardent *adj.* passionate, warm, eager, fervent, intense, keen, dedicated, enthusiastic *ant.* indifferent

arduous *adj.* hard, laborious, tough, strenuous ▷**difficult** *ant.* easy

area n. district, region, place, expanse, tract

argue v. discuss, debate, dispute, quarrel, disagree, differ, bicker

arid *adj.* parched, sterile ▷**dry** *ant.* moist

arise v. ① awaken, get up, stand up, ascend ② begin, originate, crop up

army n. troops, legion, force, soldiery, group

around *adv.* about, encircling, on every side, nearby *ant.* within

arouse v. awaken, excite, disturb, inspire *Listening to the Toronto Symphony Youth Orchestra inspires me to learn to play the cello. ant.* pacify

arrange v. sort, order, organize, place, classify

arrest v. ① capture, catch, apprehend, seize, hold, detain *ant.* release ② stop, delay, block, check *ant.* promote

arrive v. come, reach, attain, land, get to, appear *ant.* leave, depart

arrogant *adj.* proud, haughty, conceited, overconfident, overbearing, superior *ant.* modest

art n. skill, artistry, cleverness, talent, craft

artful *adj.* cunning, foxy, tricky, crafty, wily, sly *ant.* naïve

article n. ① thing, object, item ② essay, composition, story

artificial *adj.* false, fake, synthetic, imitation, invented, fabricated *ant.* real

A a A a A a A

ascend v. climb, rise, go up, move up, scale, mount *ant.* descend

ashamed *adj.* regretful, embarrassed, humiliated *ant.* proud

ask v. question, demand, query, inquire, appeal, invite ▷**request** *ant.* answer

aspect n. front, face, side, appearance, presentation, look, expression

aspire v. wish, long, desire, aim, hope, dream, crave

assault v. attack, set upon, charge, invade *ant.* defend

assemble v. ① meet, gather, convene *Star Trek fans frequently convene to share their enthusiasm for this television show.* come *ant.* disperse ② make, build, construct, fabricate *ant.* destroy

assent v. agree, comply, accept, consent *ant.* refuse

assert v. pronounce, maintain, state, promote, insist ▷**declare** *ant.* deny

assess v. estimate, evaluate, appraise, consider, review

assign v. appoint, name, allot, allocate, determine

assist v. aid, support, protect, maintain, sustain ▷**help** *ant.* hinder, frustrate

association n. union, connection, society, company, club

assortment n. variety, kind, sort, batch, arrangement, collection

assume v. ① believe, suppose ② accept, take, adopt *ant.* reject, refuse

assure v. ① promise, guarantee, pledge ② encourage, hearten, convince *ant.* deter

astonish v. startle, surprise, alarm, astound, dazzle ▷**amaze**

astound v. stagger, stupefy, amaze ▷**astonish**

astute *adj.* shrewd, knowing, sharp, acute, crafty *ant.* stupid

atrocious *adj.* monstrous, enormous, shameful, cruel, horrible, vile

attach v. fasten, bind, unite, tie, join, fix ▷**connect** *ant.* detach

attack ① v. assault, invade, raid, charge, storm ② n. invasion, strike, onslaught *ant.* retreat

attain v. accomplish, master, obtain, acquire, grasp ▷**reach** *ant.* fail

attempt v. endeavour, strive *Our athletes strive to do their best at the Olympics.* seek, tackle ▷**try** *ant.* abandon

attend v. visit, frequent, escort, accompany

attentive *adj.* mindful, particular, heedful, observant *ant.* careless

attire n. costume, robes, clothes, garments ▷**apparel**

attitude n. disposition, bearing, outlook, posture, position, pose, air, demeanour

attract v. draw, tempt, pull, fascinate, enchant, captivate, lure *ant.* repel

attractive *adj.* beautiful, lovely, handsome, pretty, tempting *ant.* repellent

avail n. benefit, advantage, use, help, profit

available *adj.* convenient, handy, ready, attainable, accessible

avenge v. retaliate, revenge, punish, pay back, take vengeance for *ant.* pardon

average *adj.* usual, ordinary, mediocre, normal, standard *ant.* unusual, extraordinary

avid *adj.* eager, greedy, grasping

avoid v. shun, elude, quit, evade, prevent ▷**dodge** *ant.* seek

awake v. wake, rouse, arouse, awaken, stir

award ① v. reward, give, bestow, grant, donate *ant.* withhold ② n. reward, trophy, medal, decoration

aware *adj.* ① conscious, sensible, attentive, alert *ant.* unaware, oblivious ② informed, knowledgeable, assured *ant.* ignorant

away *adv.* absent, not present, elsewhere *ant.* near

awe n. fear, dread, shock, amazement, wonder

awful *adj.* fearful, terrible, alarming, dreadful, horrible, shocking *ant.* wonderful, terrific

awkward *adj.* inept, cumbersome, unwieldy, bulky, graceless ▷**clumsy** *ant.* dexterous, agile

n. = noun
v. = verb
adj. = adjective
adv. = adverb
conj. = conjunction
prep. = preposition
ant. = antonym
hom. = homonym
▷ = cross-reference

B b

babble *v.* chatter, blather, jabber, blab, prattle, gossip

baby *n.* infant, child, toddler, newborn

back ① *adj.* after, rear, posterior, past, earlier *ant.* front ② *v.* support, endorse, uphold, assist

backer *n.* supporter, ally, champion, sponsor

backward *adj.* slow, shy, reluctant, unwilling, behind, underdeveloped ▷**dull** *ant.* forward

bad *adj.* ① naughty, mischievous, dishonest, wicked, evil *ant.* good ② faulty, defective, imperfect ③ rotten, spoiled *ant.* fresh

badge *n.* emblem, symbol, crest, decoration

badger *v.* bully, hassle, annoy, nag ▷**pester**

baffle *v.* perplex, confuse, bewilder, mystify *The cause of the Northern Lights continues to mystify scientists.* stun ▷**puzzle** *ant.* enlighten

bag *n.* sack, pouch, purse, knapsack

bait ① *v.* tease, badger, provoke, rib, needle ▷**pester** ② *n.* decoy, lure, snare *hom.* bate

balance *v.* weigh, adjust, equalize, compare

bald *adj.* ① hairless, bare ② severe, stark, simple

ball *n.* ① dance, prom ② globe, orb, sphere *hom.* bawl

ballot *n.* vote, election, poll

ban *v.* prohibit, forbid, prevent, outlaw, bar, exclude *ant.* allow

band *n.* ① stripe, strip, zone, belt ② orchestra, group, gang *hom.* banned

bandit *n.* outlaw, robber, thief, crook

bang *v.* crash, slam, collide, explode

banish *v.* expel, eject, exclude, exile, deport, evict, remove ▷**dismiss** *ant.* welcome

bank *n.* ① shore, ridge, coast, embankment ② safe, vault, treasury

banner *n.* pennant, streamer, ensign ▷**flag**

banquet *n.* meal, feast, reception

banter *v.* tease, joke, rib, kid

bar *v.* ① obstruct, block, forbid, ban, prohibit *ant.* permit ② fasten, bolt, lock, latch

bare *adj.* ① barren, empty, void ② naked, nude, unclothed *hom.* bear

barely *adv.* ① hardly, scarcely *There was scarcely enough time for Sean to reach his seat before the play began.* just ② simply, plainly

bargain ① *n.* deal, agreement ② *adj.* cheap, low-priced

bark ① *n.* rind, husk, peel ② *v.* growl, yap, shout

barrel *n.* cask, keg, drum, tub, cylinder

barren *adj.* bare, unfertile, empty ▷**arid** *ant.* fertile *hom.* baron

barrier *n.* fence, wall, obstacle, obstruction

barter *v.* swap, exchange, trade

base ① *adj.* low, sordid, cheap, corrupt, dishonourable, vile ② *n.* root, cause, origin ③ *n.* bottom, foundation ④ *v.* build, establish, found *The book* Obasan *was founded on a true story. hom.* bass

bashful *adj.* shy, timid, modest *ant.* bold

basin *n.* bowl, sink, tub, depression

batch *n.* bunch, group, amount, assortment

batter *v.* hurt, abuse, beat, strike, smash

battle *v.* fight, combat, struggle, clash

bawl *v.* cry, sob, wail, shout, howl

Band

Banned

B b B b B b B

n. = noun
v. = verb
adj. = adjective
adv. = adverb
conj. = conjunction
prep. = preposition
ant. = antonym
hom. = homonym
▷ = cross-reference

bay ① *n.* gulf, basin ② *v.* bark, howl, yelp
beach *n.* shore, sands, seaside, coast *hom.* beech
beacon *n.* signal, light, guide, lighthouse
beak *n.* snout, bill, nose
beam *n.* ① ray, light, glimmer ② plank, rafter, support
bear *v.* ① tolerate, endure, suffer, stand ② produce, yield *hom.* bare
bearing *n.* manner *Fatima has a gentle manner and a soft voice.* behaviour, appearance, attitude, posture *hom.* baring
bearings *n.* direction, position, location
beat ① *v.* strike, hit ▷**batter** ② *v.* win, defeat, conquer *ant.* lose ③ *n. & v.* throb, flutter, thump, pound *My heart thumped when I heard the sound of shouting in the street. hom.* beet
beautiful *adj.* attractive, lovely, ravishing, gorgeous ▷**pretty** *ant.* ugly
because *conj.* for, since, as, seeing that, due to
beckon *v.* signal, call, summon, attract, lure
before ① *prep.* ahead of, in front of, prior to ② *adv.* earlier, prior, previously *ant.* afterward
beg *v.* plead, implore, entreat, beseech, grovel, appeal
begin *v.* commence, initiate, found, launch *To launch our fund-raiser we had a magic show in the gym.* open ▷**start** *ant.* end
beginner *n.* novice, recruit, learner, trainee
beginning *n.* start, opening, origin, outset, creation, foundation, birth *ant.* end
behaviour *n.* conduct, demeanour, manner, attitude ▷**bearing**
behind ① *prep.* after, following, ② *adv.* in the rear, later, afterward
belief *n.* faith, confidence, opinion, trust *ant.* disbelief
believe *v.* ① trust, accept, have faith in *ant.* mistrust ② think, suppose
bellow *v.* roar, shout, cry ▷**bawl**
belong *v.* ① fit, match, go ② relate, pertain, be owned by
below *prep. & adv.* under, beneath, underneath *ant.* above

Bell

Bicycle bell
Church bell
Doorbell
Gong

belt *n.* strap, sash, strip, band, zone
bend *v.* curve, incline, turn, fold, flex, yield
benefit *n.* advantage, profit, good, favour, help, gain, reward *ant.* disadvantage
beside *adv.* near, next to, alongside, abreast, side by side
besides *adv.* in addition, furthermore, also, moreover
best *adj.* greatest, supreme, finest, choice, prime
bestow *v.* award, give, grant, present *ant.* withhold
betray *v.* ① deceive, double-cross, inform on ② expose, unmask, reveal *ant.* conceal
better *adj.* finer, improved, preferable
between *prep.* amid, among
beware *v.* be careful, refrain from, avoid, watch out for, guard against
bewilder *v.* confound, baffle, mystify, confuse ▷**puzzle**
beyond *prep.* over, farther, past, more than, after
bid *v.* ① ask, request, wish, order, command ② propose, tender, offer
big *adj.* ① large, great, huge, bulky, fat *ant.* small ② important, significant, influential, outstanding *ant.* insignificant
bill *n.* ① statement, account, invoice, tab ② beak, snout, nose ③ poster, advertisement, notice ④ amendment, proposal, law ⑤ money, cash
bind *v.* ① tie, fasten, secure, attach, stick *ant.* untie ② require, oblige

birth *n.* origin, beginning, source, creation *ant.* death *hom.* berth

bit *n.* morsel, piece, fragment, scrap, particle, crumb, speck

bite *v.* gnaw, chew, nibble, chomp *hom.* bight

bitter *adj.* ① sour, tart ▷**acid** *ant.* sweet ② severe, stern, harsh *ant.* mellow ▷**sarcastic**

blame *v.* rebuke, reproach, criticize, accuse, condemn

bland *adj.* mild, gentle, soothing, tasteless, dull, boring, tedious

blank *adj.* empty, bare, void, bleak *ant.* full

blare *v.* blast, boom, clang, roar

blast *v.* explode, discharge, burst, blow

blaze *v.* burn, flare, glare, glow

bleak *adj.* ① bare, open, exposed, barren *ant.* lush ② dreary, dismal, rainy, raw, desolate *ant.* bright

blemish *n.* spot, stain, mark, speck, pimple, flaw, blotch, defect

blend *v.* mix, unite, mingle, merge, fuse, combine *ant.* separate

bless *v.* praise, exalt, glorify, endow, consecrate, approve *ant.* curse

blessing *n.* benefit, approval, prayer, gift *ant.* curse, blight

blight *n.* pest, plague, disease, curse

blind *adj.* ① eyeless, sightless, unseeing ② ignorant, uninformed

blink *v.* wink, bat, twinkle, glitter, gleam

bliss *n.* joy, ecstasy, rapture, happiness *ant.* misery

block ① *n.* lump, mass, chunk, clog ② *v.* obstruct, impede, thwart, stop, bar, arrest *ant.* allow *hom.* bloc

bloom ① *n.* flower, blossom, bud ② *n.* prime, health, vigour ③ *v.* blossom, flourish *Many Canadian wildflowers can't tolerate too much sun and flourish in the shade.* flower, thrive *ant.* decay

blow ① *v.* fan, puff, gust, blast ② *v.* botch, fail ③ *n.* shock, stroke, impact, bang ④ *n.* setback, misfortune, loss

blue *adj.* ① azure, turquoise, indigo, navy, aquamarine ② sad, depressed, gloomy *ant.* happy *hom.* blew

bluff ① *n.* cliff, peak, bank ② *v.* deceive, pretend, conceal

blunder ① *n.* mistake, error, fault, oversight ② *v.* slip, fumble, stumble

blunt *adj.* ① abrupt, curt, rude ② dull, not sharp *ant.* sharp

blush *v.* redden, colour, flush *Lorna flushed with pleasure when the visitor praised her short story.*

board ① *n.* plank, beam, wood ② *n.* committee, council ③ *v.* live, lodge, accommodate *hom.* bored

boast *v.* show off, bluster, crow ▷**brag**

boat *n.* ship, vessel, craft, watercraft

body *n.* ① figure, torso, trunk, ② carcass, cadaver, corpse ③ troop, band, group, company, organization ④ volume, thickness *hom.* bawdy

bog *n.* swamp, marsh, morass

bogus *adj.* fake, false, sham, counterfeit, phony, imitation *ant.* genuine

boil *v.* cook, steam, poach, stew, bubble, seethe, foam, swelter

boisterous *adj.* stormy, loud, noisy, rowdy, unruly *ant.* serene

The Body

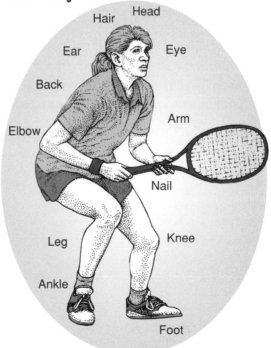

Hair
Head
Ear
Eye
Back
Arm
Elbow
Nail
Leg
Knee
Ankle
Foot

B b B b B b B

bold *adj.* fearless, courageous, confident, brash, daring *The daring Vikings were the first Europeans to settle in Canada.* ▷**brave** *ant.* fearful *hom.* bowled

bolt ① *n.* lock, latch, fastening ② *v.* run away, take flight, flee ③ *v.* devour, wolf, gobble, eat ▷**gulp**

bond *n.* tie, link, joint, band, fastening

bonus *n.* reward, benefit, award, prize

boom *n.* ① thunder, roar, rumble ② explosion, growth, surge, prosperity

boorish *adj.* crude, coarse, gross, unrefined, rude, vulgar *ant.* refined

boost *v.* ① lift, raise ② increase, strengthen

border *n.* edge, fringe, margin, boundary

bore *v.* ① tire, weary, fatigue *We were fatigued by the long bus ride home from Ottawa.* ② drill, pierce, perforate *hom.* boar

bored *adj.* uninterested, tired, fed up *ant.* fascinated *hom.* board

borrow *v.* take, copy, imitate, adopt, raise money *ant.* lend

Confusable Words

borrow means *get*

lend means *give*

boss *n.* supervisor, manager, employer

bossy *adj.* demanding, domineering, tyrannical, overbearing ▷**arrogant** *ant.* modest

bother *v.* annoy, tease, irritate, pester ▷**disturb**

bottom *n.* underside, depth, foot, floor, ground ▷**base** *ant.* top

bough *n.* branch, limb *hom.* bow

bounce *v.* leap, spring, bound, jump

boundary *n.* border, bounds, limits, perimeter *A fence marks the perimeter of the park.* ▷**barrier**

bow *v.* ① bend, nod, stoop, kneel, incline ② yield, submit *hom.* bough

box ① *n.* carton, case, chest, crate, trunk ② *v.* fight, spar, punch, hit

boy *n.* male, young man, youth, stripling, lad

brag *v.* gloat, show off, flaunt, crow ▷**boast**

branch *n.* ① limb, twig ▷**bough** ② department, office, division, section

brand ① *n.* trademark, label, stamp ② *n.* blot, stigma, stain ③ *v.* call, label, stamp

brandish *v.* flaunt, wield, flourish, swing, shake, wave

brash *adj.* brazen, bold, cocky, rude, insolent, impudent ▷**rash**

brave *adj.* fearless, daring, gallant, heroic, courageous, dauntless ▷**bold** *ant.* cowardly

break *v.* ① crack, snap, fracture, shatter, split *ant.* repair ② disobey, violate *ant.* obey ③ stop, interrupt *ant.* connect *hom.* brake

breathe *v.* draw in, gasp, inhale, exhale, sniff, gulp, wheeze, emit, pant, whisper

breed *v.* reproduce, produce, bear, rear, multiply, propagate, procreate, cultivate

bribe *v.* corrupt, buy off, fix

brief *adj.* short, little, concise, compact, curt *ant.* lengthy

bright *adj.* ① clear, cloudless, fair, sunny, brilliant *ant.* dull ② clever, intelligent, smart *ant.* stupid

brilliant *adj.* ① shining, radiant, dazzling, lustrous *The mink had a lustrous sheen to its coat. ant.* dull ② clever, intelligent

brim *n.* edge, brink, rim, lip

bring *v.* deliver, carry, bear, convey *ant.* take

Confusable Words

bring means *carry to*

take means *carry away*

bring about *v.* accomplish, achieve, cause, make happen, produce

bring up *v.* ① raise, educate, foster ② vomit

brink *n.* edge, verge, brow, limit

brisk *adj.* quick, agile, alert, energetic, active, invigorating *ant.* sluggish

brittle *adj.* breakable, fragile, delicate ▷**frail**

broad *adj.* ① wide, expansive, roomy, open, large ② vast, extensive *ant.* narrow

Bridges

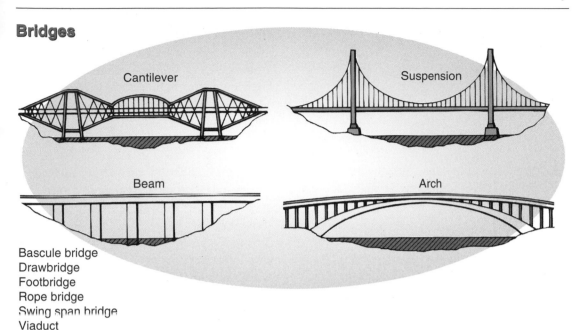

Cantilever

Suspension

Beam

Arch

Bascule bridge
Drawbridge
Footbridge
Rope bridge
Swing span bridge
Viaduct

brood *v.* fret, mope, sulk, agonize *Alexa agonized over her unkind words to her grandfather, but felt better after she apologized.* dwell upon *hom.* brewed

brook *n.* stream, creek, rivulet

brow *n.* forehead, face, front, brink, edge, summit, crest, peak

bruise *v.* hurt, discolour, blemish, injure, wound *hom.* brews

brutal *adj.* cruel, savage, mean, fierce, heartless, ruthless, vicious *ant.* humane

bubble *n.* drop, blob, bead

buckle *n.* catch, clasp, clip, fastening

bud *n.* flower, sprout, sprig, shoot

budge *v.* move, yield, push, shift, slide

build *v.* make, form, assemble, construct, erect, found *ant.* destroy *hom.* billed

bulge *n.* bump, swelling, lump, hump

bulky *adj.* big, huge, massive, large, unwieldy, cumbersome *That chair is too big and cumbersome for me to move.*

bully ① *n.* thug, brute, tormentor, tyrant ② *v.* threaten, intimidate, harass, oppress, tease

bump *v.* collide, hit, knock, strike, jolt

bunch *n.* batch, bundle, cluster, collection, group

bundle *n.* roll, sheaf, wad, package, parcel

bungle *v.* botch, mess up, ruin, fumble, spoil, flub *ant.* succeed

burden *n.* ① load, weight ② strain, hardship

burly *adj.* beefy, big, hefty, brawny, husky, muscular, stocky, strong *ant.* frail

burn *v.* blaze, flare, glow, singe, scorch, char, incinerate, sear, scald

burst *v.* crack, explode, shatter, erupt, rupture, pop, blow up

bury *v.* ① inter, entomb, lay to rest ② conceal, cover up, hide *ant.* uncover *hom.* berry

business *n.* ① occupation, career, profession, trade ② company, enterprise, firm ③ concern, interest, duty

busy *adj.* active, energetic, diligent *Theresa worked diligently all day on her project.* industrious, lively, hectic *ant.* idle

buy *v.* acquire, get, purchase, obtain, bribe, procure *With savings from his newspaper route, Marco procured a pair of inline skates.* *ant.* sell *hom.* by, bye

Confusable Words

buy means *purchase*
by means *beside* or *through*

Cc

cabin *n.* ① hut, chalet, cottage, shack ② berth, compartment

cabinet *n.* ① cupboard, hutch, storage case ② council, ministers

cackle *v.* chuckle, giggle, snicker

café *n.* restaurant, coffee shop, snack bar, bistro

cage *v.* shut up, confine, imprison *ant.* free

calamity *n.* catastrophe, disaster, trouble, misery ▷**misfortune**

calculate *v.* compute, figure, estimate ▷**count**

call *v.* ① cry out, shout, exclaim ② name, label, brand, designate ③ telephone, invite, summon

calling *n.* vocation, profession, occupation, trade, job

callous *adj.* unfeeling, harsh, insensitive, hard *ant.* sensitive *hom.* callus

calm ① *v.* soothe, ease, pacify, comfort, settle ② *adj.* still, serene, composed, quiet ▷**peaceful** *ant.* excited

cancel *v.* abolish, repeal, annul, call off, delete

candid *adj.* fair, honest, open, sincere, truthful, blunt ▷**frank** *ant.* devious

capable *adj.* talented, able, competent, clever ▷**proficient** *ant.* incompetent

capacity *n.* ① space, volume, scope ② ability, aptitude *Paul has an unusual aptitude for learning languages; he can speak four!* knack ③ position, relation

capital *n.* ① money, wealth, cash, assets, funds, resources ② city, metropolis, seat

captain *n.* chief, head, commander, master, skipper, leader, officer

capture *v.* seize, arrest, trap, apprehend, take, win ▷**catch** *ant.* release

car *n.* automobile, vehicle, sedan, limo

carcass *n.* body, corpse, skeleton, cadaver

care ① *v.* take an interest, protect, tend, watch over ② *n.* attention, protection, heed, concern, caution, wariness

careful *adj.* watchful, wary, prudent ▷**cautious** *ant.* careless

careless *adj.* thoughtless, reckless, rash, lax, sloppy *Her handwriting is sloppy, but her mind is sharp!* slack, negligent *ant.* careful

caress *v.* stroke, fondle, pet, cuddle, pat, hug, embrace, touch

carriage *n.* ① bearing, manner, behaviour, appearance ② vehicle, machine, frame

carry *v.* ① bring, convey, take ② bear ▷**support**

carry out *v.* perform, achieve, fulfil, do

carton *n.* container, case, crate ▷**box**

carve *v.* cut, slice, chisel, sculpt ▷**shape**

case *n.* ① carton, trunk, chest ▷**box** ② example, situation, instance, argument ③ lawsuit, action

cash *n.* money, funds, bills, coins *hom.* cache

cast *v.* ① mould, form, shape ② fling, pitch, toss, shed, radiate ▷**throw** *hom.* caste

casual *adj.* informal, easygoing, careless, unexpected, chance, random

catch *v.* grasp, seize, arrest, trap, hold, take ▷**capture**

cause ① *v.* produce, bring about, create, provoke, induce ② *n.* reason, motive, source, origin

caution *n.* wariness, heed, vigilance *Vigilance is necessary when riding your bicycle so you won't harm yourself or others.* prudence, warning ▷**care**

cautious *adj.* careful, wary, prudent, discreet ▷**watchful** *ant.* careless

cavity *n.* hole, hollow, gap, dent

cease *v.* stop, end, conclude, quit, finish, terminate *ant.* begin

celebrate *v.* observe, honour, glorify, rejoice, commemorate, praise, proclaim

cell *n.* cage, jail, chamber, cavity, cubicle, compartment *hom.* sell

cellar *n.* basement, vault, crypt, cave *hom.* seller

cement ① *v.* glue, stick, bind, fuse, weld ② *n.* concrete, plaster, mortar, adhesive

censor *v.* ban, cut, suppress, delete

n. = noun
v. = verb
adj. = adjective
adv. = adverb
conj. = conjunction
prep. = preposition
ant. = antonym
hom. = homonym
▷ = cross-reference

censure *v.* blame, disapprove, criticize, fault, reprimand *Don't reprimand Kim; I'm the one who ate the last apple.* ▷**scold** *ant.* praise

centre *n.* middle, core, heart, nucleus

ceremony *n.* ritual, custom, rite, observance

certain *adj.* ① positive, decided, definite, indisputable ▷**sure** *ant.* doubtful ② particular, special

certainty *n.* confidence, assurance, trust *ant.* doubt

certificate *n.* document, permit, deed, diploma, testimonial

chafe *v.* rub, grate *Amy's bossy manner grates on her classmates.* anger, irritate

chain *v.* bind, tie, shackle, handcuff, enslave

challenge *v.* dare, demand, dispute, defy, question, contest

chamber *n.* room, compartment, office

champion *n.* winner, hero, victor, master, defender *ant.* loser

chance *n.* ① fortune, risk, luck, gamble, lottery, accident ② opportunity, occasion, prospect *ant.* certainty

change *v.* alter, vary, turn, shift, reform, transform, switch, adjust *ant.* preserve

chaos *n.* turmoil, confusion, disorder, pandemonium, anarchy *ant.* order

chapter *n.* section, unit, division, part, period, phase, branch

character *n.* ① reputation *Who you hang around with affects your reputation.* disposition, nature, temperament, qualities ② letter, mark, symbol

charge *n.* ① attack, assault, advance ② cost, amount, price ③ accusation, criticism ④ care, supervision

charm *v.* delight, enchant, bewitch, fascinate, captivate, mesmerize, beguile ▷**attract**

charming *adj.* delightful, appealing, lovely, pleasant ▷**attractive** *ant.* unpleasant

chart *n.* table, graph, diagram, plan, map

chase *v.* hunt, pursue, follow, track

chastise *v.* criticize, reprimand, scold, discipline, reprove, berate, punish

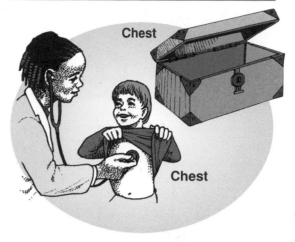

Chest

Chest

cheap *adj.* ① inexpensive, low-priced, bargain, inferior *ant.* expensive ② stingy, tight-fisted, penny-pinching *ant.* generous

cheat *v.* rip off, swindle, fool, defraud, mislead ▷**trick**

check *v.* ① inspect, compare, examine review, monitor, test ② stop, restrain, obstruct, curb *hom.* cheque

cheer *v.* ① applaud *The audience applauded the fiddler, so she played another tune.* support, root ② encourage, comfort, console, hearten

cheerful *adj.* lively, merry, joyful, glad, bright, sunny ▷**happy** *ant.* sad

cherish *v.* treasure, prize, value, appreciate

chest *n.* ① trunk, storage case ▷**box** ② torso, breast, bosom

chew *v.* bite, gnaw, grind, munch, mangle ▷**eat**

chief *adj.* main, principal *Dennis Lee is one of Canada's principal poets for children.* leading, foremost, primary, head, major *ant.* minor

child *n.* baby, infant, youth, juvenile

chilly *adj.* cool, crisp, brisk, cold, unfriendly *ant.* warm

chip *v. & n.* crack, splinter, sliver, flake

chirp *v. & n.* warble, trill, cheep, twitter

choice ① *n.* option *We had two options: mend the nets or clean the fish.* preference, alternative, pick ② *adj.* select, special, prime, superior, first-rate

choke *v.* throttle, suffocate, gag, strangle, smother, gasp, clog, repress ▷**stifle**

Churches and Places of Worship

Cathedral
Chapel
Church
Mosque
Oratory
Pagoda
Pantheon
Shrine
Stupa
Synagogue
Temple

choose *v.* pick, elect, vote, decide, prefer ▷**select** *hom.* chews

chop *v.* cut, hack, clip, mince, dice, hew

chubby *adj.* plump, fat, stocky, round, stout *ant.* slim

chuckle *v.* cackle, snicker, giggle ▷**laugh**

chunk *n.* piece, lump, mass, portion, slab

circle *n.* ① ring, band, hoop, loop, orbit, circuit ② group, clique, crowd

circular ① *adj.* round, disklike ② *n.* flyer, notice, poster, advertisement

circulate *v.* distribute, publicize *Let's make posters to publicize the plans for our science fair.* flow, mingle

cite *v.* mention, specify, name, quote *hom.* sight, site

civil *adj.* ① polite, courteous, affable, polished, suave ② civic, public

claim *v.* demand, profess, require, insist, say

clamour *n.* uproar, blare, din, hubbub, racket ▷**noise** *ant.* silence

clamp *v.* fasten, fix, hold, grasp, bind

clap ① *v.* applaud, cheer, give a hand ② *n.* bang, crack, crash

clarify *v.* ① make clear, explain, simplify, illuminate, resolve ② cleanse, purify, refine

clash *v. & n.* ① conflict, battle, quarrel, struggle ② bang, crash, clang, clatter

clasp ① *v.* grasp, grip, seize, hold, fasten, clutch ② *n.* buckle, catch, brooch, pin

class *n.* category, type, sort, grade, group, species, rank, order, quality

classical *adj.* pure, refined, scholarly, elegant, polished

classify *v.* sort, grade, arrange, catalogue

clean ① *adj.* pure, fresh, spotless, unsoiled *ant.* dirty ② *v.* cleanse, scrub, refine, purify ▷**wash**

clear *adj.* ① bright, fair, fine, light, transparent *ant.* murky ② distinct, lucid, graphic, sharp *ant.* vague ③ free, open, empty, bare, uncluttered *ant.* crowded ④ sure, obvious, apparent *ant.* obscure

cleft *n.* crack, crevice, cranny, slit, split

clever *adj.* smart, intelligent, bright, able, brainy, skilful, talented, sharp ▷**astute** *ant.* stupid

cliff *n.* precipice, height, bluff, crag, bank

climax *n.* crisis, peak, summit, turning point

climb *v.* clamber, shinny, mount, scale, ascend, soar, rise

cling *v.* adhere, attach, embrace, grasp, clutch

clip ① *n.* fastener, clasp ② *v.* trim, prune, snip, cut, mow

clog *v.* block, jam, plug, choke, fill

close ① *v.* (kloz) shut, bolt, bar, fill in, end ② *adj.* (klos) near, handy, neighbouring, adjacent *ant.* far ③ *adj.* tight, immediate, impending ④ familiar, chummy, intimate

closet *n.* cupboard, wardrobe, cabinet

clothes *n.* dress, attire, apparel, garments

cloud *n.* vapour, fog, billow, haze, shadow

clown *n.* jester, joker, comedian, buffoon

club *n.* ① bat, stick ② group, society, association, union

clue *n.* hint, sign, evidence, lead

clump *n.* cluster, group, bunch

clumsy *adj.* awkward, gawky *Northern Dancer grew from a gawky foal into a famous racehorse.* inept, blundering, graceless *ant.* graceful

clutch *v.* cling, clasp, grasp, seize, grip

clutter *n.* litter, mess, jumble, disorder

ṅ. = noun
v. = verb
adj. = adjective
adv. = adverb
conj. = conjunction
prep. = preposition
ant. = antonym
hom. = homonym
▷ = cross-reference

Clothes

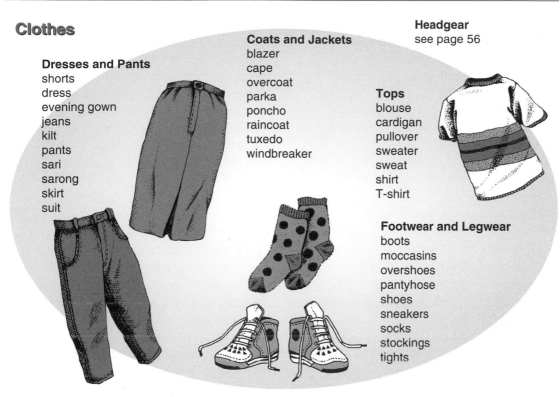

Dresses and Pants
shorts
dress
evening gown
jeans
kilt
pants
sari
sarong
skirt
suit

Coats and Jackets
blazer
cape
overcoat
parka
poncho
raincoat
tuxedo
windbreaker

Headgear
see page 56

Tops
blouse
cardigan
pullover
sweater
sweat
shirt
T-shirt

Footwear and Legwear
boots
moccasins
overshoes
pantyhose
shoes
sneakers
socks
stockings
tights

coach *n.* trainer, tutor, instructor, teacher

coarse *adj.* ① rough, unrefined, unpolished ② brutish, rude, uncivil, vulgar *ant.* refined *hom.* course

coat *n.* ① parka, jacket, blazer, windbreaker ② fur, skin, hide, fleece ③ layer

coax *v.* persuade, cajole, wheedle, urge *ant.* dissuade

coddle *v.* pamper, spoil, indulge, baby

coil *v.* twist, wind, loop, curl, spiral

coincide *v.* match, agree, be synchronized *Their watches are synchronized and show exactly the same time.* concur

cold *adj.* ① icy, chilly, frigid, freezing, frosty, frozen, wintry *ant.* hot ② cool, unfriendly, unemotional

collapse *v.* fall, crumple, disintegrate, cave in, topple

collect *v.* accumulate, compile, compose, assemble, save ▷**gather** *ant.* scatter

collide *v.* crash, smash, hit, strike, bump

colossal *adj.* enormous, gigantic, immense, massive, giant, monstrous ▷**huge** *ant.* tiny

column *n.* ① pillar, post, shaft, support, upright ② file, line, procession, rank

combat *v.* battle, contend, struggle, oppose, defy, fight, resist, clash, war

combine *v.* unite, join, link, fuse, merge, mix, bond, blend *ant.* separate

come *v.* arrive, appear, enter, reach, advance, occur, happen *ant.* go

comfort ① *v.* cheer, calm, soothe, console, reassure, relieve *ant.* torment ② *n.* ease, luxury, relief, reassurance, consolation, convenience

comfortable *adj.* restful, cosy, snug, peaceful, contented *ant.* uncomfortable

command *v.* ① order, dictate, direct, demand, require, instruct ② lead, govern, rule, head up

commence *v.* start, begin, initiate, originate, launch *ant.* finish

comment *v.* mention, remark, observe, note, respond, utter

commit *v.* ① carry out, perform, perpetrate, ② promise, entrust, obligate *Tan felt obligated to do what he had promised.*

common *adj.* ① ordinary, regular, everyday, usual, customary ② popular, general, public, social ③ shared, mutual, joint

C
C
C
C
C
C

commotion *n.* excitement, flurry, stir, uproar, riot, disturbance ▷**fuss**

communicate *v.* tell, disclose, announce, inform, reveal, transmit, say, express, report, relate

community *n.* society, neighbourhood, public, co-operation, district ▷**association**

compact *adj.* dense, close, tight, firm, condensed, concise, snug, solid

companion *n.* friend, buddy, pal, colleague, comrade, associate *ant.* rival

company *n.* ① business, firm, enterprise, corporation, association ② guest, visitor ③ group, assembly, cast, troop, band

compare *v.* match, equal, parallel, relate

compassion *n.* kindness, mercy, sympathy, charity, understanding, concern ▷**pity**

compel *v.* make, coerce, drive, force, urge

compensate *v.* pay, refund, reimburse *If you don't like the C.D. you bought, return it and you'll be reimbursed.* repay, reward, offset, balance, make up

compete *v.* contest, contend, rival, strive, oppose, challenge, vie, race, run

competent *adj.* able, skilful, proficient, capable *ant.* incompetent

competition *n.* game, match, contest, rivalry, race, tournament

compile *v.* assemble, group, put together, gather, unite ▷**collect**

complacent *adj.* self-satisfied, contented ▷**smug**

complain *v.* protest, gripe, grumble, object, whine, bellyache

complement *v.* complete, round off, add to, supplement, match *hom.* compliment

Confusable Words

complement means *supplement*

compliment means *praise*

complete ① *v.* finish, accomplish, achieve, perfect, end ② *adj.* finished, full, entire, whole, thorough, total, utter, absolute *ant.* incomplete

complex *adj.* complicated, intricate *She decorated her intricate dreamcatcher with many beads and feathers.* mixed, tangled, difficult, compound, elaborate *ant.* simple

complicated *adj.* difficult, hard, puzzling, involved ▷**complex** *ant.* easy

compliment *v.* flatter, honour, congratulate, comment ▷**praise** *ant.* insult *hom.* complement

comply *v.* agree, follow, obey, consent, conform, submit, abide by, yield *ant.* refuse

compose *v.* ① create, produce, conceive, draft, write, construct, form ② calm, quiet, collect, settle, pacify

composure *n.* assurance, calm, confidence, balance, poise

compound *n.* mixture, alloy, blend, composite, combination

comprehend *v.* know, get, fathom, grasp, discern ▷**understand**

compress *v.* condense, contract, abbreviate, cram, reduce, crowd ▷**squeeze** *ant.* expand

comprise *v.* contain, consist of, include, embody, encompass, take in, cover

compromise *v.* ① settle, give and take, meet halfway, strike a balance, adjust, agree ② imperil, weaken, jeopardize, risk, endanger, sacrifice

compulsory *adj.* required, necessary, forced, imposed, compelled, obligatory *In our home, chores are not optional, they're obligatory! ant.* voluntary

compute *v.* calculate, figure, count, tally,

conceal *v.* disguise, obscure, mask, cover, camouflage, stash, bury ▷**hide** *ant.* reveal

concede *v.* allow, admit, yield, acknowledge, recognize, grant, surrender *ant.* dispute

conceit *n.* vanity, self-importance, arrogance, egotism, pride *ant.* modesty

conceited *adj.* proud, vain, arrogant, egotistical, smug, boastful *ant.* modest

conceive *v.* create, design, devise *Sonia devised a successful way to feed the baby bird.* develop, imagine, perceive, originate

n. = noun
v. = verb
adj. = adjective
adv. = adverb
conj. = conjunction
prep. = preposition
ant. = antonym
hom. = homonym
▷ = cross-reference

concentrate *v.* focus, centralize, pay attention, collect, gather, meditate, ponder, condense

concept *n.* idea, thought, theory, view

concern ① *v.* affect, touch, distress, worry ② *n.* affair, matter, interest, business, worry

concerning *prep.* regarding, respecting, about, with reference to

concise *adj.* brief, condensed, short, pithy ▷**compact** *ant.* lengthy

conclude *v.* ① finish, terminate, close, complete, conclude, settle ▷**end** ② deduce, judge, presume, decide, infer, understand, reason

conclusion *n.* result, termination, end

concoct *v.* hatch, plan, devise, develop, invent, prepare, contrive

concrete ① *adj.* actual, definite, real, physical, tangible, solid ② *n.* cement, mortar

concur *v.* approve, agree, coincide, consent *ant.* disagree

condemn *v.* blame, denounce, reprove, criticize, rebuke, disapprove, sentence, forbid, judge *ant.* approve

condense *v.* shorten, cut, reduce, compress, concentrate, thicken, abridge *ant.* expand

condition *n.* shape, form, state, position, plight, illness, situation ▷**predicament**

condone *v.* excuse, overlook, disregard, approve, allow *ant.* censure

conduct ① *n.* (*con*-duct) behaviour, actions, manner, demeanour ② *v.* (con-*duct*) guide, direct, lead, steer, usher, behave

confer *v.* ① bestow, grant, award, give, present ② consult, advise, discuss

conference *n.* discussion, meeting, forum

confess *v.* admit, acknowledge, own up, divulge, declare *ant.* deny

confide *v.* tell, divulge, reveal, entrust, unburden

confidence *n.* ① assurance, boldness, firmness ② belief, faith, trust *ant.* doubt

confident *adj.* certain, assured, poised, sure, positive, hopeful, optimistic

confine *v.* ① restrict, limit, ② detain, imprison, cage, jail, enclose *ant.* free

confirm *v.* ① verify, assure, establish ② approve, endorse, support *ant.* deny

confiscate *v.* take and keep, seize, impound *The dogcatcher impounded the stray puppy.*

conform *v.* agree, comply, yield, adjust, adapt, follow

confound *v.* perplex, mystify, puzzle, baffle, fluster, confuse ▷**bewilder** *ant.* enlighten

confront *v.* challenge, defy, face, meet, oppose, encounter

confuse *v.* baffle, mystify, confound, puzzle, muddle, mix up ▷**bewilder** *ant.* clarify

congenial *adj.* companionable, agreeable, gracious ▷**friendly** *ant.* disagreeable

congested *adj.* jammed, crowded, clogged, packed, teeming, plugged *ant.* clear

congratulate *v.* compliment, praise, wish well, commend

congregate *v.* assemble, meet, come together, converge *ant.* disperse

conjecture *v.* guess, surmise, suspect, imagine, assume, speculate, conclude

connect *v.* unite, join, combine, fasten, link, couple, attach *ant.* disconnect

conquer *v.* beat, crush, overcome, overpower, triumph ▷**defeat** *ant.* surrender

conscientious *adj.* careful, diligent, principled, moral, scrupulous, exact ▷**honest**

conscious *adj.* ① alert, alive, aware, mindful, sensible, awake ② intentional, deliberate, knowing *ant.* unconscious

consecutive *adj.* chronological, in sequence, successive *We won three successive games in intramurals.* continuous, serial, following

consent *v.* assent, permit, concur, approve, allow ▷**agree** *ant.* oppose

conserve *v.* keep, preserve, protect, save, safeguard, maintain, sustain, support *ant.* waste

consider *v.* discuss, examine, reflect *Reflect on the story, then guess what would have happened next.* regard, judge, ponder *ant.* ignore

C
C
C
C
C
Ⓒ
Ⓒ
C

considerable *adj.* abundant, ample, great, large, important, sizable, significant *ant.* insignificant

consistent *adj.* uniform, constant, regular, steady, unchanging, same, stable *ant.* inconsistent

console *v.* comfort, sympathize, soothe

conspicuous *adj.* noticeable, marked, apparent, obvious, prominent, plain, clear, distinct, evident, visible *ant.* inconspicuous

conspire *v.* intrigue, scheme, plot

constant *adj.* ① regular, stable, uniform *The water in the fish tank must be kept at a uniform temperature.* set, fixed, firm ▷**consistent** *ant.* variable ② loyal, faithful, true, devoted, steadfast *ant.* treacherous

constitute *v.* compose, comprise, consist of, set up, fix, form, establish, found, make up

constrict *v.* tighten, strain, choke, pinch, narrow, contract, reduce *ant.* expand

construct *v.* erect, compose, create, set up, assemble, make ▷**build** *ant.* demolish

consult *v.* ask, seek advice, discuss, confer, refer to, deliberate

consume *v.* use up, absorb, eat up, devour

contact *n.* touch, connection, source, meeting, acquaintance, communication

contain *v.* comprise, consist of, hold, accommodate, enclose, include

contaminate *v.* pollute, soil, spoil, taint, infect, corrupt *ant.* purify

contemplate *v.* meditate, reflect, deliberate, consider, ponder

contempt *n.* disdain, scorn, derision, hatred *ant.* admiration

contend *v.* compete, contest, conflict, vie, struggle, argue, maintain, combat, battle *ant.* concede

content ① *adj.* (con-*tent*) satisfied, happy ② *n.* (*con*-tent) meaning, information, matter, text, subject

contest ① *n.* (*con*-test) competition, match, game, rivalry, conflict ② *v.* (con-*test*) dispute, argue, challenge, compete

continue *v.* go on, keep up, endure, persist, last, maintain, persevere, resume *ant.* stop

contract ① *v.* (con-*tract*) shrink, condense, lessen, shorten, decrease ② *n.* (*con*-tract) agreement, pact, understanding, bargain, treaty

contradict *v.* refute, oppose, challenge, dispute, conflict, deny

contrary *adj.* ① opposite, adverse, counter ② stubborn, difficult *ant.* agreeable

contrast ① *n.* (*con*-trast) difference, disparity, comparison ② *v.* (con-*trast*) compare, differ, oppose, distinguish

contribute *v.* donate, chip in, provide, assist, help, give, supply *ant.* withhold

contrive *v.* form, fashion, construct, create, design, invent, develop

control *v.* ① command, direct, dominate, lead, supervise, oversee, superintend ② regulate, restrain, keep in check, curb

convene *v.* call together, assemble *Let's assemble in the gym in ten minutes.* meet, rally *ant.* dismiss

convenient *adj.* handy, nearby, easy, accessible *ant.* inconvenient

conversation *n.* chat, communication, discussion, discourse, exchange, dialogue

convert *v.* alter, change, transform, adapt

convey *v.* ① carry, transport, conduct, bear, transmit, bring ② communicate, express, relate, relay

convict ① *n.* (*con*-vict) prisoner, captive, criminal ② *v.* (con-*vict*) find guilty, condemn, sentence

convince *v.* assure, persuade, win over, sway, influence, urge, coax, entice

cook *v.* boil, broil, heat, poach, steam, fry, stew, bake, grill, roast, prepare

cool *adj.* ① chilly, frigid ▷**cold** ② composed, calm, relaxed ③ unfriendly, distant

co-operate *v.* assist, join forces, unite, collaborate, combine, aid

copy *v.* duplicate, reproduce, photocopy, trace, imitate, mimic, simulate, ape, impersonate, follow, repeat, pirate, crib, plagiarize, emulate

cord *n.* string, rope, twine, line *hom.* chord

n. = noun
v. = verb
adj. = adjective
adv. = adverb
conj. = conjunction
prep. = preposition
ant. = antonym
hom. = homonym
▷ = cross-reference

cordial *adj.* sincere, congenial, warm, hearty, friendly, affable *ant.* hostile

core *n.* heart, kernel, crux *Once Gino helped them see the crux of their problem, they were able to find a solution.* centre, middle, essence *hom.* corps

corner *n.* nook, angle, bend, intersection

corpse *n.* body, carcass, remains

correct *adj.* true, actual, accurate, exact, precise *ant.* wrong

correspond *v.* ① fit, harmonize, agree, coincide, match ② write

corroborate *v.* confirm, certify, endorse, establish, support *ant.* contradict

corrode *v.* erode, waste, eat away, rust

corrupt ① *adj.* dishonest, fraudulent, rotten, crooked, wicked, evil, unethical, immoral ② *v.* deprave, debase, ruin, taint, entice, bribe, spoil, contaminate

cost *n.* ① charge, amount, price, expense, tab, fee ② penalty, forfeit, sacrifice, loss

costly *adj.* expensive, valuable, precious *The pirates made off with the precious jewels.*

costume *n.* suit, outfit, clothes, attire, dress, uniform, disguise, garb, get-up

cottage *n.* cabin, shack, lodge, bungalow

couch *n.* chesterfield, sofa, settee

council *n.* parliament, senate, assembly, committee, congress, convention, caucus, board *hom.* counsel

counsel ① *v.* advise, instruct, recommend *hom.* council ② *n.* advice, suggestion, recommendation, tip ③ *n.* lawyer, attorney, advocate

count *v.* calculate, compute, reckon, tally, enumerate, add up

counter ① *n.* bar, desk, table, bench ② *adj.* contrary, contradictory, opposed, incompatible

counterfeit *adj.* fake, bogus, false, phony, forged, fraudulent

Cooking Utensils

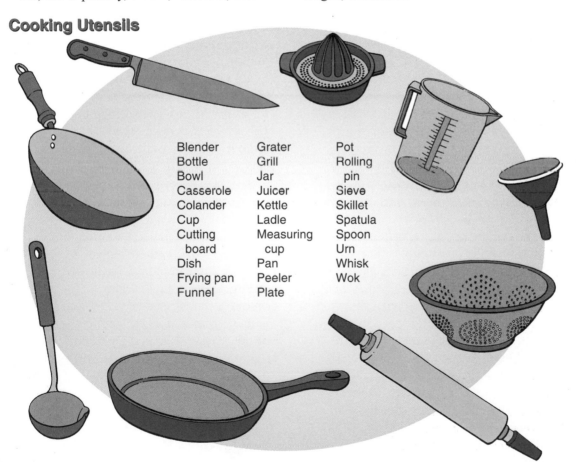

Blender	Grater	Pot
Bottle	Grill	Rolling
Bowl	Jar	pin
Casserole	Juicer	Sieve
Colander	Kettle	Skillet
Cup	Ladle	Spatula
Cutting	Measuring	Spoon
board	cup	Urn
Dish	Pan	Whisk
Frying pan	Peeler	Wok
Funnel	Plate	

C
C
C
C
C
C
C

country ① *n.* nation, people, state ② *adj.* rural, farming, rustic

couple ① *n.* pair, two ② *v.* link, unite, join, connect, combine

courage *n.* bravery, valour, boldness, gallantry, daring, nerve *ant.* cowardice

courageous *adj.* brave, bold, fearless, valiant *ant.* cowardly

course *n.* ① route, path, road, track, trail, way ② plan, manner, method, process, measure, tactic ③ subject, class ④ direction, bearing *hom.* coarse

court ① *n.* courtyard, atrium, quad ② *n.* bar, bench, tribunal ③ *n.* palace, retinue ④ *v.* date, romance, pursue, woo

courteous *adj.* considerate, polite, refined, obliging, gracious, accommodating *ant.* discourteous

courtesy *n.* politeness, civility, manners, gallantry, respect

cove *n.* inlet, bay, lagoon

cover ① *v.* conceal, hide, mask, disguise, protect, insure ② *v.* include, incorporate ③ *n.* cap, case, lid, canopy, roof, shelter, refuge, protection

coward *n.* weakling, chicken, sneak, deserter, scaredy-cat *ant.* hero *hom.* cowered

cowardice *n.* fear, faint-heartedness, gutlessness *ant.* courage

cowardly *adj.* fearful, weak, scared, spineless, timid *ant.* courageous

cower *v.* cringe, grovel, flinch, crouch

coy *adj.* demure, blushing, bashful, shy

crack ① *n.* break, split, cleft, crevice, breach ② *v.* snap, split, splinter, fracture

craft *n.* ① ability, cleverness, expertise, art ② occupation, business trade, handwork ③ boat, ship, plane

crafty *adj.* cunning, artful, wily, shrewd, clever, deceitful

cram *v.* ram, stuff, squeeze, press, jam, crowd, study

cramp *v.* restrict, hinder, confine, limit

crash *v.* ① bang, clash, clatter ② break, fall, topple, plunge, collapse, smash, collide

crass *adj.* coarse, crude, rude, unrefined, oafish, boorish, vulgar *ant.* refined

Creature

It was a huge brute–the biggest animal I'd ever seen.

crave *v.* need, desire, long for, yearn for

crawl *v.* creep, drag, slither, snake

crazy *adj.* insane, mad, berserk, deranged, demented, absurd, loony *ant.* sane

creak *v.* grate, grind, rasp, groan *hom.* creek

crease *n.* fold, pucker, line, pleat, tuck

create *v.* make, invent, devise, produce, originate, compose, concoct, cause

creation *n.* invention, handiwork, foundation, production *ant.* destruction

creature *n.* animal, beast, being, brute *It was a huge brute–the biggest animal I'd ever seen.* person, organism

credible *adj.* believable, likely, plausible, convincing *ant.* incredible

creek *n.* bay, cove, brook, stream *hom.* creak

creep *v.* crawl, slither, inch, wriggle

crest *n.* top, crown, height, brow, climax

crevice *n.* cleft, chink, cranny, split, gap

crew *n.* team, company, gang, staff

crime *n.* offence, fault, felony, violation

criminal ① *n.* culprit, convict, felon, crook, outlaw ② *adj.* illegal, unlawful, wicked

cringe *v.* cower, flinch, duck, shrink, grovel

cripple *v.* disable, mutilate, maim, injure, paralyse, weaken, damage

crisis *n.* climax, turning point, catastrophe, disaster, emergency

crisp *adj.* brittle, crunchy, firm, crusty, breakable, cold, fresh *ant.* soft, flexible

critical *adj.* ① crucial, important, pressing *This pressing decision must be made right away.* decisive, ② dangerous, serious, severe, grave ③ disapproving, negative

criticize *v.* scold, slam, censure, find fault, condemn, disapprove of, blame *ant.* praise

crooked *adj.* ① dishonest, criminal ② bent, bowed, distorted, twisted, warped, buckled, curved, slanted

crop ① *n.* harvest, gathering, yield ② *v.* graze, shorten, cut, decrease

cross ① *adj.* angry, annoyed, irritable, moody, testy, surly ② *v.* bridge, span, ford, traverse ③ *v.* cancel, strike ④ *v.* breed

crouch *v.* stoop, squat, cower, cringe

crow *v.* gloat, brag, boast, exult

crowd *n.* mob, multitude, flock, assembly, swarm, throng, horde

crowded *adj.* jammed, packed, congested, cramped

crucial *adj.* decisive, critical, key, acute, essential, all-important

crude *adj.* raw, unrefined, rustic, rude, unpolished, vulgar ▷**coarse** *ant.* polite

cruel *adj.* brutal, inhuman, ruthless, vicious, merciless, heartless ▷**savage** *ant.* kind

cruise *n.* voyage, trip, sail, crossing, spin *hom.* crews

Creek

Creak

crumb *n.* bit, morsel, scrap, shred, particle

crumble *v.* decay, grind, powder, decompose, disintegrate

crumple *v.* crinkle, crush, wrinkle, bend

crunch *v.* chew, grind, munch ▷**crush**

crush *v.* ① squash, mash, pound, compress, grind, crumple ② conquer, suppress, oppress

cry *v.* ① weep, bawl, blubber, sob, whine, lament ② exclaim, call, shout, shriek

cuddle *v.* hug, embrace, pet, snuggle, caress

cue *n.* hint, key, sign, signal *hom.* queue

culprit *n.* criminal, convict, felon, offender

cultivated *adj.* refined, civilized, cultured, educated

cumbersome *adj.* bulky, awkward, clumsy, unmanageable, unwieldy *ant.* convenient

cunning *adj.* artful, crafty, sly, shrewd, foxy

curb *v.* check, restrain, restrict, control

cure ① *n.* remedy, medicine, drug ② *v.* heal, remedy, treat, restore, preserve

curious *adj.* ① nosey, prying, inquisitive *The inquisitive stranger asked many questions.* ② odd, peculiar, strange, unusual

curl *v.* coil, twist, curve, crimp, wind

current ① *adj.* present, contemporary, modern, topical, fashionable ② *n.* stream, flow, undertow *hom.* currant

curse ① *v.* swear, condemn, cuss ② *n.* oath, denunciation ③ *v.* afflict, plague

curt *adj.* blunt, abrupt, terse, surly, crusty, gruff ▷**short**

curtail *v.* trim, shorten, clip, cut back, decrease ▷**abbreviate** *ant.* lengthen

curve *n.* loop, hook, curl, twist, coil ▷**bend**

cushion *n.* pillow, pad, support, buffer

custom *n.* habit, usage, convention, tradition, ritual, routine ▷**fashion**

customer *n.* buyer, client, patron *Moira is a daily patron of the school cafeteria.* consumer, shopper

cut *v.* carve, chisel, sever, gash, slice, shear, shave, clip, snip, chop, hew, trim, mow

cute *adj.* charming, attractive, pretty, adorable, delightful, darling, winsome

cut off *v.* disconnect, interrupt, stop

cutting *adj.* sharp, biting, bitter, sarcastic

D d

dab *v.* daub, swab, touch, pat, smear

dagger *n.* knife, bayonet, stiletto, dirk

daily *adj.* everyday, normal, common

dainty *adj.* delicate, fragile, petite

damage *n.* harm, sabotage, vandalism, injury, hurt, ruin, wreckage

damn *v.* curse, swear, condemn, criticize *ant.* bless

damp *adj.* humid, clammy, dank, wet, soaked, soggy ▷**moist** *ant.* dry

dance *v.* hop, skip, jump, prance, frolic

danger *n.* peril, hazard, risk, jeopardy, menace, threat *ant.* safety

dangerous *adj.* unsafe, risky, hazardous, perilous, precarious, reckless *ant.* safe

dangle *v.* hang, swing, sway, suspend

dank *adj.* sticky, muggy, moist, soggy ▷**damp**

dare *v.* brave, face, risk, defy, challenge, venture, confront

daring *adj.* adventurous, reckless, bold, fearless, heroic ▷**brave** *ant.* timid

dark *adj.* dusky, shady, dim, dingy, shadowy, murky, obscure, sullen, black *ant.* light

darling ① *adj.* dear, favourite, beloved, precious ② *n.* love, sweetheart, honey, pet

darn *v.* mend, sew, patch, repair

dart ① *n.* arrow, missile ② *v.* dash, flit, fly, whiz, scuttle, scurry, scramble, scamper

dash *v.* rush, gallop, run, hurry, scurry, sprint, tear, speed, race, fly, charge

date *n.* ① time, point ② appointment *Jamed has an appointment to see the doctor.* engagement ③ boyfriend, girlfriend, escort

dauntless *adj.* fearless, gallant, courageous ▷**brave** *ant.* discouraged

dawn *n.* daybreak, morning, sunrise, beginning, birth, rise *ant.* dusk, end

daze *v.* dazzle, surprise, stun, amaze, confuse, blind ▷**bewilder** *hom.* days

dead *adj.* deceased, departed, gone, lifeless, extinct, late, asleep, numb, exhausted, fallen, dull *ant.* alive

deaden *v.* paralyse, muffle, dull, numb, blunt

deadly *adj.* fatal, lethal, mortal, venomous, toxic, poisonous, malignant

deal *v.* bargain, trade, market, give out, traffic, distribute, cope

dealer *n.* merchant, trader, vendor, retailer, tradesman, trafficker

Dance

Ballet	Mazurka
Bolero	Minuet
Cha-cha	Polka
Charleston	Polonaise
Conga	Quadrille
Disco	Quickstep
Fandango	Rumba
Flamenco	Samba
Fox trot	Square dance
Gavotte	Tango
Highland fling	Tarantella
Jive	Twist
Line dance	Waltz
Mambo	

n. = noun

v. = verb

adj. = adjective

adv. = adverb

conj. = conjunction

prep. = preposition

ant. = antonym

hom. = homonym

▷ = cross-reference

dear *adj.* ① darling, beloved, loved, cherished *The drawing by Kenojuak Ashevak was their most cherished possession.* ② expensive, high-priced, costly, valuable *ant.* cheap *hom.* deer

death *n.* mortality, exinction, demise, passing, fatality, decease *ant.* life

debate *v.* argue, discuss, dispute *Players may not dispute the referee's decision.* question, contend, quarrel

debt *n.* obligation, debit, dues, liability, deficit *ant.* credit

decay *v.* ① decompose, rot, spoil, perish, wither, deteriorate, disintegrate ② decline, sink, crumble, erode, dwindle away

deceive *v.* trick, cheat, mislead, fool, delude, hoodwink, bluff, dupe ▷**betray**

decent *adj.* respectable, proper, fair, modest, right, moral, ethical, acceptable, adequate, honest, law-abiding *ant.* indecent

decide *v.* choose, settle, determine, rule, judge, resolve, conclude, fix

declare *v.* assert, state, profess, proclaim, announce, avow

decline ① *v.* descend, dwindle, decrease, drop, fall, fade ② *v.* refuse, turn down, reject *ant.* accept ③ *n.* drop, fall, descent, decrease, dip, decay, downturn, wane

decorate *v.* embellish, adorn, ornament

decoy ① *v.* entice *The smell of warm bread enticed us into the café.* ensnare, mislead, tempt ② *n.* lure, bait

decrease ① *v.* diminish, lessen, wane, fall, decline, reduce, lessen, curtail, dwindle *ant.* increase ② *n.* reduction, decline, fall

decree *n.* law, edict, manifesto, rule, decision, order, statute, proclamation

decrepit *adj.* ① weak, frail, feeble *ant.* robust ② shabby, threadbare, crumbling, timeworn, tumbledown

dedicate *v.* devote, assign, pledge, apply

deduce *v.* draw, infer, conclude, surmise, reason

deduct *v.* subtract, remove, withdraw, discount *ant.* add

deed *n.* ① act, exploit *Walking across Niagara Falls on a tightrope is a dangerous exploit.* stunt ② document, agreement, contract

deep *adj.* ① bottomless, low ② complex, wise, profound ③ serious, grave

deface *v.* disfigure, deform, injure, mar, blemish, spoil *ant.* adorn

defeat *v.* beat, conquer, overcome, vanquish, overthrow, overwhelm, subdue

defect *n.* flaw, fault, bug, blemish, error, imperfection, weakness

defective *adj.* imperfect, faulty, deficient, insufficient, flawed *ant.* perfect

defend *v.* protect, guard, fortify *Fortify your snow fort with thicker walls.* support, sustain, uphold, shield, maintain *ant.* attack

defer *v.* ① postpone, put off, adjourn, waive, delay, suspend, shelve *ant.* hasten ② yield, submit, bow

defiant *adj.* mutinous, rebellious, resistant, aggressive, unruly *ant.* submissive

deficient *adj.* wanting, imperfect, defective, faulty, lacking, flawed, inadequate

defile *v.* taint, infect, pollute, sully, disgrace, violate, spoil *ant.* purify

define *v.* explain, describe, clarify, interpret, designate, mark out, specify *ant.* obscure

definite *adj.* clear, certain, clear-cut, distinct, explicit, precise, positive ▷**sure** *ant.* vague

deform *v.* distort, contort, twist, warp, disfigure

defraud *v.* fleece, swindle, trick, deceive ▷**cheat**

defy *v.* resist, withstand, disregard, challenge, disobey, dare, rebel *ant.* obey

degrade *v.* debase, corrupt, lower, downgrade, cheapen *ant.* elevate

degree *n.* grade, measure, extent, class, step, level, standard

dejected *adj.* depressed, downcast, disheartened, disconsolate ▷**gloomy** *ant.* elated

delay *v.* postpone, put off, detain, halt, hinder, impede, defer, procrastinate, linger, loiter *ant.* hurry

D d d d d D

deliberate ① *adj.* willful, calculated, intentional, planned *ant.* unintentional ② *v.* reflect, contemplate, discuss, consider

delicate *adj.* dainty, refined, fine, fragile, tender, subtle, tactful *ant.* harsh, coarse

delicious *adj.* tasty, luscious, savoury *The savoury smell of cabbage rolls made my mouth water.* choice, mouth-watering, palatable ▷**scrumptious**

delight *n.* joy, enjoyment, pleasure, rapture, bliss ▷**happiness** *ant.* misery

delightful *adj.* enjoyable, cheery, lovely, enchanting ▷**agreeable** *ant.* horrible

deliver *v.* ① transfer, hand over, convey, courier, produce, yield, bear ② save, rescue

delude *v.* cheat, hoax, hoodwink, mislead, trick ▷**deceive**

deluge *n.* inundation *The inundation of salmon swimming upriver fed the grizzlies for days.* swamp, flood

demand *v.* request, ask, appeal, require, order, insist

demeanour *n.* bearing, manner, conduct, air

demented *adj.* irrational, foolish, insane ▷**mad** *ant.* sane

demolish *v.* destroy, wreck, ruin, smash, knock down *ant.* build

demon *n.* fiend, devil, evil spirit

demonstrate *v.* prove, exhibit, illustrate, display ▷**show**

demote *v.* degrade, downgrade, relegate, lower, reduce *ant.* promote

demure *adj.* coy, quiet, modest, proper, discreet

den *n.* ① nest, cave, hole, lair ② hideaway, retreat *This little room is my retreat, where I can sit and think alone.* study

denote *v.* designate, indicate, mean, express, stand for, convey

denounce *v.* condemn, blame, fault, criticize, brand, attack, vilify, defame ▷**accuse** *ant.* praise

dense *adj.* ① thick, solid, compact, close, crowded *ant.* sparse ② stupid, dull, foolish, ignorant *ant.* clever

dent *n.* notch, cavity, chip, hollow

Dessert

Desert

deny *v.* refuse, reject, repudiate, dismiss, refute, decline, oppose, contradict

depart *v.* quit, go, retire, withdraw, vanish, die ▷**leave** *ant.* arrive

department *n.* section, division, office, branch, area

depict *v.* describe, sketch, portray, outline, draw, represent

deplorable *adj.* distressing, disastrous, shameful, horrible, dreadful *ant.* excellent

deport *v.* banish, exile, expel, oust

deposit *v.* drop, lay, place, put, save, precipitate *ant.* withdraw, remove

depot *n.* ① warehouse, storehouse ② station, terminal

depraved *adj.* corrupt, immoral, evil, sinful, vile *ant.* upright

depreciate *v.* devalue, put down, reduce, lower, cheapen, downgrade *ant.* appreciate

depress *v.* ① sadden, dispirit, cast down *ant.* cheer ② flatten, push down *ant.* inflate

depressed *adj.* dejected, downcast, blue, dispirited *You tried your best, so don't be dispirited about losing.* despondent *ant.* glad

deprive *v.* rob, strip, starve *ant.* provide

deputy *n.* representative, agent, delegate, lieutenant, assistant, councillor

n. = noun
v. = verb
adj. = adjective
adv. = adverb
conj. = conjunction
prep. = preposition
ant. = antonym
hom. = homonym
▷ = cross-reference

derelict *adj.* ① abandoned, deserted, forlorn ② negligent, slack, careless

deride *v.* laugh at, jeer at, ridicule, scorn ▷**mock** *ant.* praise

derive *v.* develop, arise from, originate, evolve, descend, stem

descend *v.* fall, drop, lower, decline, collapse, plunge ▷**sink** *ant.* ascend

describe *v.* explain, detail, define, tell, depict

desert ① *n.* (*dez*-ert) wasteland, wilderness ② *adj.* desolate, arid, barren ③ *v.* (de-*zert*) forsake, leave ▷**abandon** *hom.* dessert

deserve *v.* be worthy of, merit, warrant *Your hard work warrants sincere congratulations!* be entitled to, earn

design *n.* ① drawing, painting, pattern, figure ② plan, scheme, intention

desirable *adj.* ① agreeable, pleasing, good ② attractive, alluring, adorable

desire *v.* wish, choose, need, want, crave, long for, yearn for, pine for *Judy still pines for her lost hamster, Alfie.*

desist *v.* refrain, avoid, break off, cease, end

desolate *adj.* lonely, forlorn, miserable, wretched, abandoned, barren, bleak

despair *n.* depression, misery, hopelessness, sorrow ▷**gloom** *ant.* hope

desperate *adj.* ① hopeless, despondent, drastic, reckless, frantic *ant.* hopeful ② critical, urgent

despicable *adj.* contemptible, low, detestable, sordid, immoral *ant.* noble

despise *v.* abhor, detest, loathe, scorn, hate *ant.* love

despondent *adj.* depressed, forlorn, hopeless, broken-hearted ▷**miserable** *ant.* cheerful

destination *n.* goal, objective, terminus, end

destiny *n.* fate, lot, fortune, future, prospect

destitute *adj.* poor, needy, bankrupt, penniless, poverty-stricken *ant.* wealthy

destroy *v.* ruin, demolish, kill, smash, exterminate, annihilate ▷**wreck** *ant.* create

destruction *n.* downfall, ruin, defeat, havoc, devastation *ant.* creation

detach *v.* separate, part, divide, loosen, split, disconnect *ant.* attach

detail *n.* item, fact, element, feature, trait, circumstance, point

detain *v.* delay, retard, restrain, arrest, hold up, hinder, keep, confine, stop *ant.* release

detect *v.* notice, discover, observe, track down, find, perceive, spot *ant.* miss

deter *v.* prevent, hold back, check, stop, prohibit, detain, discourage *ant.* encourage

deteriorate *v.* worsen, corrode, decline *If you stop practising, your skills quickly decline.* disintegrate, decay, erode *ant.* improve

determine *v.* ① find out, discover ② decide, identify, choose, judge

detest *v.* abhor *Adam is a peaceful person and abhors violence.* loathe, despise, hate *ant.* adore

devastate *v.* lay waste, ravage, overwhelm, spoil, desolate ▷**destroy**

develop *v.* ① mature, ripen, grow up, evolve ② extend, expand, increase, create, elaborate *ant.* restrict

deviate *v.* differ, vary, contrast, wander, stray, digress, diverge, depart *ant.* conform

device *n.* apparatus, instrument, appliance, machine, tool, gadget

devil *n.* evil spirit, demon, fiend, Satan

devious *adj.* tricky, sly, subtle, cunning, underhanded, crooked, deceitful *ant.* forthright

devise *v.* contrive, fashion, form, plan, conceive, design, invent

devoid *adj.* barren, empty, free, without, lacking *ant.* full

devote *v.* allocate, allot, give, assign, dedicate, apply

devoted *adj.* dedicated, affectionate, loyal, caring, faithful *ant.* indifferent

devour *v.* swallow, gulp, gobble, wolf down, consume ▷**eat**

devout *adj.* pious, holy, religious, faithful, passionate, sincere

dexterous *adj.* able, adroit, deft, nimble, handy, artful ▷**skilful** *ant.* clumsy

diagram *n.* outline, drawing, sketch, plan, draft, chart

D d d D d D

dictate *v.* ① speak, utter, say ② instruct, command, decree, rule

die *v.* expire, pass away, perish, decease, finish, end *ant.* live *hom.* dye

differ *v.* ① disagree, vary, contrast, diverge ② argue, conflict, clash

difference *n.* variance, distinction, divergence *We had a divergence of opinion, so we agreed to disagree.* contrast, disagreement *ant.* agreement

different *adj.* contrary, variant, distinct, diverse, original, unusual *ant.* same

difficult *adj.* hard, puzzling, baffling, complex, laborious, complicated, intricate *ant.* easy

difficulty *n.* trouble, hardship, predicament

diffident *adj.* bashful, reserved, retiring, timid, unsure, modest ▷**shy** *ant.* confident

dig *v.* burrow, excavate, scoop, mine, delve, nudge, rummage

digest ① *v.* (di-*gest*) absorb, assimilate, dissolve ② *n.* (*di*-gest) abridgment, condensation, précis

digit *n.* ① number, figure, cipher ② finger, toe, thumb

dignified *adj.* grave, majestic, noble, lofty, grand *ant.* undignified

dignity *n.* grandeur, merit, fame, gravity *The look of gravity on her face disappeared when she started to giggle.* nobility, honour

dilapidated *adj.* neglected, unkempt, crumbling, decayed, shabby, run-down

dilemma *n.* quandary *He was in a quandary about what to do, until he finally made up his mind.* plight, difficulty, predicament

dilute *v.* water, cut, weaken, reduce, thin

dim *adj.* dark, faint, pale, gloomy, shadowy, weak, vague, dull, faded ▷**obscure** *ant.* bright

diminish *v.* reduce, lessen, decrease, become smaller *ant.* increase

dingy *adj.* murky, dark, dreary, sombre, gloomy, shabby, dull, faded, dirty ▷**dismal** *ant.* bright, clean

dip *v.* sink, immerse, plunge

dire *adj.* alarming, critical, appalling, awful, horrible ▷**terrible** *hom.* dyer

direct ① *adj.* straight, even, through ② *adj* frank, blunt, candid ③ *v.* aim, level, train, point, show ④ *v.* order, command, instruct

direction *n.* course, trend, way, track, route

dirt *n.* impurity, filth, grime, earth, soil

dirty *adj.* ① unclean, impure, filthy, grungy, grubby, grimy ② sordid, nasty, obscene, indecent *ant.* clean

disable *v.* cripple, lame, maim, disarm

disadvantage *n.* inconvenience, obstacle, burden, damage, handicap *ant.* advantage

disagree *v.* differ, argue, dispute, deny, oppose, challenge, dissent *ant.* agree

disagreeable *adj.* unpleasant, obnoxious, offensive, ill-tempered *ant.* agreeable

disappear *v.* vanish, dissolve, fade, melt, depart, expire, evaporate *ant.* appear

Dogs

Afghan
Airedale
Bassett
Beagle
Bloodhound
Borzoi
Boxer
Bulldog
Chihuahua

n. = noun
v. = verb
adj. = adjective
adv. = adverb
conj. = conjunction
prep. = preposition
ant. = antonym
hom. = homonym
▷ = cross-reference

disappoint *v.* frustrate, disillusion, let down, dismay, dissatisfy *ant.* please

disapprove *v.* criticize, reproach, censure, object, oppose, condemn *ant.* approve

disaster *n.* calamity, catastrophe, accident, misfortune, tragedy

disbelief *n.* distrust, doubt, suspicion, incredulity *ant.* belief

discard *v.* eliminate, get rid of, reject, scrap, throw away, shed; chuck *ant.* keep

discern *v.* spot, discover, distinguish

discharge *v.* ① dismiss, excuse, expel ② detonate, emit, fire, shoot

disciple *n.* follower, learner, pupil, attendant

discipline *n.* correction, self-control, training, obedience, punishment

disclaim *v.* repudiate, disown, renounce, deny, reject *ant.* acknowledge

disclose *v.* uncover, show, reveal, expose, betray *Would you ever betray a friend's secret?* communicate ▷**divulge** *ant.* conceal

disconcert *v.* abash, confuse, confound, upset, baffle, embarrass

disconnect *v.* separate, detach, cut off, sever, uncouple, disengage *ant.* connect

discontented *adj.* displeased, disgruntled, dissatisfied, unhappy *ant.* content

discord *n.* disagreement, strife, conflict *ant.* agreement

discourage *v.* ① depress, dismay, dispirit, deject, dishearten ② prevent, deter, dissuade *ant.* encourage

discourteous *adj.* rude, ill-mannered, impolite, crude, abrupt *ant.* courteous

Chow chow
Collie
Dachshund
Dalmatian
Doberman
German shepherd

Great Dane
Greyhound
Husky
Irish setter
Labrador
Newfoundland
Pekingese

Pointer
Poodle
Pug
Retriever
Saint Bernard
Saluki
Spaniel
Terrier

D

discover v. locate, uncover, learn, reveal, determine ▷**find** *ant.* conceal

discreet *adj.* tactful, delicate, sensitive, cautious, careful, prudent *ant.* indiscreet *hom.* discrete

discriminate v. ① distinguish *Can you distinguish between male and female loons?* ② judge, favour, prejudge

discuss v. confer, consider, talk, debate, argue, negotiate, deliberate

disdain n. scorn, contempt, derision, ridicule *ant.* admiration

disease n. infection, illness, ailment, sickness, malady, plague

disfigure v. blemish, deface, deform, mar, scar, spoil *ant.* adorn

disgrace n. scandal, dishonour, shame, stigma, discredit, humiliation *ant.* honour

disguise v. conceal, mask, falsify, cloak, hide, cover up

disgust ① n. aversion, revulsion, loathing, distaste ② v. horrify, offend, sicken, repel, revolt, nauseate

dishearten v. depress, disappoint, cast down, deter, deject ▷**discourage** *ant.* encourage

dishonest *adj.* deceitful, unscrupulous, shady, crooked, corrupt, shifty *ant.* honest

disintegrate v. crumble, decompose, rot, fall apart, deteriorate

Confusable Words

disinterested means *not selfish*

uninterested means *not interested*

dislike v. hate, loathe, detest, abhor, abominate ▷**despise** *ant.* like

dismal *adj.* dreary, miserable, cheerless, depressing, gloomy, sad ▷**hopeless** *ant.* cheerful

dismiss v. release, reject, terminate, fire, discard, banish, dispel *Maya's joke helped dispel Ken's gloomy thoughts.* repudiate *ant.* appoint, welcome

disobey v. defy, transgress, resist, ignore, rebel, violate *ant.* obey

disorder n. ① confusion, disarray, commotion, chaos, turmoil, anarchy *ant.* order ② sickness, illness, disease

dispel v. disperse, drive away, dismiss, scatter *ant.* collect

dispense v. distribute, arrange, allocate *Henri allocated the markers so that everyone received four.* measure out, supply, administer

disperse v. scatter, separate, break up, spread, distribute *ant.* gather

display v. show, exhibit, expose, flaunt, express ▷**reveal** *ant.* hide

displease v. annoy, anger, irritate, upset, offend, infuriate, incense *ant.* please

dispose of v. discard, dump, destroy, eliminate, throw away *ant.* keep

dispute ① n. conflict, quarrel, argument, debate ② v. argue, refute, contest, debate

disregard v. overlook, ignore, neglect, snub *ant.* regard

disreputable *adj.* dishonourable, disgraceful, discreditable ▷**shady** *ant.* honourable

dissect v. examine, scrutinize, analyse, dismember, cut

dissent n. disagreement, opposition, conflict, disharmony *ant.* harmony

dissimilar *adj.* different, diverse, unlike, various *ant.* similar

dissolve v. ① melt, thaw, break up, fade ② end, terminate

dissuade v. deter, discourage, put off, divert *ant.* persuade

distance n. extent, remoteness, range *What's the range covered by these walkie-talkies?* reach, span, stretch, length, expanse

distinct *adj.* ① separate, independent, detached, different, contrasting ② clear, sharp, conspicuous, lucid, apparent *ant.* hazy

distinguish v. discern, discover, differentiate

distinguished *adj.* important, notable, great, famed, celebrated, eminent, exalted *ant.* ordinary

distort v. ① deform, twist, bend, buckle, warp ② misrepresent, falsify

---

n. = noun
v. = verb
adj. = adjective
adv. = adverb
conj. = conjunction
prep. = preposition
ant. = antonym
hom. = homonym
▷ = cross-reference

Domesticated Animals

Camel   Horse
Canary   Parakeet
Cat   Parrot
Cattle   Pig
Chicken   Pigeon
Dog   Sheep
Donkey
Duck
Elephant
Goat
Goose

distract *v.* ① bewilder, disturb, confuse, divert ② entertain, amuse

distress *v.* embarrass, trouble, harass, grieve ▷**worry** *ant.* soothe

distribute *v.* give out, deliver, disperse, issue, circulate, allocate, ration ▷**dispense** *ant.* collect

district *n.* area, community, locality, neighbourhood, region

distrust *v.* disbelieve, doubt, suspect, discredit *ant.* trust

disturb *v.* annoy, bother, unsettle, interrupt, upset, confuse, agitate, disrupt *ant.* calm

dive *v.* plunge, swoop, descend, drop, pitch

diverse *adj.* different, various, dissimilar, numerous, mixed *ant.* identical

divert *v.* ① alter, change, deflect, turn ② entertain, gratify, amuse

divide *v.* ① separate, dissect, part, divorce, split *ant.* join ② distribute, apportion

division *n.* ① portion, fragment, section, segment ② department, branch, unit

divorce *v.* separate, part, split up, terminate

divulge *v.* disclose, tell, announce, broadcast *If you broadcast the news, I will be so embarrassed.* uncover, betray

dizzy *adj.* giddy, confused, shaky, wobbly, muddled, staggering, unsteady, woozy

do *v.* ① carry out, perform, act, achieve, finish, execute ② be adequate, suffice, serve *hom.* dew, due

docile *adj.* gentle, tame, meek, submissive, manageable, amenable

doctrine *n.* teaching, belief, creed, dogma, article, principle, faith

document *n.* paper, deed, certificate, form

dodge *v.* avoid, duck, elude, escape, miss

doleful *adj.* sad, dismal, glum, rueful ▷**gloomy** *ant.* cheerful

domestic *adj.* ① family, homely, household *Everyone in our home helps with the household chores.* internal ② domesticated, tame ③ native

dominant *adj.* controlling, powerful, commanding, primary *ant.* subordinate

dominate *v.* rule, control, direct, command, lord it over, tyrannize, overbear

donation *n.* gift, present, contribution

doom *n.* judgment, fate, verdict, destiny

door *n.* entrance, exit, doorway, gateway

dose *n.* quantity, amount, heap, taste

doubt ① *v.* waver, suspect, mistrust, question, distrust, disbelieve ② *n.* question, suspicion, uncertainty, mistrust

doubtful *adj.* suspicious, dubious, indefinite, uncertain, unclear, sceptical, ambiguous *ant.* certain

downcast *adj.* depressed, sad, discouraged, dejected ▷**miserable** *ant.* happy

downfall *n.* ruin, overthrow, misfortune, disgrace, failure, defeat

D
d
d
d
D
d
D

n. = noun
v. = verb
adj. = adjective
adv. = adverb
conj. = conjunction
prep. = preposition
ant. = antonym
hom. = homonym
▷ = cross-reference

downright *adj.* ① blunt, candid, forthright *He was a forthright person who always said what he thought.* straightforward ② thorough, complete, positive, absolute

doze *v.* sleep, drowse, nap, snooze, slumber *hom.* does

drab *adj.* colourless, cheerless, dull, gloomy, grey, dingy, flat ▷**dreary** *ant.* bright

draft *v.* outline, draw up, design, compose

drag *v.* draw, pull, haul, tug, tow, lug

drain ① *v.* strain, drip, empty, dry, drink up, exhaust, decrease ② *n.* outlet, sewer, pipe

dramatic *adj.* theatrical, exciting, surprising, sensational, spectacular *ant.* ordinary

drape *v.* hang, suspend, droop, cover, sprawl

drastic *adj.* extreme, desperate, harsh, radical, dire *ant.* mild

draw *v.* ① sketch, illustrate, design, depict ② pull, tug, drag, attract

drawback *n.* weakness, shortcoming, failing, defect, handicap, disadvantage *ant.* advantage

dread *n.* fear, terror, horror, alarm, awe, dismay, anxiety ▷**fright**

dream *n.* trance, vision, fancy, reverie, fantasy, illusion

dreary *adj.* ① dingy, gloomy, sombre, cheerless ▷**dismal** *ant.* bright ② boring, tiresome

drench *v.* wet, saturate, soak, flood

dress ① *n.* clothing, costume, garb, apparel, attire ② *v.* clothe, attire, array

drift *v.* float, flow, wander, stray, slide, meander *The people meandered here and there through the fairground.*

drill *v.* ① teach, exercise, train, discipline ② bore, penetrate, pierce

drink *v.* sip, swallow, gulp, guzzle, imbibe, absorb

drip *v.* drop, ooze, percolate, drizzle, trickle

drive *v.* ① force, make, compel, oblige, prod, goad ② guide, direct, propel, operate

drizzle *v.* sprinkle, shower, spit ▷**rain**

droll *adj.* amusing, whimsical, comical ▷**funny**

droop *v.* sag, wilt, sink, decline, languish, drop, bend, wither

drop ① *v.* fall, sink, dip, plunge, tumble, collapse ② *n.* bead, droplet, drip, globule ③ *v.* abandon, release, discard, reliquish

drown *v.* sink, immerse *Immerse the egg in water and see if it will float.* swamp, submerge, flood

drowsy *adj.* sleepy, dazed, tired, somnolent

drug *v.* dope, sedate, deaden, stupefy, poison

dry *adj.* ① arid, parched, moistureless, dried up, thirsty *ant.* wet ② dull, boring, uninteresting, tedious, monotonous

dubious *adj.* suspicious, fishy, suspect, untrustworthy, distrustful ▷**doubtful** *ant.* trustworthy

duck ① *n.* water fowl ② *v.* plunge, submerge, dip ③ *v.* dodge, evade, avoid

due *adj.* ① owing, unpaid, payable ② scheduled, expected ③ just, fair, proper, fit *hom.* dew

duel *n.* combat, contest, battle

dull *adj.* ① blunt, not sharp ② boring, uninteresting, tedious, monotonous, lifeless ③ flat, drab

dumb *adj.* ① mute, silent, speechless ② foolish, stupid ▷**dense**

dummy ① *n.* mannequin, puppet, doll ② *adj.* artificial, fake, false

dump *v.* dispose of, discard, ditch, empty, throw away, unload, abandon

dungeon *n.* cell, prison, jail, vault

duplicate *n.* copy, facsimile, replica, reproduction, double, likeness

durable *adj.* lasting, enduring, solid, tough, sturdy, stable, reliable *ant.* fragile

dusk *n.* twilight, nightfall, evening *ant.* dawn

dusty *adj.* gritty, dirty, filthy, grubby

duty *n.* ① obligation, responsibility, allegiance, trust, task, charge ② tax, excise, custom

dwell *v.* ① stay, rest, linger ② live, reside, occupy, inhabit ③ brood, reflect, meditate

dwindle *v.* diminish, decrease, decline, waste, shrink *ant.* increase

dye *n.* colour, stain, tint, pigment *hom.* die

E e

eager *adj.* avid, enthusiastic, ambitious, ardent, zealous ▷**keen** *ant.* indifferent

early *adj.* ① previous, prior, initial, first *ant.* latter ② premature, untimely *ant.* late

earn *v.* gain, get, make money, deserve, rate, merit, win, acquire *ant.* spend *hom.* urn

earnest *adj.* serious, sincere, determined, eager, zealous, ardent

earth *n.* ① soil, dirt, ground, dust ② world, globe, sphere

ease *n.* ① calm, rest, quiet, peace, comfort, security, well-being *ant.* tension ② knack, effortlessness, deftness *ant.* difficulty

easy *adj.* effortless, simple, uncomplicated, elementary, comfortable *ant.* difficult

eat *v.* consume, dine, chew, swallow, gorge

eccentric *adj.* different, strange, odd, erratic, unusual, weird ▷**peculiar** *ant.* normal

echo *v.* repeat, mimic, reverberate, imitate, parrot

economical *adj.* moderate, reasonable, frugal *Be frugal and save some of your allowance.* prudent, stingy ▷**thrifty** *ant.* extravagant

ecstasy *n.* joy, happiness, delight, elation, thrill, rapture ▷**bliss** *ant.* misery

edge *n.* border, boundary, brim, rim, brink, side, limit ▷**end**

edit *v.* revise, correct, adapt, censor, publish

educate *v.* instruct, teach, tutor, coach, train

educated *adj.* learned, knowledgeable, literate, well-informed *ant.* ignorant

eerie *adj.* weird, mysterious, strange, unearthly, creepy

effect ① *n.* result, end, outcome *Mix sand and water, and what is the outcome?* consequence ② *v.* produce, make, bring about, accomplish

effective *adj.* operative, productive, efficient, competent

efficient *adj.* competent, proficient, able, productive ▷**effective** *ant.* inefficient

effort *n.* exertion, labour, toil, energy, attempt

eject *v.* expel, evict, oust, dismiss, throw out, discharge, drive out, force out

elaborate ① *adj.* complex, elegant, ornate *Should she bring her pet goose into such an ornate room?* intricate, detailed, fancy *ant.* simple ② *v.* develop, expand, flesh out

elated *adj.* delighted, ecstatic, excited, gleeful, overjoyed *ant.* downcast

elderly *adj.* old, aged, ancient *ant.* young

elect *v.* vote, pick, select, choose, opt for

elegant *adj.* refined, polished, delicate, exquisite ▷**graceful** *ant.* coarse

elementary *adj.* easy, effortless, basic, beginning, clear ▷**simple** *ant.* complex

elevate *v.* raise, exalt, glorify, hoist, boost, heighten ▷**lift** *ant.* lower

eligible *adj.* qualified, suitable, acceptable, proper ▷**fit** *ant.* unfit

eliminate *v.* rule out, remove, abolish, erase, delete *ant.* keep

elude *v.* evade, avoid, dodge, escape

Eating Verbs

binge, bolt, breakfast
chew, chomp, consume
devour, dig in, dine
eat, eat up
feast, feed, finish off
gobble, gorge, gulp, guzzle
lap up, lunch
masticate, munch
nibble
partake, pick at
relish

sample, savour, snack, sup, swallow
taste, tuck in
wolf down

E
e
E
e
E
e
E

embarrass v. shame, humiliate, confuse, disconcert, fluster

emblem n. badge, mark, brand, sign, crest, symbol

embrace v. ① hug, squeeze, cuddle, caress, hold ② contain, include, encompass, enclose ③ accept, adopt

emerge v. come out, exit, appear, arise, turn up, develop *ant.* disappear

emergency n. crisis, danger, dilemma, problem, difficulty, predicament ▷**plight**

eminent adj. famous, noted, renowned *People from all over came to meet the renowned artist.* well-known, esteemed, prominent ▷**important** *ant.* unknown

emit v. give off, release, radiate, discharge, vent, issue *ant.* absorb

emotion n. sentiment, feeling, fervour, passion

emotional adj. moving, sensitive, responsive, temperamental *ant.* cold

emphasize v. accent, intensify, highlight, magnify ▷**stress** *ant.* underrate

employ v. engage, hire, retain, enlist, apply, adopt ▷**use**

empty ① adj. bare, barren, vacant, unoccupied, void, blank, meaningless *ant.* full ② v. discharge, drain, unload, pour out *ant.* fill

enchant v. enthral, bewitch, delight, fascinate ▷**charm** *ant.* bore

enclose v. surround, encircle, encompass, contain, include, confine, wrap

encounter v. meet, experience, face, confront

encourage v. cheer, inspire, motivate, promote, hearten, console, comfort, support ▷**urge** *ant.* dissuade

end ① n. result, purpose, goal, conclusion, finish, limit, boundary ② v. stop, cease, complete, close, terminate ▷**finish**

endanger v. jeopardize, expose, threaten, imperil *ant.* protect

endeavour v. attempt, aspire, strive, struggle, try ▷**aim**

endless adj. infinite, perpetual, continuous, everlasting, limitless, vast

endowed adj. talented, gifted, enhanced

endure v. bear, tolerate, suffer, go through, experience, cope with, persist

enemy n. opponent, rival, competitor *If I had no competitors, I might not do as well.* foe, adversary, antagonist *ant.* friend

energetic adj. dynamic, lively, strenuous, vital, spirited, brisk, peppy, animated, active ▷**vigorous** *ant.* sluggish

energy n. vitality, force, power, spirit, strength, vim, pep, vigour, endurance, stamina

enforce v. apply, administer, carry out

engage v. ① pledge, betroth ② involve, occupy *That new book has occupied my mind for weeks.* operate

engine n. motor, machine, locomotive, turbine

engrave v. etch, sculpt, carve, chisel, stamp, cut

engrossed adj. absorbed, occupied, fascinated, enthralled *ant.* bored

enhance v. increase, intensify, strengthen, amplify, improve, enrich *ant.* decrease

enigma n. mystery, puzzle, riddle, problem

enjoy v. like, appreciate, savour, admire, have ▷**relish**

enjoyable adj. likable, pleasant, delicious ▷**agreeable** *ant.* disagreeable

enlarge v. increase, grow, expand, extend, broaden, magnify, augment ▷**swell** *ant.* shrink

enlighten v. inform, teach, explain to, educate, instruct *ant.* confuse

enlist v. ① conscript, employ, engage ② join, sign up, volunteer

enormous adj. immense, vast, tremendous, massive, gigantic ▷**huge** *ant.* tiny

enough adj. sufficient, adequate, ample, plenty, satisfactory *ant.* insufficient

enrage v. aggravate, incite, incense, infuriate, provoke ▷**anger** *ant.* soothe

enrich v. enhance, embellish, adorn, improve, fertilize *ant.* impoverish

enrol v. sign up, enlist, register, join

ensue v. develop, follow, result, arise, occur ▷**happen** *ant.* precede

n. = noun
v. = verb
adj. = adjective
adv. = adverb
conj. = conjunction
prep. = preposition
ant. = antonym
hom. = homonym
▷ = cross-reference

Engines

Diesel engine
Internal combustion engine
Jet engine
Piston engine
Steam engine
Turbojet engine
Turboprop engine
Wankel engine

ensure *v.* confirm, guarantee, insure, protect, secure

entangle *v.* involve, catch, tangle, snarl, ensnare, complicate ▷**mix up** *ant.* free

enter *v.* go in, arrive, enrol, invade, intrude, commence, penetrate, start, join *ant.* leave

enterprise *n.* endeavour, adventure, undertaking, concern, establishment

entertain *v.* amuse, charm, cheer, please, divert *ant.* bore

enthusiasm *n.* fervour, ardour, interest, spirit, passion, eagerness

entice *v.* attract, beguile, coax, lead on, tempt

entire *adj.* complete, intact, total, whole, full *ant.* partial

entirely *adj.* completely, absolutely, wholly, utterly *ant.* partially

entitle *v.* ① allow, authorize, empower, enable ② call, christen, term, name

entrance ① *n.* (*en*-trance) way in, access, doorway, gate, opening, admission ② *v.* (en-*trance*) bewitch, captivate, charm *ant.* repel

entry *n.* access, admission, admittance ▷**entrance** *ant.* exit

envelop *v.* wrap, wind, roll, cloak, conceal *A thick scarf concealed most of his face.* enfold

envious *adj.* jealous, grudging, covetous resentful *ant.* content

environment *n.* surroundings, scene, locale *Let's film this scene on locale at the docks, and not in the studio.* vicinity, background, atmosphere

envy *v.* covet, begrudge, desire, crave, resent

episode *n.* incident, event, occasion, affair, circumstance, happening, instalment

equal *adj.* ① matching, like, alike, same, identical, equivalent *ant.* different ② fair, even, impartial *ant.* unfair

equip *v.* furnish, provide, supply, prepare, rig

equipment *n.* gear, supplies, stores, outfit, apparatus, implements, tackle *When they reached the lake, they discovered they'd left all their fishing tackle behind.*

equivalent *adj.* same, equal, comparable, alike, similar, interchangeable, synonymous *ant.* unlike

era *n.* age, period, time, epoch, generation

erase *v.* cancel, rub out, delete, obliterate, eliminate ▷**remove**

erect ① *adj.* upright, straight, vertical, tall ② *v.* build, construct, put up *ant.* demolish

err *v.* be mistaken, blunder, misjudge, miscalculate, deviate, go astray, slip up

errand *n.* mission, assignment, duty, job, chore ▷**task**

erratic *adj.* eccentric, irregular, unstable, unreliable, wandering *ant.* stable

erroneous *adj.* untrue, false, faulty, inaccurate, incorrect ▷**wrong** *ant.* correct

error *n.* mistake, fault, flaw, fallacy, failing ▷**blunder** *ant.* truth

erupt *v.* explode, burst, spew, vent, blow up

escape *v.* break free, get away, dodge, elude, evade, avoid ▷**flee** *ant.* face, endure

escort ① *n.* (*es*-cort) guard, aide, attendant, date ② *v.* (es-*cort*) accompany, conduct, guide

especially *adv.* particularly, chiefly, principally, notably

Confusable Words

especially means *particularly*
specially means *uniquely*

E e E e e E

n. = noun
v. = verb
adj. = adjective
adv. = adverb
conj. = conjunction
prep. = preposition
ant. = antonym
hom. = homonym
▷ = cross-reference

essay ① *n.* (*es*-say) composition, story, manuscript ② *v.* (es-*say*) attempt, endeavour, undertake

essence *n.* ① extract, juice, perfume ② substance, core, pith, heart, character

essential *adj.* necessary, needed, vital, key, basic, fundamental, important *ant.* superfluous

establish *v.* situate, place, start, found, organize, set up, institute *ant.* upset

estate *n.* ① inheritance, fortune ② land, property

esteem *v.* honour, respect, admire, regard ▷**like** *ant.* dislike

estimate *v.* approximate, count, consider, calculate, figure, assess, reckon, appraise, evaluate, judge

eternal *adj.* everlasting, endless, ceaseless, immortal, undying, infinite, continual *ant.* temporary

evacuate *v.* leave, desert, quit, empty, vacate ▷**abandon** *ant.* occupy, fill

evade *v.* elude *When you play tag, you must try to elude the player who is "it."* avoid, dodge, escape from *ant.* face

evaporate *v.* vanish, dissolve, disappear, condense, dry up, vaporize, boil away

even *adj.* ① smooth, level, straight, flat, flush ② balanced, equal *ant.* uneven ③ calm, still, constant, steady, regular

evening *n.* eve, sunset, twilight, nightfall ▷**dusk** *ant.* morning

event *n.* incident, occurrence, occasion, thing

ever *adv.* always, forever, perpetually *ant.* never

everlasting *adj.* continual, endless, permanent, enduring *ant.* temporary

everyday *adj.* common, frequent, daily, familiar *ant.* rare

evict *v.* expel, eject, remove, kick out

evidence *n.* proof, testimony, facts, sign, grounds

evident *adj.* obvious, apparent, plain, visible, conspicuous *ant.* obscure

evil *adj.* wicked, sinister, wrong, bad, hurtful, sinful, immoral *ant.* good

Confusable Words

evoke means *call forth*

invoke means *appeal to*

exact *adj.* accurate, precise, definite, correct ▷**right** *ant.* approximate

exaggerate *v.* overstate, inflate *She inflated the truth so often that no one believed her any more.* stretch, magnify, overestimate *ant.* underrate

examine *v.* check, inspect, scrutinize *Joe scrutinized every detail carefully.* test, quiz, question, investigate, search, probe, study, analyse

example *n.* case, sample, specimen, pattern, model, illustration, instance, lesson

exasperate *v.* provoke, anger, annoy, aggravate *ant.* soothe

excavate *v.* dig up, shovel, mine, quarry, discover, unearth, remove *ant.* bury

exceed *v.* excel, surpass, better, beat, top,

excellent *adj.* great, superior, exceptional, superb, exquisite ▷**splendid** *ant.* poor

except *prep.* save, saving, omitting, barring, excluding

exceptional *adj.* unique, unusual, rare, uncommon, outstanding, excellent *ant.* ordinary

excess *n.* overabundance, glut, extreme, extravagance ▷**surplus** *ant.* scarcity

exchange *v.* trade, barter, swap, change, substitute, replace, interchange

excite *v.* inflame, inspire, provoke, rouse, thrill, stimulate, whet, agitate *ant.* calm

excited *adj.* wild, ecstatic, frantic, thrilled, restless, exhilarated, frenzied *ant.* bored

exclaim *v.* yell, shout, call, blurt, declare, cry out, squeal

exclude *v.* bar, shut out, prevent, boycott, rule out, prohibit, banish *ant.* include

exclusive *adj.* only, choice, particular, special, select, fancy *ant.* inclusive

excuse *v.* forgive, pardon, absolve, exempt, release, free, condone *ant.* accuse

execute *v.* ① accomplish, do, carry out, achieve, fulfil, perform ② put to death, kill

exempt *v.* excuse, release, discharge, relieve

exercise ① *n.* activity, practice, performance, lesson, drill, training ② *v.* use, drill, apply, train, practise *We have been practising our soccer skills for months.*

exert *v.* apply, exercise, strain, put forth, use

exhale *v.* breathe out, expel, expire

exhaust *v.* ① use up, consume, finish, deplete *We have depleted our supply of videotapes.* empty ② tire, weaken, fatigue, tax, strain

exhibition *n.* spectacle, show, fair, pageant, display, exposition

exhilarate *v.* invigorate, animate, stimulate, thrill, elate *ant.* discourage

exile *v.* deport, banish, expel, dismiss

exist *v.* be, live, breathe, subsist, survive

exit *n.* way out, outlet, door, gate, departure

expand *v.* inflate, spread, dilate, extend, amplify, stretch, increase, enlarge, strengthen, elaborate ▷**swell** *ant.* contract, reduce

expansive *adj.* genial, friendly, open, outgoing

expect *v.* anticipate, assume, foresee, contemplate, await, hope

expedition *n.* ① outing, excursion, exploration, quest *The thirst for gold inspired many quests in the Yukon Territory in 1896.* foray ② speed, haste

expel *v.* evict, eject, discharge, throw out, banish, exile *ant.* admit

expend *v.* spend, waste, consume, use up ▷**exhaust** *ant.* save

expensive *adj.* costly, dear, pricey, valuable *ant.* cheap

experience ① *n.* event, activity, incident, ordeal, adventure ② *n.* training, practice, wisdom, skill, knowledge ③ *v.* encounter, try, undergo, endure, meet, know, taste, live through, feel

experiment *n.* trial, test, check, venture

expert *n.* specialist, master, authority, professional, veteran *ant.* novice

expire *v.* ① exhale, breathe out ② die, lapse, run out, disappear *ant.* begin

explain *v.* define, describe, interpret, clarify, solve, resolve, teach

explanation *n.* definition, outline, answer, meaning, clarification, account, interpretation

explode *v.* detonate, blow up, erupt, blast, burst, discharge

exploit ① *n.* (*ex*-ploit) deed, feat, act, stunt ② *v.* (ex-*ploit*) abuse, take advantage of, manipulate, use

expose *v.* show, reveal, exhibit, lay bare, present, betray, uncover, disclose *ant.* cover

express ① *v.* phrase, voice, utter, tell, declare, communicate ② *adj.* speedy, fast, non-stop

expression *n.* ① phrase, figure of speech, idiom ② look, face, countenance, appearance

exquisite *adj.* dainty, subtle, fine, refined, delicate ▷**beautiful** *ant.* coarse

extend *v.* stretch, reach, lengthen, prolong, spread ▷**expand** *ant.* shorten

extent *n.* breadth, expanse, width, degree, reach, size, stretch, range, duration

exterior ① *n.* outside, surface, appearance ② *adj.* external, outer, outdoor *ant.* interior

extinct *adj.* defunct, dead, exterminated, finished, ended, vanished, gone *ant.* living

extinguish *v.* put out, blow out, abolish, destroy, quench, douse, snuff, suppress

extract *v.* take out, select, remove, withdraw, glean, pull *ant.* insert

extraordinary *adj.* ① unusual, incredible, strange, uncommon, marvellous, rare, odd, peculiar ② remarkable, amazing, exceptional, important *ant.* ordinary

extravagant *adj.* wasteful, reckless, prodigal, lavish, spendthrift, excessive *ant.* stingy, frugal

extreme *adj.* ① excessive, outrageous, intense *ant.* moderate ② farthest, final, remote, outermost *ant.* middle

exultant *adj.* rejoicing, jubilant, joyous, triumphant ▷**elated** *ant.* depressed

F f

fable *n.* myth, legend, story, fantasy *ant.* fact

fabric *n.* cloth, textile, material

fabulous *adj.* imaginary, legendary, mythical, marvellous ▷**wonderful**

face ① *n.* expression ② *n.* front, surface, façade ③ *v.* confront, defy, encounter

facetious *adj.* frivolous, jocular, witty, humorous, comical, amusing ▷**funny** *ant.* serious

facility *n.* ① ease, readiness, quickness, knack, skill ② convenience, building, installation, amenity

facsimile *n.* replica *You can see life-size replicas of dinosaurs in many Canadian museums.* copy, likeness, representation

fact *n.* truth, deed, occurrence, event, reality, actuality, certainty *ant.* fiction

factory *n.* plant, mill, shop

factual *adj.* true, actual, accurate, correct ▷**real** *ant.* false

fad *n.* craze, fashion, trend, mania, vogue

fade *v.* discolour, bleach, dwindle, dim, pale, weaken, wither, die, disappear, melt

fail *v.* collapse, fall, miss, slip, lose, flop, flunk *ant.* succeed

failing *n.* frailty, weakness, fault, flaw, shortcoming ▷**defect**

failure *n.* flop, collapse, crash, fiasco, downfall, disaster *ant.* success

faint ① *adj.* indistinct *The crayon marks on the wall were so indistinct that Dad could hardly see them.* soft, low, dim, feeble, weak, unclear, faded ② *v.* swoon, pass out, drop, collapse, crumple, black out *hom.* feint

fair *adj.* ① just, equal, reasonable, honest, neutral, impartial *ant.* unfair ② mediocre, average, moderate ③ blond, light-skinned, comely ④ beautiful, sunny, clear

faith *n.* ① trust, confidence, ② belief, creed

faithful *adj.* ① loyal, constant, true, devoted, trustworthy *ant.* faithless ② accurate, dependable, exact, close *ant.* inaccurate

faithless *adj.* false, unfaithful, untrue, disloyal *ant.* faithful

fake *adj.* false, fictitious, artificial, synthetic, fraudulent, counterfeit, phony, sham ▷**bogus** *ant.* genuine

fall *v.* ① drop, stumble, topple, slip, trip, descend ② decline, dwindle, lower, decrease, diminish *ant.* rise ③ collapse, fail, founder

fallacy *n.* error, mistake, illusion, deception

false *adj.* ① untrue, wrong, inaccurate *ant.* true ② fake, counterfeit *ant.* genuine

falsehood *n.* lie, fib, fiction, fable, untruth, fabrication *ant.* truth

falter *v.* reel, totter, stumble, waver, tremble, hesitate, lurch

fame *n.* glory, distinction, honour, eminence, renown, repute, celebrity, reputation

familiar *adj.* ① common, well-known, frequent ② friendly, intimate *I tell my most intimate friend all my secrets.* close, dear

famine *n.* scarcity, hunger, shortage, starvation

famished *adj.* hungry, starving, ravenous

famous *adj.* famed, well-known, celebrated, prominent, popular, legendary, notorious *ant.* unknown

fan ① *v.* cool, blow, stimulate ② *n.* supporter, admirer, follower

fanatic *n.* enthusiast, zealot, devotee, extremist

fancy ① *adj.* decorative, ornate, ornamental *Her handwriting is full of ornamental flourishes.* ② elegant, refined, lavish

fantastic *adj.* strange, bizarre, marvellous, wonderful, imaginary *ant.* ordinary

far *adj.* distant, faraway, remote *ant.* near

fare ① *n.* charge, cost, fee, price ② *n.* food, meals, menu, rations, provisions ③ *v.* manage, get along, turn out *hom.* fair

farm ① *v.* cultivate, raise, grow ② *n.* farmstead, homestead, ranch

fascinate *v.* bewitch, beguile, engross *She was so engrossed by the scene outside her window, she didn't hear the phone ring.* charm, enchant, intrigue *ant.* bore

n. = noun
v. = verb
adj. = adjective
adv. = adverb
conj. = conjunction
prep. = preposition
ant. = antonym
hom. = homonym
▷ = cross-reference

fashion ① *n.* style, fad, vogue, craze, trend, mode ② *v.* make, create, build, shape, form

fast ① *adj.* rapid, quick, speedy, swift, express ② *v.* starve, famish, go hungry

fasten *v.* fix, tie, attach, bind, hitch, hook, clasp, secure *ant.* unfasten

fat ① *adj.* stout, chubby, chunky, obese, overweight ▷**plump** *ant.* thin ② *n.* grease, oil

fatal *adj.* deadly, lethal, destructive, mortal, terminal, disastrous *ant.* harmless

fate *n.* fortune, destiny, future, luck, chance, doom

fatigue ① *n.* exhaustion, tiredness, weariness ② *v.* tire, exhaust, drain, tax, wear out

fault *n.* ① defect, flaw, imperfection, blemish ② blame, responsibility, error, mistake

faulty *adj.* imperfect, defective *It is unwise to drive with defective brakes.* unreliable, unsound, broken *ant.* perfect

favour ① *n.* kindness, courtesy, benefit, help, support ② *v.* indulge, prefer, approve *ant.* disapprove

Fare

Fare

favourite ① *n.* choice, darling, preference, pet ② *adj.* best-liked, chosen, preferred, popular, adored

fear ① *n.* fright, alarm, terror, panic, shock, horror *ant.* courage ② *v.* dread, be afraid, doubt, tremble, shudder

fearful *adj.* timid, anxious, alarmed, worried, cowardly ▷**afraid** *ant.* courageous

fearless *adj.* gallant, courageous, daring, valiant *The injured player made a valiant effort to keep going.* ▷**brave** *ant.* cowardly

feast *n.* banquet, dinner, meal, spread

feat *n.* deed, exploit, achievement, stunt, performance, accomplishment *hom.* feet

feature *n.* quality, characteristic, distinction, peculiarity, mark

fee *n.* charge, cost, payment, bill, fare

feeble *adj.* ① sickly, unhealthy, frail, faint ▷**weak** *ant.* strong ② useless, hopeless, ineffective

feed *v.* nourish, sustain, foster *My work at the veterinary clinic is fostering my love of animals.* nurse, nurture

feel *v.* ① touch, handle ② perceive, comprehend, know, suffer, understand

fellow *n.* human being, man, guy, peer, companion, associate, colleague, mate

female *adj.* feminine, womanly, girlish *ant.* male

fence ① *n.* barrier, barricade, wall ② *v.* wall, enclose, surround

ferocious *adj.* fierce, savage, brutal, vicious, wild, violent, cruel *ant.* gentle

fertile *adj.* fruitful, productive, rich, abundant *ant.* barren

fervent *adj.* warm, passionate, enthusiastic, zealous ▷**ardent**

festival *n.* celebration, carnival, jubilee, holiday, feast, ceremony

festive *adj.* gleeful, merry, glad, joyful, convivial, holiday, celebratory, jovial *ant.* sombre

fetch *v.* bear, bring, carry, deliver, convey

feud *n.* dispute, grudge, conflict, discord, quarrel, argument, spat, fight, squabble *ant.* harmony

F f f F f F F f F

fever *n.* ① illness, infection ② passion, excitement, heat, ecstasy

few *adj.* scanty, scarce, rare, infrequent

fiasco *n.* disaster, failure, scandal

fib *n.* lie, untruth ▷**falsehood**

fickle *adj.* unstable, changeable, flighty, unpredictable, moody, faithless, disloyal *ant.* constant

Flags

Yukon Territory

Northwest Territories

British Columbia

Alberta

Saskatchewan

Manitoba

Prince Edward Island

New Brunswick

Québec

Newfoundland

Ontario

Nova Scotia

n. = noun
v. = verb
adj. = adjective
adv. = adverb
conj. = conjunction
prep. = preposition
ant. = antonym
hom. = homonym
▷ = cross-reference

fiction *n.* story, fable, myth, legend, fantasy, yarn, tale, invention *ant.* fact

fidget *v.* fret, fuss, wiggle, squirm, wriggle, writhe, fiddle

field *n.* farmland, grassland, green, meadow, prairie, paddock, area

fiend *n.* devil, demon, beast, brute, monster

fiendish *adj.* cruel, devilish, diabolical, sinister, vicious

fierce *adj.* cruel, brutal, merciless, vicious, barbarous, intense ▷**savage** *ant.* gentle

fiery *adj.* blazing, hot, spirited, passionate, inflamed, excitable, flaming *ant.* mild

fight ① *n.* conflict, argument, encounter, scuffle ② *v.* contest, battle, quarrel, feud, brawl, argue, combat, struggle, strive, oppose, resist, squabble

figure ① *n.* symbol, character, numeral, digit ② *n.* form, shape, pattern, model ③ *v.* calculate *Lorna has calculated the amount correctly.* count, total, add, reckon

file ① *v.* scrape, grind, grate, rasp ② *n.* binder, case, folder

fill *v.* load, pack, cram, heap, pile, stuff, stock *ant.* empty

filter *v.* sift, strain, purify, clarify, screen, percolate

filth *n.* dirt, soil, slime, smut, grime, muck

filthy *adj.* unclean, impure, nasty, foul, squalid, polluted ▷**dirty** *ant.* pure

final *adj.* terminal, closing, ultimate, conclusive ▷**last**

find *v.* discover, achieve, locate, uncover, spot, perceive *ant.* lose *hom.* fined

fine ① *adj.* thin, minute, tiny, smooth, slender ② *adj.* excellent, sharp, keen, acute, choice ③ *n.* penalty, punishment, fee

finesse *n.* skill, competence, deftness

finger ① *v.* feel, handle, touch ② *n.* digit

finish *v.* accomplish, complete, close, conclude, achieve, terminate ▷**end** *ant.* begin

fire ① *n.* blaze, heat, flame, flare, glow ② *v.* ignite, light, discharge, shoot

firm ① *adj.* stable, steady, solid, fixed, hard, substantial ② *n.* company, business

first *adj.* beginning, earliest, leading, initial *Alexander Graham Bell made the initial telephone call to his uncle in Brantford, Ontario.* original, chief, principal

fishy *adj.* suspicious, dubious *We listened politely to his story about seeing the Abominable Snowman, but we really thought it sounded dubious.* shady, doubtful *ant.* honest

fissure *n.* breach, cleft, crack, cranny *hom.* fisher

fit *adj.* ① appropriate, suitable ② healthy, sturdy

fitting *adj.* proper, suitable, appropriate, correct *ant.* unsuitable

fix ① *v.* repair, cure, heal, mend ② *n.* predicament, jam, pickle, plight

flabby *adj.* baggy, drooping, sagging, slack, limp

flag ① *v.* signal, hail ② *n.* pennant, banner, ensign, colours

flagrant *adj.* blatant *No one could help noticing his blatant cruelty to others.* bold, brazen, obvious, shocking, outrageous

flair *n.* knack, talent, ability, gift *hom.* flare

flame *n.* fire, blaze, radiance

flap *v.* flutter, waggle, flop, fly, wave, swing

flare ① *v.* blaze, burn, flash, glow, break out ② *n.* signal, beacon *hom.* flair

flash *v.* ① gleam, glimmer, sparkle, twinkle, glint, glitter, shimmer, blink ② rush, streak, dash

flat *adj.* level, smooth, even, horizontal, prone

flatter *v.* praise, compliment, butter up, sweet-talk, soft-soap *ant.* criticize

flavour *n.* taste, savour, tang, aroma, quality, seasoning

flaw *n.* fault, defect, blemish, mark, weakness

flawless *adj.* perfect, immaculate, faultless, clear, excellent *ant.* imperfect

flee *v.* escape, abscond *She absconded with the ring, and no one ever saw it again.* vanish, run away *ant.* stay *hom.* flea

fleeting *adj.* passing, brief, momentary, temporary *ant.* permanent

flexible *adj.* bendable, floppy, pliant, pliable, supple *The supple gymnast could do the splits.* elastic, adaptable, versatile

flicker *v.* waver, glitter, flash, burn, sparkle

flimsy *adj.* slight, fragile, rickety, weak, frail, feeble *ant.* sturdy

flinch *v.* cower, cringe, shrink, wince

fling *v.* throw, pitch, cast, heave, toss, hurl

float *v.* drift, glide, hover, sail, swim

flock *n.* herd, crowd, group, gaggle

flog *v.* beat, chastise, lash, whip

flood *v.* deluge, engulf, inundate, drown, swamp, overwhelm, surge

floor *n.* deck, base, bottom, platform, level, storey, ground

flop *v.* flap, fall, drop, droop, fail

flounder ① *v.* stumble, fail, falter, fumble, wallow ② *n.* flatfish

flourish *v.* ① shake, brandish, flaunt ② bloom, blossom, sprout, prosper ▷**thrive**

flow *v.* run, stream, glide, sweep, swirl ▷**gush** *hom.* floe

flower *n.* & *v.* blossom, bloom, bud *hom.* flour

fluent *adj.* vocal, articulate *Two-year-old Jordan knows many words and is very articulate.* eloquent, smooth, flowing, fluid

fluid *adj.* watery, flowing, liquid, runny *ant.* solid

flush ① *v.* glow, blush ② *v.* swab, drench, rinse ③ *adj.* level, even, flat

fluster *v.* bother, rattle, startle, agitate, confuse, ruffle, disconcert *ant.* calm

flutter *v.* wave, flap, flitter, hover, flit

fly *v.* ① glide, soar, float, hover ② escape, flee ③ rush, whiz, dash, zoom

foam *n.* fizz, froth, scum, lather, suds, surf

foe *n.* enemy, opponent, rival, adversary *ant.* friend

fog *n.* mist, vapour, haze, cloud, daze

foil *v.* frustrate, prevent, thwart

fold *n.* & *v.* crease, crimp, pleat, bend

follow *v.* ① pursue, trail, chase, track, succeed, come after ② understand, catch on to, comprehend ③ obey, conform, observe

fond *adj.* tender, loving, devoted ▷**affectionate** *ant.* hostile

fondle *v.* pet, stroke, cuddle, caress, touch

food *n.* nourishment, provisions, fare, sustenance, cuisine

fool ① *n.* idiot, dunce, clown, blockhead, simpleton ② *v.* cheat, hoax, deceive, trick, dupe

foolhardy *adj.* reckless, impetuous *Without even saying goodbye, she impetuously ran off to join the circus.* madcap ▷**rash** *ant.* cautious

foolish *adj.* absurd, ridiculous, senseless, frivolous ▷**silly** *ant.* wise

forbid *v.* bar, ban, prohibit, deter, disallow, deny, refuse, prevent *ant.* allow

force ① *n.* energy, strength, might, power, vigour, impact ② *v.* make, compel, coerce *No matter what you do, you can't coerce me into going.* push, drive, urge, bully

forecast *v.* foresee, predict, foretell, prophesy

foreign *adj.* alien, strange, remote, exotic, unfamiliar, imported, outlandish *ant.* familiar

foremost *adj.* chief, leading, principal

forfeit *v.* abandon, give up, lose, relinquish, sacrifice *ant.* gain

forge *v.* ① counterfeit, falsify, copy, fake ② construct, form, make, fashion, create

forgery *n.* fake, counterfeit, imitation, phony, sham, fraud

forget *v.* overlook, neglect, lose sight of, disregard *ant.* remember

forgive *v.* pardon, excuse, release, reprieve, clear, acquit, let off, overlook *ant.* blame

forlorn *adj.* lonely, desolate, miserable, wretched *ant.* hopeful

Flower

Flour

form ① *v.* make, shape, fashion, contrive, create ② *n.* type, fashion, style ③ *n.* shape, figure

formal *adj.* stiff, solemn, ceremonial, dignified, dressy *ant.* informal

former *adj.* earlier, previous, prior, first *ant.* latter

formidable *adj.* awesome, terrible, alarming, fearsome, terrifying, serious *ant.* trivial

forsake *v.* abandon, give up, desert, discard, leave ▷**quit** *ant.* resume

forth *adv.* ahead, forward, onward, outward

forthright *adj.* frank, candid, direct, sincere, bald, blunt *ant.* devious

fortify *v.* ① strengthen, confirm, hearten ② garrison, protect, buttress *The farmer buttressed the crumbling wall with large rocks. ant.* weaken

fortitude *n.* courage, endurance, stamina ▷**strength** *ant.* cowardice

fortunate *adj.* happy, favourable, auspicious, rosy, felicitous ▷**lucky** *ant.* unfortunate

fortune *n.* ① affluence, wealth, riches, treasure ② chance, destiny, fate, luck

forward ① *adv.* onward, forth, ahead ② *adj.* aggressive, bold, audacious *ant.* modest ③ *v.* advance, send, transmit

foster *v.* help, promote, aid, cherish, nurse

foul *adj.* rotten, vile, rancid, nasty, filthy, dirty, murky *ant.* fair *hom.* fowl

found *v.* start, create, build, erect, establish

foundation *n.* base, basis, groundwork *He knew Spanish, and this formed the groundwork for studying Italian.*

fountain *n.* spring, well, reservoir, source, origin

fowl *n.* bird, chicken, poultry *hom.* foul

foxy *adj.* crafty, slick, cunning, tricky, deceitful, sly ▷**artful** *ant.* naïve

fraction *n.* portion, part, piece, division ▷**fragment**

fracture *n.* break, cleft, crack, fissure, rupture, breach, opening, split

fragile *adj.* brittle, frail, delicate, weak, breakable, dainty ▷**flimsy** *ant.* robust

fragment *n.* portion, bit, chip, morsel, piece, shard ▷**fraction**

fragrance *n.* aroma, smell, odour, bouquet, perfume ▷**scent**

frail *adj.* weak, feeble, infirm ▷**fragile**

frame *n.* framework, casing, shape, chassis

frank *adj.* direct, straightforward, sincere, candid, open, honest, blunt ▷**truthful** *ant.* insincere

frantic *adj.* excited, furious, distracted, wild, delirious, agitated, mad ▷**frenzied** *ant.* calm

fraud *n.* cheat, deceit, fake, extortion, swindle ▷**forgery**

fraudulent *adj.* sham, fake, counterfeit ▷**bogus** *ant.* genuine

freak *adj.* abnormal, bizarre *A snowstorm in Victoria would be a bizarre event.* odd, unusual *ant.* common

free ① *adj.* unhindered, liberated, loose, untied, independent, unrestricted ② *adj.* complimentary, gratis, without cost ③ *v.* let loose, unleash, release, liberate, emancipate, discharge

freeze *v.* ice, chill, congeal, refrigerate, harden, immobilize *hom.* frees, frieze

frenzied *adj.* agitated, excited, furious, hysterical *He was suddenly seized with hysterical laughter.* ▷**frantic** *ant.* placid

frequent *adj.* repeated, numerous, recurrent, persistent, common ▷**regular** *ant.* rare

frequently *adv.* often, many times, commonly *ant.* seldom

fresh *adj.* new, young, vigorous, blooming, recent, wholesome, pure, novel, healthy *ant.* stale

friction *n.* ① rubbing, grating, contact, abrasion ② ill feeling, discord, dispute, conflict, disharmony

friend *n.* buddy, companion, associate, ally, chum, crony, pal *On Saturdays, my father plays boccie with some of his pals.*

friendly *adj.* warm, sociable, personable, amicable, kindly, cordial, outgoing ▷**genial** *ant.* hostile

friendship *n.* affection, fellowship, fondness, harmony, concord

fright *n.* alarm, dread, dismay, terror, panic ▷**fear** *ant.* calm

F f F f F f F

frighten *v.* dismay, scare, alarm, shock, threaten, petrify ▷**terrify** *ant.* reassure

frigid *adj.* frosty, cold, chilly, icy, frozen, wintry *ant.* warm

fringe *n.* edge, border, limits, outskirts

frisky *adj.* lively, spirited, playful, active *ant.* quiet

frivolous *adj.* foolish, giddy, silly, flippant, frothy ▷**trivial** *ant.* serious

front *n.* fore, face, façade, beginning, pretence, appearance *ant.* back

frontier *n.* border, boundary, edge, limit

frosty *adj.* chilly, frigid, frozen, freezing, unfriendly ▷**cold** *ant.* warm

froth *n.* scum, bubbles ▷**foam**

frown *v.* glower, grimace *She grimaced when she heard her sister practising violin.* glare, pout, mope, sulk ▷**scowl** *ant.* smile

frugal *adj.* thrifty, economical, careful, simple *ant.* wasteful

fruitful *adj.* fertile, productive, flourishing, plentiful, abundant, profitable *ant.* barren

fruitless *adj.* unprofitable, sterile, barren, pointless, futile *ant.* fruitful

frustrate *v.* discourage, foil, hinder, defeat *ant.* fulfil

fugitive *n.* escapee, runaway, deserter

fulfil *v.* perform, accomplish, achieve, finish, complete, carry out, realize, satisfy *ant.* frustrate

full *adj.* loaded, packed, stuffed, filled, crammed, abundant, complete *ant.* empty

fumble *v.* ① grope ② botch, spoil, mismanage, flub ▷**bungle**

fun *n.* entertainment, amusement, enjoyment, play

function ① *n.* job, role, purpose, use, duty ② *n.* affair, party, gathering ③ *v.* act, operate, work, behave

fund *n.* stock, supply, pool, store, treasury *Her stories are a treasury of information about Canada's past.* kitty, reserve

fundamental *adj.* basic, essential, primary *ant.* unimportant

funny *adj.* comical, entertaining, hilarious, amusing, ridiculous, droll ▷**humorous** *ant.* solemn, sad

furious *adj.* enraged, angry, fierce, intense, irate ▷**frantic** *ant.* calm

furnish *v.* supply, provide, offer, give, equip

furrow *n.* groove, channel, hollow, seam, rib, line

further ① *adj.* extra, more, other, additional, supplementary ② *v.* help, promote, facilitate *I can facilitate your party preparations by helping you blow up balloons.* ease, advance, aid

furtive *adj.* secretive, sly, hidden ▷**stealthy** *ant.* open

fury *n.* anger, frenzy, ferocity, passion, wrath ▷**rage** *ant.* calm

fuse *v.* glue, melt, smelt, combine, merge, solder, weld, integrate ▷**join**

fuss *n.* stir, excitement, tumult, bustle, commotion, worry, disquiet, unrest, ado ▷**uproar** *ant.* calm

fussy *adj.* fancy, fastidious, finicky, exacting, impatient, cranky *ant.* plain

futile *adj.* useless, vain, hopeless *It was hopeless—the bear was too big for Zak to carry.* barren, ineffective *ant.* effective

future *adj.* forthcoming, coming, impending, eventual, next, imminent

fuzzy *adj.* murky, foggy, misty, unclear

Futile

It was hopeless—the bear was too big for Zak to carry.

G g

gain *v.* get, win, earn, obtain, acquire, attain, profit

gale *n.* storm, wind, hurricane, tornado, cyclone

gallant *adj.* courageous, noble, valiant, heroic, chivalrous ▷**brave**

gallop *v.* dash, run, ride, hurry, rush

gamble *v. & n.* bet, risk, wager, chance *hom.* gambol

game *n.* ① sport, match, contest, competition, amusement *ant.* work ② quarry, prey

gang *n.* crew, team, troop, crowd, mob, clique, band, party

gap *n.* space, blank, hole, break, cranny *The spider slipped through the cranny in the wall.* chink, opening, crack, interval

gape *v.* stare, gaze, gawk ▷**look**

garbage, *n.* trash, rubbish, refuse, waste, litter, debris, junk

garden *n.* flower bed, vegetable patch, park

garment *n.* dress, attire, costume ▷**clothes**

gas *n.* fuel, gasoline, vapour, fume

gasp *v.* wheeze, heave, puff, gulp, pant, choke ▷**breathe**

gather *v* ① collect, pick, amass, assemble, accumulate, acquire *ant.* scatter ② understand, assume, infer

gathering *n.* meeting, assembly, function, affair, collection

gaudy *adj.* flashy, cheap, vulgar, loud, showy, garish, tacky

gauge ① *n.* measure, meter, rule, standard ② *v.* judge, measure, estimate *Estimate the number of leaves still left on the maple tree.* guess, probe

gaunt *adj.* thin, lean, skinny, wasted ▷**haggard** *ant.* plump

gaze *v.* stare, look, gape, gawk, ogle, regard

gear *n.* tackle, accessories, machinery, harness, equipment, outfit

gem *n.* jewel, stone, treasure

general *adj.* usual, common, popular, customary, widespread, broad, indefinite, universal *ant.* specific

generous *adj.* free, unselfish, kind, lavish *ant.* selfish

genial *adj.* cheerful, cheery, sunny, cordial, pleasant, warm, friendly, jolly *ant.* cold

genius *n.* brilliance, intelligence, talent, skill, cleverness, brains

gentle *adj.* ① easy, mild, soft, kind, tender, humane, harmless, inoffensive, light, low ② gradual, moderate, slight *Jogging up even a slight slope made her puff.*

gentleman *n.* man, male, squire, fellow, master

genuine *adj.* ① real, authentic, true, actual ② sincere, honest, candid, frank *ant.* false

germ *n.* bug, microbe, seed, embryo, origin

gesture *n.* sign, signal, motion, nod, shrug

get *v.* ① acquire, obtain, gain, win, receive, secure, achieve, accomplish *ant.* forfeit ② understand, catch on, figure out, learn ③ grow, become

get rid of *v.* discard, reject, throw away, scrap, trash, delete

ghastly *adj.* shocking, hideous, horrible, terrible, fightening, appalling

ghost *n.* spook, spirit, vision, bogey, phantom, apparition, spectre, goblin

ghostly *adj.* eerie, weird, haunted, spooky

giant *adj.* huge, colossal, enormous, tremendous, immense, vast, mammoth, monstrous, big, gigantic *ant.* tiny

gibberish *n.* nonsense, double talk, babble, mumbo jumbo

giddy *adj.* dizzy, whirling, reeling, unsteady, wild, reckless, silly, flighty

gift *n.* ① present, donation, prize, award ② talent, skill, ability, aptitude

gigantic *adj.* huge, enormous, immense, colossal ▷**giant** *ant.* minute

giggle *v.* chuckle, snicker, cackle, titter ▷**laugh**

girder *n.* beam, rafter, joist *The floor boards were nailed to the joists.*

girl *n.* female, young woman, maiden, lass, miss

G
g
g
g
G
g
G

girlish *adj.* feminine, maidenly, youthful

girth *n.* circumference, perimeter, fatness

gist *n.* essence, substance, core, drift, significance, heart

give *v.* ① donate, grant, distribute, endow ② move, budge, bend, yield *We've made up our minds and we won't yield.* ③ produce, supply, provide *ant.* take

give back *v.* return, restore, send back

give in *v.* surrender, quit, yield, concede

give off *v.* emit, exude, discharge

give up *v.* surrender, give in, relinquish, hand over, cease, abandon

glad *adj.* joyful, joyous, delighted, pleased, contented, elated ▷**happy** *ant.* sad

glamour *n.* romance, prestige, fascination, attraction, enchantment

glance ① *n.* look, glimpse, peep ② *v.* scan, skim, check ③ rebound, graze *Luckily, the puck only grazed Lea's leg!* ricochet

glare *v.* ① blaze, glow, flare, sparkle, dazzle ② frown, glower, stare, scowl

glaring *adj.* ① sparkling, dazzling ② blatant, conspicuous, flagrant

glass *n.* ① tumbler, goblet, beaker ② windowpane, lens

glaze *n. & v.* shine, polish, gloss, varnish

gleam *v. & n.* sparkle, glitter, twinkle, glow, shine, flash

glib *adj.* fluent, slick, smooth, talkative, plausible, flip, facile, articulate

glide *v.* slide, slither, slip, soar, sail, skate, skim, flow, sneak

glimmer *v. & n.* sparkle, flicker, glow, gleam, shine, blink, flash

glimpse *v.* spy, spot, glance, notice

glisten *v.* shine, glitter, glow, gleam, sparkle

glitter *v.* gleam, sparkle, flash, glint, glisten

gloat *v.* crow, revel, exult, triumph

globe *n.* ball, sphere, planet, earth, world

gloom *n.* ① darkness, shade, dusk, shadow, bleakness *ant.* light ② sadness, grief

gloomy *adj.* cheerless, black, dark, bleak, cloudy, overcast, dismal, dour, glum, sad, melancholy ▷**dreary** *ant.* happy

glorious *adj.* brilliant, magnificent, noble, exalted, renowned ▷**splendid**

glory *n.* brilliance, pride, fame, honour, ▷**splendour**

gloss *n.* lustre, sheen, shimmer, polish, shine ▷**glaze**

glossy *adj.* shiny, sleek, slick, polished, lustrous, glassy

glow *n. & v.* glare, glitter, bloom, blush, flush, shine, gleam, twinkle, beam

glue ① *n.* paste, gum, cement, mortar, adhesive ② *v.* stick, fasten

glum *adj.* sullen, sulky, morose, miserable, dejected, downcast, moody ▷**gloomy**

glut *n.* surplus, plenty, abundance, excess

gnash *v.* grind, chomp, bite, crunch

gnaw *v.* chew, nibble, bite, eat, consume

go *v.* ① leave, pass, move, travel, advance, depart, proceed ② run, stretch, reach, extend *The prairies extend to the Rockies.*

go after *v.* pursue, chase, follow

go ahead *v.* progress, proceed, continue

go away *v.* leave, depart, vanish, disappear

go back *v.* return, resume, retreat

go in *v.* enter, advance, invade, penetrate

go off *v.* explode, blow up, detonate

go on *v.* ① continue, advance, proceed, move ahead, keep up, endure ② chatter

go up *v.* climb, mount, rise ▷**ascend**

goad *v.* prod, incite, impel, drive, urge, sting, provoke

goal *n.* target, aim, object, end, purpose, destination, intention, ambition

gobble *v.* devour, wolf, swallow, gulp

goblin *n.* sprite, demon, gnome ▷**ghost**

golden *adj.* excellent, precious, brilliant, bright

good *adj.* ① satisfactory, adequate, admirable, fine ② favourable, agreeable ③ virtuous, moral, true ④ clever, skilful, expert ⑤ appropriate, correct, valid *Your valid arguments have convinced me.* proper, suited *ant.* bad

Confusable Words

good means *correct*

well means *correctly*

goodness *n.* excellence, merit, honesty, worth, kindness ▷**virtue** *ant.* wickedness

goods *n.* merchandise, wares, commodities, material, belongings

gorge ① *v.* gobble, stuff oneself, binge, devour, pig out ② *n.* canyon, valley, ravine

gorgeous *adj.* beautiful, ravishing, superb, stunning, magnificent, attractive, radiant

gossip ① *v.* chat, chatter, prattle, tattle ② *n.* rumour, hearsay, whispering

gouge *v.* ① excavate, groove, dig out ② extort, overcharge

govern *v.* rule, reign, manage, direct, guide, control, conduct, command, lead, administer

government *n.* rule, administration, supervision, management, parliament, legislature

governor *n.* director, manager, leader, chief, overseer, head of state

gown *n.* dress, robe, nightgown

grace *n.* ① elegance, refinement, polish, beauty ② mercy, decency, kindness

graceful *adj.* beautiful, lovely, refined, tasteful, cultured, polished ▷**elegant**

gracious *adj.* amiable, kind, suave *His suave manner hides his nervousness well.* urbane, elegant, cordial, sociable *ant.* rude

grade *n.* ① class, rank, degree, category, level, stage, mark ② slope, gradient, incline, slant

gradual *adj.* step-by-step, continuous, slow, gentle, moderate, easy *ant.* sudden

graft ① *v.* splice, insert, implant ② *n.* bribery, corruption

grain *n.* fibre, crumb, seed, particle, atom, bit, drop

grand *adj.* splendid, impressive, stately, magnificent, wonderful, superb, majestic, lofty, dignified, regal

grandeur *n.* splendour, majesty, glory, magnificence

grant ① *n.* award, subsidy ② *v.* give, allow, donate, confer, bestow

grasp *v.* ① grip, seize, take, grab, hold, clasp, cling to, clutch ② understand, comprehend, fathom

Great

Grate

grasping *adj.* greedy, selfish, tight-fisted, miserly *ant.* generous

grate ① *v.* rasp, file, clash, rub, grind, scrape ② *v.* annoy, irritate ③ *n.* grill, frame, bars *hom.* great

grateful *adj.* thankful, appreciative, obliged, indebted

gratify *v.* delight, satisfy, please, content, indulge, favour, humour *ant.* displease

gratitude *n.* thankfulness, appreciation, recognition

grave ① *adj.* solemn, sober, dignified, sombre ② *adj.* serious, severe, urgent *We are in urgent need of assistance.* critical, dire ③ *n.* tomb, crypt, vault, shrine

gravity *n.* ① seriousness, solemnity, importance, significance ② gravitation, pull, weight

graze *v.* ① scrape, brush, shave, glance ② browse, crop, nibble

great *adj.* ① large, considerable, bulky, huge, big ② important, distinguished, noted *Canada is a noted producer of animated films.* ③ main, chief, principal *hom.* grate

G g g G g G g G g G

greedy *adj.* selfish, grasping, piggish, acquisitive *ant.* unselfish

green *adj.* ① emerald, jade, turquoise, olive, lime ② young, inexperienced, immature, raw, untrained *ant.* mature

greet *v.* welcome, accost, hail, salute, address

grief *n.* woe, sadness, regret, distress, anguish, misery, agony ▷**sorrow** *ant.* joy

grievance *n.* injury, complaint, wrong

grieve *v.* lament, deplore, mourn, sorrow, weep, suffer, pine, brood *ant.* rejoice

grievous *adj.* lamentable, deplorable *"Please apologize for your deplorable behaviour!"* grave, critical, severe, mortal, dangerous

grill ① *v.* fry, broil, barbecue ② *v.* question, interrogate, quiz ③ *n.* grate, grid

grim *adj.* ① serious, stern, harsh, solemn, severe, dour, forbidding ② horrid, dreadful, terrible, awful ▷**ghastly**

grime *n.* filth, dust, soot, soil ▷**dirt**

grin *n. & v.* smile, beam, smirk

grind *v.* ① crunch, crush, powder, trample ② sharpen, grate, scrape, file, gnash

grip *v.* grasp, grab, clutch, clasp, cling to, seize ▷**hold** *ant.* drop

grisly *adj.* horrid, horrible, dreadful, ghastly, shocking, repellent ▷**grim**

grit *n.* ① powder, dust, sand, gravel ② nerve, pluck ▷**courage**

groan *v.* moan, complain, grumble, creak *hom.* grown

groom ① *n.* husband, bridegroom ② *n.* stable hand, servant ③ *v.* spruce, tidy, preen

groove *n.* furrow, ridge, ditch, trench, channel, rut, score

grope *v.* feel, finger, fumble *He fumbled his way through the dark passage.* search

gross *adj.* ① broad, general ② disgusting, repulsive, vulgar, crude ③ outrageous, glaring, flagrant

grotesque *adj.* deformed, malformed, misshapen, freakish, abnormal, bizarre

ground *n.* ① land, soil, earth, dust ② bottom, base, foundation

grounds *n.* ① foundation, cause, basis, reason ② dregs, sediment, silt ③ land, gardens, premises, estate

group *n.* ① gang, throng, bunch, class, band, troop, team, club, association ② division, section, branch, category

grovel *v.* fawn, crouch, crawl, cringe, wallow, cower

grow *v.* ① increase, advance, expand, extend, develop, mature, evolve, sprout, germinate ② raise, produce, cultivate

Groups of Animals

A sloth of bears
A swarm of bees
A flock of birds
A cloud of blackflies
An obstinacy of buffaloes
A gang of caribou
A brood of chicks
An army of caterpillars
A kennel of dogs
A parade of elephants
A shoal of fish

A skulk of foxes
A gaggle of geese
A skein of geese (in flight)
A drove of horses
A mob of kangaroos
A litter of kittens
A pride of lions
A troop of monkeys
A colony of seals
A flock of sheep
A knot of toads
A school of whales
A pack of wolves

n.= noun
v.= verb
adj.= adjective
adv.= adverb
conj.= conjunction
prep.= preposition
ant.= antonym
hom.= homonym
▷ = cross-reference

Growls, Grunts, and Other Animal Noises

Bees buzz.
Cats meow.
Cockerels crow.
Cows moo.
Dogs bark.
Dogs also growl.
Ducks quack.
Horses neigh.
Lions roar.
Mice squeak.
Owls hoot.
Pigs grunt.
Seals bark.
Snakes hiss.
Wolves howl.

growl *v.* snarl, snap, threaten, thunder, rumble

growth *n.* expansion, development, advance, extension ▷**increase**

grubby *adj.* messy, dirty, filthy, stained

grudge *n.* envy, dislike, spite, resentment

gruesome *adj.* shocking, hideous, ghastly ▷**grisly**

gruff *adj.* ① husky, throaty, croaky, hoarse ② abrupt, bad-tempered, crusty, curt

grumble *v.* complain, gripe, murmur, growl, protest

grumpy *adj.* irritable, bad-tempered, cross, crotchety, surly, sour, sullen, disgruntled, dissatisfied *ant.* cheerful

grunt *n. & v.* snort, groan, mutter, growl

guarantee *n.* warranty, assurance, security, pledge, promise

guard ① *n.* protector, sentry, guardian, watchman, lookout ② *v.* protect, defend, watch over, be vigilant

guess *v.* surmise, conjecture, judge, think, suspect, suppose, estimate, predict

guest *n.* visitor, company *hom.* guessed

guide ① *n.* pilot, director, leader, controller, escort ② *v.* steer, navigate, lead, direct, manage, administer, supervise, conduct
The guide conducted our tour through the fortress at Louisbourg.

guilty *adj.* ① responsible, at fault, sinful, wicked *ant.* innocent ② sorry, repentant

guise *n.* garb, dress, façade, appearance *hom.* guys

gulf *n.* ① bay, basin, inlet ② chasm, opening, abyss, depths

gullible *adj.* innocent, naïve, trusting, suggestible

gully *n.* trench, ditch, channel, ravine

gulp *v.* swallow, consume, guzzle, devour, swill, wolf, gobble

gurgle *v.* ripple, murmur, babble

gush *v.* stream, spurt, spout, flow, run, pour out, emit

gust *n.* blast, puff, squall, wind, outburst

gusto *n.* relish, zest, eagerness, zeal, pleasure

gutter *n.* ditch, drain, gully, channel, groove, moat, dike

guzzle *v.* gulp, imbibe, drink, swill, quaff

H h

habit *n.* ① custom, practice, routine, way, style ② mannerism *One of my sister's mannerisms is playing with the ends of her braids.* trait, characteristic ③ addiction

hack *v.* chop, mangle, gash, slash

haggard *adj.* drawn, wan, pinched, thin, worn ▷**gaunt** *ant.* healthy

haggle *v.* bargain, bicker, dispute, wrangle

hail ① *v.* salute, honour, welcome, greet, signal, come from ② *n.* sleet, frozen rain, ice storm ③ *n.* barrage *hom.* hale

hair *n.* locks, mane, tresses, strand

half *n.* part, division, fraction, segment, share

hall *n.* entrance, foyer, corridor, lobby, passage, vestibule *Please leave your wet boots in the vestibule when you come to our apartment. hom.* haul

hallucination *n.* illusion, fantasy, delusion, mirage, dream *ant.* fact

halt *v.* end, pause, rest, cease, arrest, curb ▷**stop** *ant.* start

halting *adj.* faltering *Her faltering steps brought her slowly to the stage.* hestitating, wavering, awkward

hammer ① *v.* beat, pound, bang, hit, slap ② *n.* mallet, gavel

hamper ① *v.* hinder, interfere with, impede, curb, shackle, restrict *ant.* further ② *n.* container, basket

hand ① *v.* give, pass, present, return ② *n.* fist, palm, paw, mitt ③ *n.* applause ④ *n.* labourer, worker

handicap *n.* defect, disability, drawback *In Canada, not knowing any French can be a real drawback.* restriction, disadvantage *ant.* advantage

handicraft *n.* skill, hobby, art, craft

handle ① *n.* shaft, holder, grip ② *v.* feel, touch, finger, work, wield, manipulate, fondle, operate ③ manage, cope with, deal with, stand

Habitations

Apartment
Bungalow
Cabin
Castle
Château
Condominium
Cottage
Duplex
Estate
Flat
Hacienda
Hut
Igloo
Lodge
Mansion
Palace
Ranch
Shack
Shanty
Villa

handsome *adj.* ① attractive, beautiful, graceful, good-looking *ant.* ugly ② generous, lavish *The solid gold bracelets were a lavish gift—thank you!*

handy *adj.* ready, convenient, skilful, practical, adept *ant.* clumsy

hang *v.* ① dangle, suspend, sag, droop, swing, sling ② attach ③ hover, float

haphazard *adj.* accidental, random, aimless, casual ▷**careless** *ant.* deliberate, orderly

happen *v.* occur, take place, result, transpire *What transpired here while I was gone?* arise, develop, fall

happiness *n.* delight, ecstasy, gaiety, joy, enjoyment, mirth, merriment ▷**bliss** *ant.* misery

happy *adj.* cheerful, content, joyous, jubilant, jolly, satisfied, glad ▷**merry** *ant.* unhappy

harass *v.* annoy, bother, pester, badger, hassle

harbour ① *n.* port, anchorage, mooring ② *n.* refuge, shelter, cover, haven, safety ③ *v.* give shelter to ④ *v.* hold, bear, nurse

hard *adj.* ① firm, stony, rocky, solid *ant.* soft ② difficult, tough, complicated *ant.* easy ③ stern, severe, callous *Was she being callous or was she trying not to show her real feelings?* ruthless, harsh

hardly *adv.* seldom, rarely, scarcely, slightly, barely

hardship *n.* trouble, suffering, want ▷**difficulty** *ant.* ease

hardy *adj.* rugged, sturdy, tough, healthy, sound, durable, strong ▷**robust** *ant.* weak

harm ① *n.* damage, mischief, ruin, injury, abuse *ant.* benefit ② *v.* abuse, damage, hurt, injure

harmful *adj.* dangerous, bad, injurious *Too much loud noise can be injurious to your ears.* evil, wicked, damaging *ant.* harmless

harmless *adj.* safe, gentle, innocuous, innocent, inoffensive *ant.* harmful

harmony *n.* agreement, conformity, accord, unity, goodwill, peace, tranquillity *ant.* discord

harsh *adj.* ① jarring, coarse, grating, rasping, rough ② severe, strict, ruthless *ant.* mild

harvest *v.* reap, pick, gather

hassle *n.* argument, bother, difficulty, squabble, struggle, annoyance

haste *n.* rush, bustle, dispatch, urgency, swiftness, speediness, hurry

hasten *v.* hurry, hustle, quicken, accelerate, speed up, rush *ant.* delay

hasty *adj.* hurried, rushed, quick, prompt, swift, fast, abrupt

hate *v.* abhor, detest, loathe ▷**despise** *ant.* love

hateful *adj.* abominable, loathsome, odious, despicable, horrid *ant.* pleasing

haughty *adj.* arrogant, disdainful, scornful, snobbish *ant.* humble

haul *v.* pull, draw, tug, drag, heave *hom.* hall

have *v.* possess, occupy, own, sport, boast, keep, hold, enjoy

haven *n.* harbour, port, refuge, retreat, shelter, home

havoc *n.* wreckage, ruin, destruction, disorder, mayhem

hay *n.* silage, grass, straw

haze *n.* cloud, vapour, fog, mist, smog, film

hazy *adj.* foggy, misty, murky, vague, uncertain, unclear *ant.* clear

head ① *n.* skull, cranium, noggin ② *n.* top, front ③ *n.* person, individual ④ *adj.* chief, main, principal, leading

heading *n.* caption, headline, title, inscription

heal *v.* cure, mend, restore, remedy, fix, soothe, treat *hom.* heel, he'll

healthy *adj.* fine, fit, hearty, sound, vigorous, well ▷**hardy** *ant.* sick

heap *n.* pile, mass, mound, collection

hear *v.* listen, heed, discover, learn, catch *hom.* here

Confusable Words

hear means *listen*

here means *at this place*

heartless *adj.* brutal, callous, cold ▷**unkind** *ant.* kind

hearty *adj.* cordial, sincere, earnest, honest, jovial, healthy

heat *n.* ① warmth, temperature ② passion *Francesca spoke with passion about her favourite music.* ardour, excitement, fervour

heave *v.* fling, cast, hurl, hoist, pull, tug, throw, toss

heavenly *adj.* beautiful, blessed, divine, lovely, marvellous *ant.* abominable

heavy *adj.* ① weighty, hefty, loaded, bulky, cumbersome *ant.* light ② difficult, troublesome, burdensome, oppressive ③ sorrowful, grieving

hectic *adj.* excited, fast, frenzied, wild, fervid, intense ▷**frantic** *ant.* leisurely

heedless *adj.* thoughtless, reckless, unwary, rash, mindless ▷**careless** *ant.* careful

Headgear

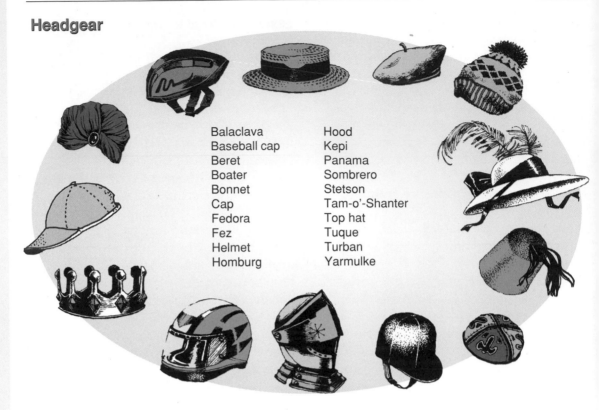

Balaclava
Baseball cap
Beret
Boater
Bonnet
Cap
Fedora
Fez
Helmet
Homburg
Hood
Kepi
Panama
Sombrero
Stetson
Tam-o'-Shanter
Top hat
Tuque
Turban
Yarmulke

height *n.* ① altitude, stature, elevation ② top, apex, peak, zenith *The zenith of Sir Frederick Banting's career was the discovery of insulin.* climax, crown, summit *ant.* bottom

help ① *n.* aid, support, assistance, relief ② *v.* aid, assist, support, benefit *ant.* hinder

helpful *adj.* caring, beneficial, supportive, neighbourly, considerate ▷**useful**

helping *n.* serving, share, portion, piece *Mike would like a second piece. He's still hungry.*

helpless *adj.* dependent, vulnerable, incapable, powerless, unfit, forlorn ▷**weak** *ant.* strong

herd *n.* crowd, drive, flock, group, mass, mob, horde *hom.* heard

heritage *n.* ① tradition ② inheritance, legacy, birthright

hermit *n.* recluse, solitary, loner, monk

hero *n.* champion, star, idol, celebrity, winner *ant.* villain

heroic *adj.* bold, fearless, gallant ▷**brave** *ant.* cowardly

heroine *n.* celebrity *Roberta Bondar, the first Canadian woman in space, has become a celebrity.* goddess, idol, star, lead

hesitate *v.* falter, vacillate, waver, pause, wait

hidden *adj.* concealed, covered, veiled, unseen, obscure *ant.* visible

hide *v.* conceal, cover, obscure, bury, cloak, mask, disguise *ant.* reveal

hideous *adj.* repulsive, unsightly, gruesome, horrible ▷**ugly** *ant.* beautiful

high *adj.* ① tall, towering, lofty, elevated ② shrill *He covered his ears when the shrill whistle blew.* piping, squeaky ③ steep, exorbitant, excessive *ant.* low

hijack *v.* raid, kidnap, seize, snatch, steal

hilarious *adj.* amusing, sidesplitting, entertaining ▷**funny** *ant.* serious

hill *n.* rise, height, elevation, slope, incline, mound, knoll

hinder *v.* hamper, impede, obstruct, retard, frustrate, inhibit ▷**block** *ant.* help

hindrance *n.* impediment, obstruction, bar, barrier, handicap *ant.* aid, advantage

n. = noun
v. = verb
adj. = adjective
adv. = adverb
conj. = conjunction
prep. = preposition
ant. = antonym
hom. = homonym
▷ = cross-reference

hint *n.* clue, inkling *Not even the organizer had an inkling of what was really going to happen.* sign, whisper, tip, suggestion, pointer

hire *v.* employ, contract, use, retain, engage *ant.* dismiss *hom.* higher

history *n.* past, background, narration, account, saga, story, chronicle *The photo essay is the chronicle of one grey whale's migration along the coast.*

hit ① *v.* strike, slap, beat, batter, whack ② *v.* collide, strike, crash *ant.* miss ③ *n.* collision, blow ④ *n.* success, triumph

hitch ① *v.* attach, connect, fasten ② *n.* delay, holdup, problem, snag *The work went smoothly until we hit a snag.*

hoard *v.* accumulate, save, squirrel away, collect, stash *ant.* squander *hom.* horde

hoarse *adj.* husky, throaty, croaky, harsh *hom.* horse

hoax *n.* trick, deception, fraud, lie, cheat, swindle

hobby *n.* interest, recreation, pursuit, amusement, pastime

hoist *v.* lift, raise, erect, heave, elevate

hold *v.* ① have, possess, own, retain *Retain any leftover wood and we'll use it to build a tree house!* keep, grasp, grip, clutch, clasp ② contain, store, accommodate ③ stop, arrest *hom.* holed

hole *n.* opening, cavity, gap, pit, hollow, outlet, slit, aperture, slot, perforation, rip *hom.* whole

Confusable Words

hole means *hollow*

whole means *entire*

hollow ① *adj.* concave, empty, vacant ② *adj.* false, insincere, hypocritical ③ *adj* muffled, dull, flat ④ *n.* indentation, basin, depression *Rainwater has filled the shallow depressions in the lawn.* crater

holy *adj.* sacred, pure, blessed, hallowed, saintly, pious, devout *ant.* wicked *hom.* wholly

home *n.* house, dwelling, residence, household

homely *adj.* plain, unattractive

homey *adj.* cosy, humble, unpretentious, comfortable, modest, ordinary, simple, domestic, rustic

honest *adj.* truthful, trustworthy, just, good, fair, honourable, reputable, scrupulous, sincere, upright *ant.* devious

honesty *n.* integrity, honour, sincerity, morality, truth *ant.* fraud

honour *n.* morality, honesty, reputation, integrity, uprightness, virtue

honourable *adj.* honest, respectable, high-minded, virtuous, noble *ant.* corrupt

hook *n.* clasp, link, catch, fastener, barb

hoop *n.* loop, ring, band, circle

hoot *v.* cry, howl, shout, shriek, yell, call

hop *v.* jump, leap, skip, spring, vault, bound

hope ① *v.* wish, anticipate, desire, expect, foresee *I foresee only good things ahead.* ② *n.* heart, confidence, optimism, anticipation *ant.* despair

hopeful *adj.* expectant, confident, optimistic, encouraging *ant.* pessimistic

hopeless *adj.* impossible, despondent *The despondent boy cheered up when his grandmother arrived.* desperate, downhearted, unattainable *ant.* hopeful

horde *n.* crowd, gang, band, throng, swarm *hom.* hoard

horrible *adj.* awful, atrocious, ghastly, terrible, dreadful, frightening ▷**horrid** *ant.* agreeable

horrid *adj.* beastly, gruesome, dreadful, frightening ▷**horrible** *ant.* pleasant

horror *n.* dread, fear, fright, outrage, panic, loathing, disgust, alarm *ant.* pleasure

horse *n.* mount, charger, stallion, mare, filly, colt, foal, steed, nag, pony, yearling

hospitable *adj.* sociable, neighbourly, charitable, welcoming *ant.* hostile

host *n.* ① emcee, entertainer ② crowd, army, band, legion, horde

hostile *adj.* unfriendly, antagonistic, aggressive, belligerent *ant.* friendly

H h H h H h H

Hue

A hue is a variety of a colour.

Blue: aquamarine, azure, beryl, indigo, navy, royal, sapphire, turquoise, ultramarine

Brown: amber, beige, chocolate, dun, fawn, khaki, taupe

Green: apple, chartreuse, emerald, jade, moss, olive, pea, sea

Purple: amethyst, fuchsia, lilac, magenta, mauve, violet

Orange: apricot, carrot, peach, sand, tangerine

Red: cardinal, cerise, cherry, crimson, pink, salmon, scarlet, terra cotta

Yellow: canary, citron, lemon, primrose, saffron, sulphur

hot ① *adj.* warm, fiery, scalding, roasting, heated, scorching, blazing, sweltering, sizzling *ant.* cold ② spicy, piquant, peppery, sharp

hotel *n.* motel, resort, inn, tavern

house *n.* home, residence, dwelling, abode, apartment, shelter

hover *v.* float, hang, linger, flutter

howl *v.* hoot, cry, wail, bawl ▷**scream**

hub *n.* centre, heart, focal point, pivot

huddle *v.* cluster, flock, gather, herd, nestle, crouch, stoop *ant.* scatter

hue *n.* colour, dye, shade, tinge, tint *hom.* hew

huff *n.* mood, temper, snit, rage, sulk

hug *v.* clasp, embrace, enfold ▷**cuddle**

huge *adj.* enormous, monstrous, colossal, immense, gigantic, tremendous ▷**vast** *ant.* tiny

hum *v.* drone, whir, buzz, pulsate, throb

humane *adj.* benevolent, compassionate, gentle, lenient, kind *ant.* inhuman

humble *adj.* lowly, meek, unassuming, respectful, unpretentious ▷**modest** *ant.* arrogant

humdrum *adj.* boring, everyday, commonplace, monotonous *Life in this village is monotonous and slow, but we like it.* ▷**dreary** *ant.* thrilling

humid *adj.* damp, moist, wet, muggy, sticky, sultry, clammy, oppressive *ant.* dry

humiliate *v.* embarrass, humble, shame, degrade, deflate *ant.* boost

humorous *adj.* amusing, comical, whimsical, witty, droll ▷**funny** *ant.* serious *hom.* humerus

humour ① *n.* comedy, fun, banter, whimsy, wit ② *v.* pamper, spoil, indulge, oblige

hunch ① *n.* feeling, guess, idea, inkling ② *v.* crouch, curl up, stoop, squat

hunger ① *n.* appetite, craving, desire ② *v.* crave, desire, long, yearn

hungry *adj.* famished, voracious *The bear had just wakened from its winter hibernation and was voracious.* ravenous

hunt *v.* chase, seek, search, stalk, trail, pursue, track

hurdle *n.* barrier, obstacle, obstruction

hurl *v.* cast, fling, heave, pitch, throw, propel, toss

hurry *v.* rush, speed, race, dash, hustle, quicken, accelerate ▷**hasten** *ant.* delay

hurt ① *v.* injure, abuse, mistreat, harm, wound, sting, smart, ache, throb ② *v.* upset, grieve, distress ③ *adj.* sad, offended

hurtful *adj.* cutting, cruel, distressing, harmful, painful, wounding *ant.* kind

hush *v.* silence, calm, soothe *ant.* disturb

husky *adj.* ① croaking, gruff, harsh, grating, hoarse ② sturdy, chunky

hustle *v.* rush, dash, bustle, speed ▷**hurry**

hut *n.* cabin, shelter, shanty, shack, shed

hypnotize *v.* mesmerize, fascinate, spellbind *We stood spellbound as he danced in the fountain.* bewitch

hypocrite *n.* fraud, deceiver, impostor, phony

hysterical *adj.* ① distraught, delirious, raving ② comical, hilarious, farcical

n. = noun
v. = verb
adj. = adjective
adv. = adverb
conj. = conjunction
prep. = preposition
ant. = antonym
hom. = homonym
▷ = cross-reference

I i

icy *adj.* freezing, frozen, cold, frigid, frosty

idea *n.* notion, thought, belief, impression, image, opinion, view, concept

ideal *adj.* perfect, ultimate, supreme, best, model, flawless

identical *adj.* same, alike, twin, duplicate, equal *ant.* different

identify *v.* detect, recognize, know, distinguish, spot

identity *n.* existence, self, individuality

idiot *n.* imbecile, moron, fool, dimwit

idiotic *adj.* stupid, inane ▷**foolish**

idle *adj.* ① unoccupied, unemployed, unused, empty ② lazy, sluggish, slothful *ant.* industrious ③ frivolous, vain, silly, meaningless *hom.* idol

idol *n.* ① image, icon, god, fetish ② hero, favourite, celebrity, star *hom.* idle

ignite *v.* light, kindle, spark, catch fire, burn

ignorant *adj.* unknowing, uninformed, unread, uneducated, backward *ant.* educated

ignore *v.* disregard, neglect, omit, overlook, pass over, snub, slight *ant.* recognize

ill *adj.* sick, ailing, unhealthy, diseased, frail, infirm *ant.* well

ill-mannered *adj.* coarse, crude, boorish, uncivil ▷**rude** *ant.* polite

ill-tempered *adj.* sour, grumpy, curt, irritable, cranky, crabby *ant.* happy

illegal *adj.* unlawful, wrong, villainous, illicit, criminal, forbidden *ant.* legal

illegible *adj.* unreadable, indecipherable, obscure, indistinct *ant.* legible

illegitimate *adj.* illegal, unauthorized, improper, wrongful *ant.* legitimate

illiterate *adj.* uneducated, unlearned, unlettered, unread, ignorant *ant.* literate

illness *n.* sickness, ailment, disorder, complaint, disease,

illuminate *v.* ① brighten, light up *ant.* obscure ② clarify, enlighten, instruct

illusion *n.* apparition, fantasy, mirage, vision, hallucination, dream *ant.* fact

illustration *n.* picture, drawing, explanation, sketch, example

image *n.* ① likeness, representation, portrait, replica, reflection ② idea, concept, notion, impression

imaginary *adj.* unreal, fanciful, fictitious, make-believe, invented, made-up, mythical *ant.* real

imagination *n.* ① mind's eye, invention, make-believe, illusion, fantasy *ant.* fact ② vision, creativity, resourcefulness

imagine *v.* ① assume, believe, think ② conceive, pretend, dream, make believe, visualize ▷**invent**

imitate *v.* copy, emulate, follow, reproduce, simulate, mock, duplicate, mimic, ape
If you do it first, then we will try to ape your movements. echo

immaculate *adj.* clean, spotless, faultless, stainless ▷**pure** *ant.* dirty

immature *adj.* young, childish, green, unripe, undeveloped *ant.* mature

immediate *adj.* ① instant, instantaneous, prompt *ant.* late ② close, nearest, next, next-door *Saskatchewan and Manitoba are next-door neighbours.* direct, first-hand *ant.* indirect

immediately *adv.* at once, directly, promptly, without delay

immense *adj.* tremendous, enormous, vast, colossal, giant ▷**huge** *ant.* tiny

immerse *v.* ① plunge, dip, douse, submerge, duck, sink ② absorb, engross

imminent *adj.* impending, approaching, looming, close

immobile *adj.* motionless, unmoving, fixed, at rest *ant.* moving

immoral *adj.* evil, unscrupulous, vicious, wrong, corrupt, warped, perverted, vile, depraved ▷**wicked** *ant.* moral

immortal *adj.* undying, eternal, everlasting, constant, endless *ant.* mortal

immune *adj.* exempt, resistant, safe, protected, inoculated *ant.* vulnerable

impact *n.* blow, shock, stroke, collision, crash, knock, force, wallop

impair *v.* damage, spoil, devalue, cheapen, harm, injure ▷**hinder** *ant.* enhance

impartial *adj.* unbiassed, fair, impersonal, neutral *ant.* prejudiced

impatient *adj.* ① eager, uneasy, anxious, restless ② intolerant, irritable, curt, short, rude *ant.* patient

impede *v.* hamper, interfere with, obstruct, stop ▷**hinder** *ant.* aid

impel *v.* goad, move, urge, push, motivate ▷**drive** *ant.* dissuade

impending *adj.* approaching, coming, looming, imminent

imperfect *adj.* defective, blemished, flawed ▷**faulty** *ant.* perfect

imperial *adj.* majestic, lofty, regal, royal, sovereign, grand, august

imperious *adj.* arrogant, domineering, overbearing *The overbearing team captain forced them all to do what she wanted.* dictatorial *ant.* humble

impersonal *adj.* unemotional, aloof, detached, remote, neutral, cold *ant.* warm

impersonate *v.* imitate, mimic, pose as, portray, act like

impertinent *adj.* rude, insolent, impudent, discourteous, disrespectful *ant.* polite

impetuous *adj.* sudden, unexpected, impulsive, spontaneous, rash ▷**hasty** *ant.* careful

implement ① *v.* put into practice, bring about, use, enforce, carry out ② *n.* instrument, tool, device

implicate *v.* connect, entangle, involve, throw suspicion on

implicit *adj.* ① implied, understood, tacit, insinuated *Even his compliments were full of insinuated criticism.* inferred, unexpressed ② undoubting, whole-hearted

implore *v.* beg, crave, plead, appeal, beseech

imply *v.* hint at, intimate, insinuate, suggest

impolite *adj.* discourteous, ill-mannered, boorish, insolent, tactless ▷**rude** *ant.* polite

import ① *v.* (im-*port*) bring in, introduce ② *n.* (*im*-port) meaning, sense, importance, drift *I caught the drift of Robin's speech, but I didn't understand all the details.*

important *adj.* significant, essential, substantial, necessary, vital, urgent, serious, prominent ▷**great** *ant.* trivial

imposing *adj.* impressive, massive, grand, large, magnificent ▷**stately** *ant.* modest

impossible *adj.* hopeless, unacceptable, inconceivable, unworkable, unthinkable *ant.* possible

impostor *n.* impersonator, deceiver, fraud, fake, pretender, phony, charlatan

impoverish *v.* bankrupt, diminish, weaken, ruin, deplete *ant.* enrich

impractical *adj.* impossible, unworkable, idealistic, unusable *ant.* practical

impress *v.* awe, move, influence, affect, sway, inspire, please, surprise

impression *n.* ① belief, concept, feeling, image ② dent, imprint, stamp

imprison *v.* jail, lock up, confine *ant.* free

improbable *adj.* doubtful, unlikely, implausible ▷**dubious** *ant.* probable

impromptu *adj.* spontaneous, improvised, ad lib, unrehearsed *ant.* planned

improper *adj.* incorrect, unsuitable, inappropriate, indiscreet, tactless *It was tactless to invite me in front of him without asking him, too.* immoral, indecent ▷**wrong** *ant.* proper

improve *v.* enhance, fix, correct, better, sharpen, hone, refine, enrich, progress

impudent *adj.* disrespectful, insolent, impertinent, brazen, saucy, smart-alecky ▷**rude** *ant.* polite

impulse *n.* urge, wish, motive, drive, force, inclination, stimulus

impulsive *adj.* sudden, unexpected, spontaneous, reckless, rash, thoughtless, impetuous *ant.* cautious

impure *adj.* contaminated, foul, defiled, polluted, unclean, corrupt *ant.* pure

inaccessible *adj.* remote, isolated, unattainable, unreachable, inconvenient *ant.* handy

n. = noun
v. = verb
adj. = adjective
adv. = adverb
conj. = conjunction
prep. = preposition
ant. = antonym
hom. = homonym
▷ = cross-reference

Incline

inaccurate *adj.* false, wrong, incorrect, imprecise ▷**faulty** *ant.* accurate

inactive *adj.* idle, sleeping, inert, static, dormant, quiet *ant.* lively

inadequate *adj.* deficient, insufficient, lacking, unsatisfactory, incapable ▷**unfit** *ant.* adequate

inane *adj.* absurd, ridiculous, stupid, senseless ▷**silly** *ant.* sensible

inappropriate *adj.* improper, wrong, incorrect, unsuitable, unfitting *ant.* appropriate

inattentive *adj.* unheeding, indifferent, careless, negligent *ant.* attentive

incapable *adj.* helpless, inadequate, unable, unfit, weak, powerless *ant.* capable

incense ① *v.* (in-*cense*) enrage, infuriate, outrage, anger ② *n.* (*in*-cense) fragrance aroma, perfume

incentive *n.* motivation, attraction, stimulus, encouragement, enticement, spur, lure

incident *n.* event, happening, episode, circumstance, occurrence, occasion, experience

incidental *adj.* casual, chance, accidental, random, minor

incite *v.* encourage, urge, drive, goad, spur, stir up, provoke ▷**prompt** *ant.* restrain

incline ① *n.* (*in*-cline) slant, slope, grade, gradient ② *v.* (in-*cline*) list, tilt ③ *v.* (in-*cline*) tend, lean, favour

inclined *adj.* ① liable, prone, disposed, favourable, apt, willing ② sloping, tilted

include *v.* contain, incorporate *Incorporate all these details into your project and it will be complete.* embody, comprise, involve, embrace, enclose *ant.* exclude

inclusive *adj.* general, comprehensive, all-embracing *ant.* exclusive

income *n.* earnings, royalty, revenue, receipts, profits, wages, proceeds *ant.* cost

incomparable *adj.* unique, one-of-a-kind, exceptional, unequalled, extraordinary ▷**unrivalled** *ant.* ordinary

incompetent *adj.* incapable, inadequate, inept, helpless, unskilful, fumbling, unfit, unqualified ▷**clumsy** *ant.* competent

incomplete *adj.* unfinished, partial, imperfect, wanting, deficient, lacking *ant.* complete

incomprehensible *adj.* unintelligible, perplexing, puzzling, confusing *ant.* simple

inconceivable *adj.* incredible, unlikely, unthinkable, unheard of, unbelievable, strange ▷**extraordinary** *ant.* credible

inconsiderate *adj.* tactless, careless, insensitive ▷**thoughtless** *ant.* thoughtful

inconsistent *adj.* unpredictable, capricious, incongruous *Your kind actions are incongruous with your harsh words.* unstable *ant.* consistent

inconspicuous *adj.* indistinct, ordinary, faint, hidden *ant.* conspicuous

inconvenient *adj.* annoying, awkward, difficult, troublesome, inopportune, cumbersome, untimely *ant.* convenient

incorrect *adj.* false, untrue, inaccurate, erroneous, imprecise, mistaken ▷**wrong** *ant.* correct

increase ① *v.* (in-*crease*) gain, grow, expand, enlarge, extend, add to, magnify, heighten ② *n.* (*in*-crease) addition, rise, enlargement, raise, hike, growth *ant.* decrease

I

n. = noun

v. = verb

adj. = adjective

adv. = adverb

conj. = conjunction

prep. = preposition

ant. = antonym

hom. = homonym

▷ = cross-reference

incredible *adj* unbelievable, amazing, far-fetched, improbable, impossible, fabulous, wonderful, fantastic *ant.* ordinary

incriminate *v.* implicate, accuse, indict ▷**blame** *ant.* acquit

indecent *adj.* immodest, improper, coarse, obscene, shameful *ant.* decent

indeed *adv.* actually, truly, really, very much, positively, even

indefinite *adj.* uncertain, unsure, imprecise, undetermined, unclear, dubious ▷**vague** *ant.* certain

indelicate *adj.* coarse, immodest, indecent, tactless, insensitive, unseemly ▷**gross** *ant.* delicate

independent *adj.* free, self-reliant, separate, self-governing, autonomous

indicate *v.* ① show, point out, signal, designate ② denote, suggest, imply, symbolize

indifference *n.* disinterest, unconcern, apathy, coldness *ant.* interest

indifferent *adj.* uninterested, cold, casual, apathetic, detached *ant.* attentive

indignant *adj.* annoyed, resentful, wrathful ▷**angry** *ant.* calm, pleased

indirect *adj.* roundabout, incidental, circuitous, oblique *ant.* direct

indiscreet *adj.* thoughtless, incautious, ill-advised ▷**hasty** *ant.* discreet

indiscriminate *adj.* haphazard, blind, purposeless, careless ▷**random** *ant.* deliberate

indispensable *adj.* necessary, crucial, vital ▷**essential** *ant.* unnecessary

indistinct *adj.* faint, dim, unclear, obscure, murky ▷**vague** *ant.* distinct

individual ① *adj.* single, distinctive, separate, special, exclusive *Each girl had a room for her own exclusive use.* ② *n.* person, being, creature, body, thing

indulge *v.* gratify, humour, pamper, satisfy, spoil, baby

industrious *adj.* busy, hardworking, diligent, conscientious *ant.* lazy

inedible *adj.* unpalatable, uneatable, rancid, rotten, off, poisonous, harmful *ant.* tasty

inefficient *adj.* disorganized, incapable ▷**incompetent** *ant.* efficient

inept *adj.* awkward, unskilled, incompetent, inefficient ▷**clumsy** *ant.* skilful

inert *adj.* inactive, unmoving, passive, static, sluggish, listless, dead *ant.* active

inevitable *adj.* unavoidable, certain, sure, necessary *ant.* uncertain, unlikely

inexpensive *adj.* low-priced, reasonable, economical ▷**cheap** *ant.* expensive

inexperienced *adj.* inexpert, unskilled, untrained, untried, amateur, naïve ▷**green** *ant.* adept

infallible *adj.* perfect, unerring, faultless, sure ▷**reliable** *ant.* faulty

infamous *adj.* notorious, shady *He was a shady character whom no one trusted.* scandalous, shameful, disgraceful, shocking, vile *ant.* glorious

infant *n.* baby, child, nursling

infatuated *adj.* in love, enamoured, charmed, fascinated, smitten, bewitched, beguiled

infect *v.* contaminate, defile, pollute, taint, poison, blight *ant.* clean

infectious *adj.* catching, contagious, communicable

infer *v.* reason, conclude, gather, understand, deduce, guess

inferior *adj.* second-rate, lesser, lower, poor, mediocre, imperfect, ordinary, bad, shoddy, worthless, substandard *ant.* superior

infinite *adj.* eternal, unending, endless, immense, unbounded

inflame *v.* ignite, provoke, excite, stimulate, arouse, irritate *ant.* calm

inflate *v.* ① dilate, swell, pump up, blow up ② exaggerate, build up, jack up, overstate *ant.* contract

inflict *v.* impose, wreak, deal, deliver, force

influence ① *n.* effect, sway, control, guidance, force, power, leadership ② *n.* importance, prestige, clout ③ *v.* affect, sway, change, alter, transform, manipulate, impress, inspire, prejudice

inform *v.* tell, enlighten, advise, notify, brief, let know, acquaint, warn

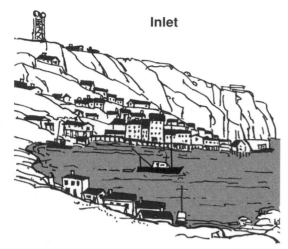
Inlet

informal *adj.* casual, easygoing, familiar, relaxed, simple, unceremonious *ant.* formal

information *n.* facts, data, knowledge, news, intelligence, advice

infrequent *adj.* rare, sporadic *Ferry service was sporadic, so he stayed near the dock until noon.* irregular, unusual, uncommon ▷**occasional** *ant.* frequent

infuriate *v.* anger, enrage, madden, incense, vex ▷**annoy** *ant.* calm

ingenious *adj.* clever, resourceful, shrewd, inventive, creative

ingratiate oneself *v.* curry favour, grovel, flatter

ingredient *n.* component, element, part, factor

inhabit *v.* live in, reside in, dwell in, occupy, populate, settle, colonize

inherit *v.* ① acquire, receive, come into ② succeed to, take over

inhospitable *adj.* ① unfriendly, unkind, unsociable *ant.* hospitable ② forbidding, desolate, austere

inhuman *adj.* barbaric, brutal, beastly, heartless, savage, fierce

initiate *v.* start, launch, establish, found, pioneer, introduce ▷**begin**

initiative *n.* resourcefulness, ambition, drive, enterprise, first step

injure *v.* hurt, harm, wound, abuse, damage, bruise, blemish, deform, disfigure, mar

inkling *n.* suspicion, notion, clue, hint

inlet *n.* bay, gulf, basin, estuary, harbour, fiord

inn *n.* hotel, motel, lodge *hom.* in

innocent *adj.* ① guiltless, faultless, pure, clean, blameless, virtuous *ant.* guilty ② naïve, ignorant, artless

inoffensive *adj.* harmless, safe, gentle, quiet ▷**innocent** *ant.* malevolent

inquire *v.* ask, examine, inspect, check, question, probe, query, investigate, explore

inquisitive *adj.* nosey, snooping, inquiring, questioning ▷**curious**

insane *adj.* demented, mad, crazy, wild, lunatic, deranged, unbalanced *ant.* sane

inscription *n.* heading, caption, legend, epitaph, label

insecure *adj.* ① perilous, unsafe, hazardous, dangerous ② shy, timid, unsure, anxious, apprehensive *ant.* secure

insensitive *adj.* cold, indifferent, unfeeling, dull, thick-skinned, hard, impassive, uncaring, thoughtless *ant.* sensitive

inseparable *adj.* indivisible, one, intertwined, devoted, intimate, close

insert *v.* put in, introduce, add, place, ease, enclose, slip *ant.* remove

insight *n.* awareness, understanding, judgment, knowledge ▷**wisdom**

insignificant *adj.* unimportant, little, measly, irrelevant, dispensable, expendable *ant.* important

insincere *adj.* dishonest, deceptive, two-faced, false, underhanded, hypocritical *ant.* sincere

insinuate *v.* suggest, imply, work in, get at, hint, intimate

insipid *adj.* ① bland, tasteless, flat, flavourless ② banal *I found the whole conversation utterly banal.* colourless, dull, lifeless, trite

insist *v.* assert, maintain, hold to, require, demand, persist, swear *ant.* waive

insolent *adj.* impudent, impertinent, discourteous, insulting, rude, disrespectful *ant.* respectful

inspect *v.* examine, check, study, evaluate, review, search, scan, analyse, scrutinize

Musical Instruments

Accordion
Bagpipes
Balalaika
Banjo
Bassoon
Bells
Bongo drum
Bugle
Castanets
Cello
Clarinet
Cornet
Cymbals
Didgeridoo
Double bass
Drum
Dulcimer
Electric guitar

Fiddle
Fife
Flute
French horn
Glockenspiel
Guitar
Harmonica
Harp
Harpsichord
Kazoo
Kettledrum
Keyboard
Lute
Lyre
Mandolin
Maraca
Oboe
Organ

Piano
Piccolo
Recorder
Saxophone
Steel drum
Synthesizer
Tambourine
Tom-tom
Triangle
Trombone
Trumpet
Tuba
Ukelele
Viola
Violin
Whistle
Xylophone
Zither

inspiration *n.* brain wave, brainstorm, stimulus, motivation, revelation, encouragement

inspire *v.* stimulate, excite, motivate, instigate, stir, provoke, prompt ▷**encourage** *ant.* deter

install *v.* establish, plant, set up, position, introduce, settle, admit

instance *n.* example, case, occasion, occurrence *hom.* instants

instant ① *adj.* immediate, instantaneous *Touch the ant's nest, and there is instantaneous activity.* rapid, sudden, snap ② *n.* moment, minute, flash, second, point

instantly *adv.* at once, right away, immediately, in a flash

instead *adv.* rather, preferably, alternatively

instinct *n.* ① impulse, intuition, feeling, drive, sixth sense ② talent, gift, flair, ability, knack

institute ① *n.* association, college, establishment, organization ② *v.* begin, start, introduce, found, establish

instruct *v.* ① teach, educate, coach, drill, train, tutor ② command, order, direct

instrument *n.* device, gadget, implement, contraption, tool, utensil

insufferable *adj.* unbearable, intolerable, impossible *ant.* tolerable

insufficient *adj.* inadequate, scarce, lacking *Supplies were lacking after the hurricane.* wanting, deficient ▷**short** *ant.* sufficient

insulate *v.* protect, shield, isolate, set apart

insult ① *n.* (*in*-sult) slander, snub, abuse, outrage ② *v.* (in-*sult*) offend, ridicule, humiliate, jeer, mock, taunt, belittle, tease, affront *ant.* compliment

insure *v.* guarantee, protect, cover

intact *adj.* whole, complete, unharmed, uncut, in one piece, sound *ant.* faulty

integrity *n.* honour, honesty, goodness, purity *There is no question about the purity of her intentions.* character, quality, uprightness

intellectual *adj.* scholarly, studious, thoughtful ▷**intelligent**

intelligent *adj.* bright, quick-witted, astute *I can tell from your astute comments that you really understand this.* brainy, brilliant, intellectual ▷**clever** *ant.* stupid

intend *v.* mean, aim, determine, plan, project, resolve, propose, choose, contemplate

intense *adj.* ① extreme, severe, harsh, violent ② ardent, earnest, passionate, vehement ▷**keen** *ant.* mild *hom.* intents

intention *n.* aim, intent, design, end, goal, purpose, target

intercept *v.* stop, arrest, check, obstruct, head off, block ▷**thwart**

interest *n.* ① appeal, fascination, zest, curiosity, concern ② benefit, advantage ③ share, piece, part, stake

interesting *adj.* appealing, fascinating, absorbing, entertaining, compelling *I've been unable to put down this compelling book. ant.* dull

interfere *v.* meddle, intrude, butt in, tamper, intervene, hamper, block *ant.* further

interior *adj.* internal, inner, inside, inward *ant.* exterior

interpret *adj.* explain, decode, construe

interrogate *v.* question, examine, ask, inquire, quiz, grill

interrupt *v.* break in, butt in, disturb, disrupt, suspend, stop, disconnect, sever, discontinue, interfere

interval *n.* space, period, term, intermission

intervene *v.* ① break in, intrude, come to the rescue ▷**interfere** ② mediate, arbitrate

interview *n.* meeting, talk, dialogue, consultation, conference

intimate ① *adj.* (*in*-ti-mit) near, close, familiar, private, secret *ant.* formal ② *v.* (in-ti-*mate*) hint, suggest ▷**insinuate**

intimidate *v.* threaten, scare off, bully, frighten, browbeat

intolerant *adj.* biassed, inflexible, bigoted, narrow-minded, dogmatic *ant.* tolerant

intoxicated *adj.* drunk, inebriated, tipsy

intrepid *adj.* daring, heroic, bold, gallant, brave, courageous, unafraid ▷**fearless**

intricate *adj.* complex, complicated, elaborate, tricky, difficult *ant.* simple

intrigue ① *n.* plot, scheme *Their scheme to crash the computer network failed.* affair ② *v.* attract, fascinate, captivate

introduce *v.* ① acquaint, present, offer ② start, begin, originate, initiate ③ put in, insert, inject

intrude *v.* interrupt, interfere, invade, trespass, meddle, infringe, butt in *ant.* withdraw

inundate *v.* flood, deluge, engulf, immerse, submerge, swamp

invade *v.* attack, raid, storm, overrun, break in, penetrate, assault, assail, enter *ant.* withdraw

invalid ① *adj.* (in-*val*-id) null, void *These tickets are void, because they are more than a year old.* useless ② *n.* (*in*-val-id) patient, sick person, disabled person

invaluable *adj.* precious, costly, priceless *ant.* worthless

invent *v.* create, fabricate, conceive, devise, make up, originate, concoct, coin

invention *n.* creation, discovery, brainchild, device, gadget, contrivance

investigate *v.* probe, analyse, examine, explore, research, inquire, search, study

invisible *adj.* hidden, concealed, out of sight, unseen, masked, imperceptible *ant.* visible

invite *v.* ① ask, request, bid, summon, urge ② attract, entice, tempt, lure

involve *v.* ① concern, engage, mean, include, take in, entail ② complicate, entangle, implicate

irate *adj.* incensed, cross, annoyed, furious, infuriated ▷**angry** *ant.* calm

ironic *adj.* ① satirical, mocking, cynical, derisive ② curious, revealing, telling, apt, surprising

irregular *adj.* ① uncertain, unsettled *The unsettled weather alternated between sun and rain.* unusual ▷**odd** ② disordered, uneven, crooked *ant.* regular

irrelevant *adj.* immaterial, unnecessary, unrelated *ant.* relevant

irresistible *adj.* compelling, fascinating, overpowering, charming *ant.* repulsive

irresponsible *adj.* undependable, unreliable, reckless, flighty *ant.* responsible

irritable *adj.* testy, touchy, grumpy, grouchy, crabby, moody, bad-tempered, edgy, peevish ▷**cross** *ant.* cheerful

irritate *v.* annoy, vex, offend, provoke, chafe, pester, disturb, goad ▷**bother** *ant.* please

issue ① *v.* flow, ooze, discharge, emit ② *v.* bring out, circulate, publish, distribute ③ *n.* edition, printing, publication *After a final edit, Kevin Major's book was ready for publication.* ④ *n.* problem, question, concern

itch ① *v.* prickle, tingle, irritate, tickle ② *n.* impulse, urge, desire

item *n.* detail, feature, ingredient, element, point, thing, object, article

Confusable Words

it's means *it is*

its means *belonging to it*

n. = noun
v. = verb
adj. = adjective
adv. = adverb
conj. = conjunction
prep. = preposition
ant. = antonym
hom. = homonym
▷ = cross-reference

J j

jab *v.* poke, prod, push, stab, dig, thrust

jabber *v.* chatter, mumble, babble

jagged *adj.* rough, broken, notched, uneven, irregular *ant.* smooth

jail *n.* prison, penitentiary, brig

jam ① *n.* predicament *Losing my voice just before the school concert put me in a terrible predicament.* tight spot, pickle ② *n.* jelly, preserve, marmalade ③ *v.* crowd, pack, crush, squeeze, sandwich, cram, block, ram *hom.* jamb

jar ① *n.* jug, bottle, flask, vase, pitcher, pot ② *v.* jog, jangle, grate, jolt

jealous *adj.* envious, green, grudging *With a grudging look, my sister took off my new basketball shoes.* resentful, possessive

jealousy *n.* envy, resentment, spite

jeer *v.* laugh at, deride, mock, ridicule, insult ▷**taunt**

jeopardize *v.* risk, compromise, threaten, endanger *ant.* protect

jerk *n. & v.* yank, pull, drag, jog, jolt, tug, wrench

jest *n.* joke, teasing, playfulness, banter

jester *n.* clown, joker, comedian, buffoon, prankster

jet *n. & v.* spurt, squirt, flow, gush, stream

jewel *n.* gem, stone, trinket, treasure

jiffy *n.* instant, flash, twinkling, moment

jilt *v.* abandon, desert, drop, forsake

jingle *v.* tinkle, clink, ring, jangle

job *n.* ① task, work, chore ② office, post, position, occupation, profession, trade

jog *v.* ① prod, nudge, shake ② run, sprint, trot, exercise

join *v.* ① unite, link, combine, connect, attach, merge, couple *ant.* separate ② enlist, enrol, enter, sign up

joint ① *n.* junction, knot, union, connection, seam, bond, link ② *adj.* shared, common, united, mutual *It's in our mutual interest to study together.*

joke *n.* gag, trick, frolic, lark, prank, antic, laugh ▷**jest**

jolt *n. & v.* jar, shock, shove, rock, jerk, bump

jostle *v.* push, shove, shoulder, thrust, elbow

jot *v.* note, scribble, take down

journal *n.* ① diary, ledger, account book ② newspaper, magazine

journey *n.* trip, voyage, excursion, expedition, tour

jovial *adj.* jolly, festive, good-humoured,

Jewels

Agate	Lapis lazuli
Amber	Moonstone
Amethyst	Onyx
Aquamarine	Opal
Bloodstone	Pearl
Carnelian	Ruby
Coral	Sapphire
Diamond	Sardonyx
Emerald	Topaz
Garnet	Tourmaline
Jade	Turquoise
Jasper	Zircon

cheerful, light-hearted ▷**merry** *ant.* sad

joy *n.* happiness, delight, pleasure, charm, rapture, enchantment ▷**bliss** *ant.* sorrow

joyful *adj.* happy, glad, elated, merry, joyous, delighted, exultant, blissful *ant.* sorrowful

judge ① *n.* justice, magistrate, referee, umpire, arbitrator ② *v.* assess, decide, find, appraise, estimate, evaluate ③ *v.* blame, criticize, condemn

judgment *n.* ① decision, ruling, sentence, verdict *The jury gave a verdict of not guilty.* decree, finding ② intelligence, understanding, taste, discretion, good sense ③ opinion, view, estimation

judicious *adj.* prudent, shrewd, discreet, expedient, wise

jug *n.* pitcher, urn, vase ▷**jar**

juice *n.* essence, extract, sap, fluid, nectar

jumble *n.* disorder, assortment, collection, mixture, muddle, tangle, clutter

jump *v. & n.* spring, bound, hop, skip, vault ▷**leap**

junction *n.* crossroads, intersection, juncture, crossing, connection, union, combination, joint

jungle *n.* forest, bush, wilderness, thicket, tangle

junior *adj.* lesser, lower, younger, subordinate *ant.* superior

junk *n.* garbage, trash, debris, rubbish, waste, clutter, litter, scrap, refuse

just ① *adj.* exact, fair, honest, impartial, lawful, reasonable, appropriate ② *adv.* exactly, precisely ③ *adv.* only, merely, simply

justice *n.* equity, impartiality, fairness, right, legitimacy *ant.* prejudice, wrong

justify *v.* vindicate, acquit, defend *What I did is wrong and I know I can't defend it.* explain, clear, account for, excuse

jut *v.* bulge, extend, stick out, overhang, project *ant.* recede

juvenile ① *adj.* adolescent, youthful, young, childish, immature *ant.* mature ② *n.* boy, girl, child, youngster, youth

K k

keen *adj.* ① eager, enthusiastic, earnest, diligent ② sharp, acute, fine, clever *ant.* dull, poor

keep *v.* ① hold, save, reserve, retain, collect, possess *ant.* abandon ② care for, maintain, protect, guard, tend, preserve, shelter *The raccoon sheltered her young from the rain.* protect, guard, tend ③ detain, confine

keep on *v.* continue, go on, endure, persist *ant.* give up

keepsake *n.* souvenir, token, memento, reminder, relic

keg *n.* barrel, cask, tub, drum, container

kerchief *n.* scarf, shawl, cloth

kernel *n.* seed, core, heart, hub, centre, gist, nub *hom.* colonel

key ① *n.* opener ② *n.* solution, clue, answer ③ *n.* isle, reef, atoll ④ *adj.* essential, fundamental, vital, crucial, primary, significant *hom.* quay, cay

kick *v.* boot, punt, strike

kidnap *v.* abduct, hijack, carry off, seize, snatch, capture, steal

kill *v.* slay, assassinate, destroy, massacre, slaughter, execute, exterminate, butcher, murder

kin *n.* kindred, people, clan, family, relation, relative

kind ① *adj.* thoughtful, considerate, friendly, gentle, merciful, good-natured, amiable *ant.* unkind ② *n.* type, breed, category, class, character, sort, variety

kindle *v.* ① light, ignite, set fire to ② inflame *Being ignored inflamed their angry feelings even more.* excite, provoke, rouse

kindness *n.* good nature, charity, amiability, affection, tenderness, sympathy, compassion, benevolence *ant.* spite

king *n.* monarch, sovereign, his majesty, ruler, emperor

kink *n.* knot, loop, bend, coil

kiss *v & n.* caress, smack, peck, brush

kit *n.* tools, equipment, outfit, gear

knack *n.* flair, talent, ability, genius, gift ▷**skill**

knead *v.* form, squeeze, mould, shape, press, mix, work *hom.* need

knife *n.* scalpel, blade, dagger, cutter

knight *n.* cavalier, champion, soldier, warrior *hom.* night

knit *v.* weave, crochet, spin, link, loop

knob *n.* ① handle, opener, button ② bump

knock *v.* hit, slap, punch, bang, strike, thump, tap

knoll *n.* hill, mound, hillock, rise, pingo

knot ① *v.* tie, secure, join ② *n.* tangle, kink ③ *n.* group, cluster *hom.* not

know *v.* perceive, discern, notice, identify, determine, grasp, experience, recognize ▷**understand** *hom.* no

know-how *n.* skill, knowledge, expertise, ability

knowing *adj.* astute, knowledgeable, intelligent, perceptive, wise, shrewd *ant.* ignorant

knowledge *n.* ① understanding, acquaintance, learning, wisdom, scholarship, education ② information, data, facts

kudos *n.* prestige, distinction, fame, glory, recognition, praise

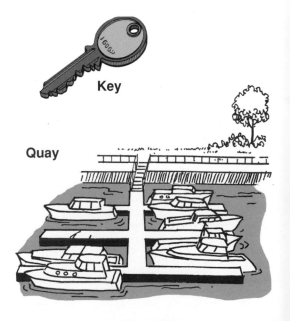

Key

Quay

L l

label *n.* badge, tag, ticket, sticker, slip

laborious *adj.* strenuous, arduous *Building Canada's railways was arduous work.* tiring, difficult *ant.* easy

labour *n. & v.* toil, work, drudge, strain, struggle, slog, sweat

lack ① *n.* need, want, absence, deficiency, shortage, deficit, scarcity *There was a scarcity of empty seats at the popular concert.* ② *v.* need, require, want, miss

laden *adj.* loaded, burdened, hampered, weighed down *ant.* empty

ladle *v.* dip, scoop, dish, shovel

lady *n.* woman, female, damsel, matron

lag *v.* dawdle, loiter *Please come straight home without loitering!* trail, delay ▷**linger** *ant.* hurry

lagoon *n.* pool, pond, lake, basin

lair *n.* den, nest, retreat, hideout, hole

lake *n.* lagoon, pond, pool, reservoir, slough

lame *adj.* ① crippled, hobbled, disabled ② weak, feeble, inadequate, unconvincing

lament *v.* mourn, grieve, deplore ▷**regret** *ant.* rejoice

lamp *n.* lantern, light, flare

lance ① *n.* spear, pike, javelin, shaft ② *v.* puncture, pierce, cut

land ① *n.* country, earth, tract, area, nation, region, property, estate ② *v.* alight, arrive, catch, touch down, snag, dismount

landmark *n.* milestone, beacon, monument, signpost

landscape *n.* scenery, view, prospect, countryside, panorama

lane *n.* alley, driveway, passage, path *hom.* lain

language *n.* ① tongue, speech, dialect ② jargon, slang, vocabulary

languid *adj.* leisurely, unhurried, sluggish, slow, easy, lackadaisical, apathetic, listless *ant.* lively

languish *v.* decline, droop, flag, pine, yearn, wither, fade *ant.* flourish

lanky *adj.* tall, rangy, gangling, scrawny, thin *ant.* stout

lantern *n.* lamp, flashlight, light

lap ① *v.* lick, drink, gobble ② *n.* circuit, course, leg, length ③ *n.* thighs, knees

lapse *v.* expire, die, pass, fail, flag *When his little sister's interest flagged, he suggested that they play a different game.* fall, deteriorate, run out *hom.* laps

large *adj.* bulky, substantial, great, broad, vast, extensive, roomy, spacious, important, general ▷**huge** *ant.* small

lash ① *v.* beat, whip, flay, flog ② *v.* prod, goad, drive ③ *n.* whip

last ① *adj.* final, concluding, latest, utmost *Fresh bamboo is of the utmost importance in the diet of panda bears.* ultimate, recent, latter, previous *ant.* first ② *v.* remain, linger, endure, stay, continue, persist, survive

latch *n.* bolt, catch, padlock, fastener

late *adj.* ① overdue, belated, tardy *ant.* early ② departed, former, past, previous, dead

lately *adv.* recently, of late, formerly

lather *n.* suds, foam, bubbles, froth, sweat

latter *adj.* final, last, later, recent, second *ant.* former

laud *v.* extol, praise, applaud, glorify, honour

laugh *v.* chuckle, giggle, guffaw, snicker, titter, cackle *ant.* cry

launch *v.* start, begin, commence, establish, initiate *If you initiate the conversation, others will join in.* introduce

lavish ① *adj.* abundant, generous, liberal, extravagant, luxurious ② *v.* waste, squander *Squander all your energy on the preparations and you'll be too tired to enjoy the party!* ③ *v.* give, shower

law *n.* rule, ordinance, regulation, edict, decree, statute, act, standard, principle

lawful *adj.* legal, legitimate, rightful, innocent *ant.* illegal

lawyer *n.* attorney, counsel, jurist, advocate, Crown attorney, QC

lax *adj.* careless, casual, slack, relaxed, tolerant, loose, negligent *ant.* strict *hom.* lacks

L

lay *v.* ① put, set, deposit, place, prepare, spread, rest, park ② charge, assign

Confusable Words

lay means *put*
lie means *recline*

learn means *understand*
teach means *instruct*

let means *allow*
leave means *abandon*

layer *n.* coat, sheet, thickness, tier, seam *The quarry walls showed seams of different kinds of rock.* vein, deposit

lazy *adj.* idle, inactive, slothful, sluggish, passive, slack *ant.* energetic

lead *v.* conduct, guide, escort, direct, command, govern, pilot, steer *ant.* follow

leader *n.* boss, chief, head, director, manager, captain, master, front-runner, guide, pilot, conductor

leaf *n.* ① frond, blade ② sheet, page

league *n.* band, association, society, group, federation, coalition, alliance, conference, class

leak *v.* trickle, ooze, seep, flow out, filter, dribble *hom.* leek

lean ① *adj.* slim, thin, gaunt, skinny ② *adj.* spare, poor, non-productive ③ *v.* tilt, incline, slant, slope, depend, rely, prop *hom.* lien

leap *v.* spring, bound, jump, hop, skip

learn *v.* understand, absorb, assimilate, digest, master, discover, ascertain *Looking at the map will help us ascertain where we are.* determine

learned *adj.* educated, scholarly, literate, lettered, cultivated, cultured *ant.* ignorant

learning *n.* scholarship, education, knowledge ▷**wisdom**

least *adj.* fewest, smallest, slightest, lowest, tiniest *ant.* most *hom.* leased

leave ① *v.* go, depart, exit, quit, abandon, desert, retire, forsake ② *n.* will, bequeath, pass ③ *n.* vacation, furlough

lecture *n.* talk, speech, address, sermon, lesson

ledge *n.* shelf, ridge, step

legacy *n.* bequest *Connor's stamp collection was a bequest from his late Aunt Brenda.* inheritance, gift, birthright

legal *adj.* legitimate, lawful, valid, sound, authorized, rightful, permissible, proper *ant.* illegal

legend *n.* ① fable, myth, tale, fiction, lore *According to Nova Scotian lore, Oak Island is the site of buried treasure.* ② inscription, heading, caption

legible *adj.* clear, readable, understandable, distinct *ant.* illegible

legitimate *adj.* legal, lawful, proper, rightful, true ▷**genuine** *ant.* illegitimate

leisurely *adj.* unhurried, slow, easy, carefree, tranquil *ant.* hectic

lend *v.* loan, advance, provide, supply, grant, lease *ant.* borrow

lengthen *v.* extend, stretch, draw out, prolong, spin out, elongate *ant.* shorten

lengthy *adj.* long, drawn out, rambling, wordy, verbose, long-winded *ant.* brief

lenient *adj.* tolerant, merciful, sparing, indulgent, compassionate, humane, mild *ant.* severe

less *adj.* fewer, smaller, inferior, lower

lessen *v.* reduce, decrease, cut, diminish, shrink, taper, subside *ant.* increase *hom.* lesson

lesson *n.* ① instruction, lecture, unit, teaching, exercise, seminar, class, course ② warning, example *hom.* lessen

let *v.* allow, permit, authorize *The principal authorized our class to go on a field trip to the fort.* entitle, enable *ant.* forbid

let down *v.* ① betray, abandon, disappoint ② lower, take down

letter *n.* ① dispatch, communication, message, note, epistle ② character *In Cree syllabic script, each character stands for a whole syllable.* sign, symbol

n. = noun
v. = verb
adj. = adjective
adv. = adverb
conj. = conjunction
prep. = preposition
ant. = antonym
hom. = homonym
▷ = cross-reference

Lights

Arc lamp
Candle
Chandelier
Desk lamp
Flashlight
Floor lamp
Fluorescent lamp
Footlights
Headlight
Lantern
Night light
Reading light
Spotlight
Table lamp
Torch

level ① *n.* floor, plane, grade, degree
② *adj.* even, flat, equal, smooth *ant.* uneven
③ *v.* aim, direct, point ④ *v.* demolish
*They rebuilt the houses demolished by
the tornado.* destroy, raze

liable ① *adj.* answerable, accountable,
responsible ② prone, likely, inclined,
subject, apt *My parents are apt to be
pleased when I help out in the yard.*

liar *n.* deceiver, fibber, perjurer, fabricator

libel *v.* slander, malign, slur, defame, vilify,
blacken *ant.* praise

liberal *adj.* ① generous, open-hearted, free,
lavish ② progressive, broad-minded

liberate *v.* set free, save, release *ant.* restrict

liberty *n.* freedom, independence, release
ant. slavery

license *v.* allow, permit, entitle, approve,
sanction *ant.* ban

lie ① *n.* fib, fiction, untruth, falsehood
② *v.* recline *Tired Annie reclined on the
chesterfield.* lounge, repose, rest, loll, be
situated ▷**sprawl** ③ *v.* fib, invent, falsify,
perjure oneself, deceive *hom.* lye

life *n.* being, existence, activity, energy, pep,
breath, animation *ant.* death

lift *v.* ① raise, erect, hoist, elevate, pick up,
boost, support *ant.* lower ② end, revoke

light ① *n.* radiance, glow, shine, glare,
brightness, illumination ② *n.* lamp, beacon,
flame ③ angle, viewpoint, slant ④ *v.* ignite,
illuminate, kindle *The scouts kindled a fire
to cook their food.* ⑤ *adj.* light-coloured,
fair, pale, sunny *ant.* dark ⑥ *adj.* airy,
lightweight, buoyant *ant.* heavy

like ① *prep.* similar to, resembling, akin to
Our love of snakes is akin to a mania.
ant. unlike ② *v.* admire, approve of,
esteem, respect, enjoy, relish, prefer
ant. dislike

likely *adj.* probable, expected, liable

likeness *n.* ① resemblance, similarity
② image, copy, photograph, portrait

likewise *adv.* also, too, similarly, equally

limb *n.* leg, arm, extension, branch, bough

limit ① *n.* barrier, boundary, border, edge,
end, restraint, perimeter, extremity
② *v.* reduce, restrict, confine *Our cattle
are confined to the barn during this storm.*
bound, curb, inhibit, control *ant.* free

limited *adj.* restricted, reduced, narrow,
confined, local *ant.* unrestricted

L

n. = noun

v. = verb

adj. = adjective

adv. = adverb

conj. = conjunction

prep. = preposition

ant. = antonym

hom. = homonym

▷ = cross-reference

limp ① *adj.* flabby, droopy, drained, flaccid ② *v.* hobble, falter, shuffle, stagger

line *n.* ① stripe, streak, dash, bar, crease, furrow ② cord, thread, string ③ row, queue, file, rank, procession ④ occupation, business

linger *v.* loiter, lag, dally, tarry, delay, pause, stay, procrastinate, dawdle ▷**remain** *ant.* depart

link ① *n.* bond, tie, connection, joint, relation ② *v.* unite, join, couple, combine, associate *ant.* separate

liquid *n.* fluid, solution, juice, sap, liquor

list ① *n.* schedule, table, catalogue, register, roll, roster ② *v.* record, enumerate, tabulate, index, itemize ③ tilt, lean, heel *The* Bluenose *heeled over as it turned into the offshore wind.*

listen *v.* ① hear, hark ② heed, obey

listless *adj.* languid, dull, lethargic, lifeless, apathetic ▷**sluggish** *ant.* lively

literally *adv.* actually, word for word, narrowly, precisely, really

literate *adj.* educated, learned *She has studied for many years and is very learned.* lettered *ant.* illiterate

litter *n.* clutter, jumble, rubbish, mess ▷**trash**

little ① *adj.* tiny, short, slight, miniature, petite ② petty, trivial, minor ▷**small** *ant.* large ③ *adv.* hardly, rarely, seldom *We seldom play with those toys.* infrequently

live ① *adj.* alive, living, existing *ant.* dead ② *adj.* in concert, on stage ③ *v.* be, subsist, exist, survive, remain, persist, endure *ant.* die

lively *adj.* active, brisk, vivacious, animated, agile, energetic, spry, frisky *ant.* listless

livid *adj.* ① angry, enraged, furious, incensed ② ashen, greyish, pale, leaden

living ① *adj.* alive, existing, live ② *n.* job, occupation, work, livelihood

load ① *n.* freight, cargo, goods, burden, shipment ② *v.* fill, pack, burden, pile up, stack, charge, arm *hom.* lode, lowed

loaf ① *v.* waste time, idle, dally ② *n.* block, cube, lump, cake

loan ① *n.* credit, advance, allowance ② *v.* allow, lend, advance *Her parents advanced her the money, and she promised to pay it back. hom.* lone

loathe *v.* detest, despise, dislike, abhor ▷**hate** *ant.* like

lobby *n.* foyer, vestibule, entrance, hallway

local *adj.* regional, district, provincial, isolated, limited, neighbourhood

locate *v.* find, discover, detect

lock ① *n.* bolt, fastener, latch, clasp ② *v.* bolt, fasten, secure ③ *n.* floodgate ④ *n.* curl, braid, tress

lodge ① *v.* stay, put up, shelter, remain ② *v.* get stuck ③ *n.* inn, hotel

lofty *adj.* ① tall, high, noble, great, towering, exalted ② proud, arrogant, snobbish, haughty *ant.* modest

logical *adj.* fair, reasonable, sound, rational, clear, lucid *ant.* absurd

loiter *v.* linger, trail, dawdle, hang around, dally, lag, delay, idle

lone *adj.* ① one, single, sole, lonely, separate, solitary, unaccompanied *hom.* loan

lonely *adj.* alone, forlorn, lonesome, solitary, forsaken, friendless, remote, deserted, abandoned

long ① *adj.* lengthy, extended, expanded, elongated *The giraffe has an elongated neck.* prolonged *ant.* short ② *v.* crave, hanker, yearn, desire, want, pine

look ① *v.* appear, seem ② *v.* peer, glance, watch, stare, gape, gawk ③ *n.* appearance, expression, glance, gaze ④ *v.* examine, inspect, consider ⑤ *v.* search, seek, hunt

loom *v.* menace, rise, emerge, threaten

loop *n.* bend, circle, coil, noose, twist, ring

loophole *n.* escape, way out, excuse

loose *adj.* ① slack, limp, relaxed, flimsy, flabby, baggy ② free, unconfined ③ vague, indefinite

Confusable Words

loose means *not tight*

lose means *misplace*

Loot   Lute

loosen *v.* slacken, relax, undo, detach, release, unfasten, ease *ant.* tighten

loot *n.* booty, haul, spoils, prize, plunder *hom.* lute

lord *n.* noble, ruler, duke, marquis, earl, viscount, baron

lose *v.* ① mislay, misplace, miss *ant.* find ② be defeated, fail, sacrifice, yield, forfeit *ant.* win

loser *n.* failure, dud, flop *ant.* winner

loss *n.* damage, harm, forfeit *Missing the hike was the forfeit he suffered for sleeping late.* ruin, misfortune *ant.* profit

lost *adj.* ① mislaid, missing, gone, vanished, disappeared, strayed, ruined *ant.* recovered ② forgotten, erased

lot *n.* ① group, batch, assortment, allotment, heap ② fate *Do you believe you can change your fate?* fortune ③ plot, patch, land, parcel, tract

lotion *n.* balm, salve, ointment, liniment

loud *adj.* ① noisy, blatant, shrill, blaring, deafening, boisterous, clamorous, rowdy *ant.* quiet ② gaudy, vulgar, tasteless

lounge ① *v.* recline, lie, loll, sprawl, laze, idle ② *n.* parlour, reception room, sitting room

lovable *adj.* adorable, charming, attractive, delightful, winsome *ant.* hateful

love ① *v.* adore, idolize, worship, dote on, cherish, treasure, admire, revere *ant.* hate ② *n.* affection, passion, devotion, ardour, romance, adoration

lovely *adj.* charming, delightful, beautiful, adorable, attractive, comely, magnificent *ant.* hideous

low *adj.* ① base, vulgar, crude ② not high, short, sunken ③ soft, faint, muffled, deep *ant.* high ④ glum, depressed *hom.* lo

lower ① *v.* let down, drop, reduce, depress ② *adj.* inferior, lesser, smaller, minor, subordinate

loyal *adj.* constant, staunch, true, devoted, reliable ▷**faithful** *ant.* treacherous

lucid *adj.* clear, rational, intelligible *Choose your words more carefully and your argument will be more intelligible.* coherent ▷**transparent** *ant.* murky

luck *n.* chance, fortune, success, fate, risk *ant.* misfortune

lucky *adj.* fortunate, successful, blessed, charmed, favoured, happy, promising *ant.* unlucky

ludicrous *adj.* absurd, foolish, silly, laughable, outlandish ▷**ridiculous**

lug *v.* pull, draw, drag, haul, tow, heave, carry, move

luggage *n.* baggage, suitcases, trunks, boxes

lull ① *v.* calm, hush, soothe, quiet, subside ② *n.* calm, slowdown, break, stillness

lumber ① *n.* timber, wood, boards, logs ② *v.* plod, shuffle, clump

luminous *adj.* shining, radiant, bright

lump *n.* bit, piece, chunk, block, knob, swelling

lunatic *n.* maniac, psychopath, fool

lunge *v.* rush, thrust, plunge, charge, pounce

lurch *v.* lean, list, reel, rock, stagger, stumble

lure *v.* attract, draw, decoy, ensnare, invite, entice ▷**tempt** *ant.* repulse

lurid *adj.* ghastly, disgusting, grim, grisly, melodramatic, sensational, garish

lurk *v.* slink, skulk *Is that a burglar skulking about in the dark?* sneak, crouch, hide, prowl, snoop

luscious *adj.* juicy, succulent, mellow, delicious, scrumptious, delightful

lush *adj.* wild, green, rich, abundant, thick, profuse, luxuriant

lust *n.* desire, passion, craving, greed, hunger

lustre *n.* brightness, brilliance, gleam, sheen

luxury *n.* wealth, richness, comfort, affluence, splendour, abundance, opulence

M m

macabre *adj.* morbid, ghastly, grisly, hideous, horrible, sinister

machine *n.* apparatus, appliance, tool, device

mad *adj.* ① furious, cross, annoyed, enraged ▷**angry** ② lunatic, crazy ▷**insane** *ant.* sane

magic ① *n.* witchcraft, hocus-pocus, sorcery, wizardry ② *n.* spell, trance, charm ③ *adj.* bewitching, fascinating, entrancing, enchanting, miraculous, magical

magician *n.* wizard, witch, sorcerer, juggler, conjuror

magistrate *n.* judge, justice, bailiff, official

magnanimous *adj.* forgiving, generous, charitable *It was charitable of him to forgive you.* liberal

magnate *n.* industrialist, merchant, tycoon, VIP, leader *hom.* magnet

magnet *n.* attraction, bait, draw, lodestone *The Olympic Games is the lodestone that draws together the world's finest athletes.* *hom.* magnate

magnetic *adj.* charismatic, attractive, absorbing, entrancing, alluring, mesmerizing ▷**charming** *ant.* repulsive

magnificent *adj.* majestic, noble, grand, stately, regal, brilliant, superb ▷**splendid**

magnify *v.* ① enlarge, increase, amplify, intensify ▷**enhance** *ant.* diminish, reduce ② exaggerate, overstate

maid *n.* ① servant, domestic, help, employee ② girl, maiden, lass, damsel *hom.* made

mail *n.* ① letters, post, correspondence ② armour *hom.* male

maim *v.* mutilate, injure, mangle, crush, cripple ▷**disable** *ant.* heal

main ① *adj.* leading, principal, central, chief, major, primary, key, head ② *n.* channel, duct, line, pipe *hom.* mane

mainly *adv.* generally, mostly, usually, on the whole, chiefly

Mail

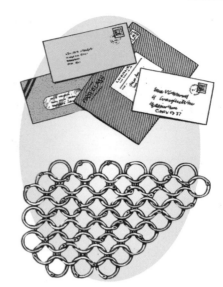

Mail

maintain *v.* ① look after, keep, support, preserve ② declare, affirm, argue *She argued that fairness was more important than popularity.* insist, assert ③ continue, keep up, sustain

majestic *adj.* dignified, grand, noble, regal, stately, royal, splendid, magnificent

major *adj.* senior, chief, leading, important, primary, principal, greater, larger *ant.* minor

majority *n.* ① greater number, most part, bulk, mass ② adulthood, legal age

make *v.* ① build, construct, fabricate, manufacture, produce, prepare *ant.* destroy ② force, compel, drive, coerce ③ appoint, designate *Regina was designated the Queen's City.*

make up *v.* ① invent, fabricate, create, improvise ② reconcile, forgive and forget ③ atone, compensate

makeshift *adj.* improvised, temporary, stopgap *ant.* permanent

male *adj.* masculine, manly, boyish *ant.* female

malevolent *adj.* evil, hateful, wicked, vicious, nasty, malicious ▷**hostile** *ant.* sympathetic

malice *n.* hatred, bitterness, spite, malevolence, enmity, rancour *His heart was filled with rancour after his best friends betrayed him.* *ant.* kindness

n. = noun
v. = verb
adj. = adjective
adv. = adverb
conj. = conjunction
prep. = preposition
ant. = antonym
hom. = homonym
▷ = cross-reference

malicious *adj.* spiteful, vicious, hostile, malevolent ▷**hurtful** *ant.* kind

mammoth *adj.* giant, enormous, massive, colossal ▷**huge** *ant.* small

man ① *n.* humankind ② *n.* male, fellow, guy ③ *v.* crew, staff, operate

manage *v.* ① direct, control, administer, supervise, run ② handle, manipulate ③ get along, cope, fare, fend

manager *n.* director, supervisor, boss, administrator, superintendent, overseer, executive

mandate *n.* task, authority, command, instruction

mangle *v.* crush, destroy, batter, maul, deform ▷**maim**

mania *n.* craze, fad, enthusiasm, passion, madness, delirium, craziness

manifest *v.* reveal, demonstrate, prove, display, exhibit *She exhibits a friendly concern for her lonely classmate at recess.* ▷**show** *ant.* hide

manipulate *v.* work, handle, wield, control, manage, use, exploit ▷**operate**

manly *adj.* masculine, macho, brave, bold, strong

manner *n.* ① fashion, style, form, mode, method ② behaviour, appearance, attitude, demeanour, bearing *hom.* manor

manoeuvre *v.* direct, drive, guide, scheme, wangle, navigate, move ▷**manipulate**

manor *n.* estate, mansion, château, hall *hom.* manner

mansion *n.* house, castle, residence, estate ▷**manor**

mantle *n.* cape, covering, hood, cloak, shroud *hom.* mantel

manual ① *adj.* hand-operated *We saw hand-operated machinery at the pioneer museum.* physical ② *n.* guide, guidebook, handbook

manufacture *v.* make, build, construct, fabricate, create, produce

many *adj.* numerous, varied, various, frequent, countless, abundant, myriad *ant.* few

map *n.* chart, plan, diagram, outline

mar *v.* deface *The graffiti defaced the bridge.* disfigure, injure, blemish, damage ▷**spoil** *ant.* enhance

march *v.* walk, stride, pace, step, strut, swagger, parade, file, trek, advance

margin *n.* edge, border, rim, side, brim, brink, boundary

mark ① *n. & v.* blemish, stain, smudge, smear, scratch ② *n.* imprint, indentation, impression *The Mounties studied the impression left in the dirt by the thief's shoe.* ③ *n.* brand, trademark, stamp, seal ④ *v.* indicate, show, notice

marked *adj.* noticeable, apparent, clear, striking, conspicuous

market *n.* store, supermarket, grocery, bazaar, fair

maroon *v.* desert, leave stranded, abandon, beach, cast away *ant.* rescue

marry *v.* wed, get married, mate, unite, join, betroth *ant.* separate *hom.* merry

marsh *n.* swamp, bog, wetland, morass

marshal *v.* gather, group, assemble, mobilize, muster *hom.* martial

martial *adj.* military, militant, warlike *ant.* peaceful *hom.* marshal

marvel *n.* miracle, wonder, spectacle, sensation, phenomenon

marvellous *adj.* wonderful, fabulous, spectacular, superb, astounding, amazing, astonishing ▷**remarkable** *ant.* ordinary

mash *v.* crush, squash, grind, pulverize

mask ① *n.* disguise, camouflage, veil ② *v.* conceal, disguise, veil, cover *ant.* uncover

mass *n.* ① matter, body, lump, heap ② batch, load, quantity, crowd

massacre *v.* murder, kill, slaughter, butcher, exterminate

massive *adj.* immense, enormous, giant, bulky, heavy ▷**huge** *ant.* small

master ① *n.* lord, owner, leader, captain, chief, champion ② *adj.* main, controlling, original ③ *v.* tame, control, subdue, conquer, learn, overcome

match ① *n.* light, fuse ② *n.* game, contest ③ *v.* copy, pair, mate, equal

M m M m M m M

mate ① *n.* spouse, husband, wife, partner ② *n.* friend, companion, chum ③ *v.* breed, join, wed, marry

material ① *n.* matter, substance, stuff, data, literature ② *n.* fabric, cloth, textile ③ *adj.* actual, relevant, real, concrete *This is concrete evidence for our theory.*

maternal *adj.* motherly, parental, kind, affectionate, protective

matter ① *n.* stuff, material, substance ② *n.* subject, topic, concern, issue ③ *n.* trouble, problem ④ *v.* signify, count, be important

mature *adj.* adult, grown, ripe, developed, seasoned, mellowed *ant.* immature

maul *v.* batter, molest, paw ▷**mangle**

maxim *n.* saying, motto, axiom, proverb

maximum *adj.* supreme, highest, greatest, most, top, largest, ultimate *ant.* minimum

maybe *adv.* possibly, perhaps, conceivably

Confusable Words

maybe means *perhaps*

may be means *could be*

maze *n.* puzzle, tangle, confusion, labyrinth ▷**muddle** *hom.* maize

meadow *n.* field, pasture, grassland

meagre *adj.* thin, slight, paltry, sparse *Food for the caribou is sparse in the winter.* ▷**scanty** *ant.* substantial

meal *n.* dinner, lunch, breakfast, supper, repast, feed, banquet ▷**feast**

mean ① *v.* indicate, signify, denote, express, suggest, imply ② *adj.* cruel, unkind, nasty ③ *adj.* stingy, miserly *ant.* generous ④ *adj.* average, medium *hom.* mien

Measurements

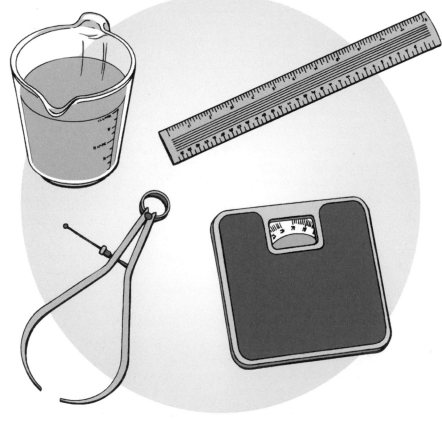

Millimetre	(mm)
Centimetre	(cm)
Metre	(m)
Kilometre	(km)
Millilitre	(mL)
Litre	(L)
Milligram	(mg)
Gram	(g)
Kilogram	(kg)
Tonne	(t)

n. = noun
v. = verb
adj. = adjective
adv. = adverb
conj. = conjunction
prep. = preposition
ant. = antonym
hom. = homonym
▷ = cross-reference

meaning *n.* significance, explanation, sense, definition, purpose, implication

means *n.* ① resources, money, wealth ② tool, instrument, technique, method, pathway, strategy

measure ① *n.* limit, extent, amount, size, dimension, standard ② *v.* estimate, value, gauge, survey, rate, determine, quantify, appraise ③ *n.* step, action

mechanical *adj.* ① machine-driven ② routine, wooden *We were disappointed in the actor's wooden performance.* automatic, unthinking

medal *n.* award, prize, decoration, ribbon, trophy *hom.* meddle

meddle *v.* interfere, intrude, tamper, butt in *hom.* medal

medicine *n.* remedy, cure, antidote, drug, prescription, pill, tablet, ointment

mediocre *adj.* average, medium, common, unimpressive ▷**ordinary** *ant.* excellent

meditate *v.* ponder, puzzle over, think, reflect, contemplate, consider

medium ① *adj.* average, fair, middle ▷**mediocre** ② *n.* setting, environment *The quiet of the library makes it an excellent environment for study.* ③ *n.* means, agent, material

medley *n.* assortment, jumble, collection

meek *adj.* docile, humble, quiet, patient, uncomplaining, gentle ▷**mild** *ant.* arrogant

meet *v.* ① intersect, converge, join up ② flock, assemble, congregate ③ face, encounter, confront *hom.* meat, mete

meeting *n.* gathering, assembly, convention, appointment, date

melancholy *adj.* mournful, unhappy, depressed, blue, gloomy, glum ▷**miserable** *ant.* cheerful

mellow *adj.* ① ripe, rich, mature, full-flavoured *ant.* unripe ② smooth, soothing, laid-back, relaxed

melodious *adj.* melodic, musical, resonant, sweet, mellow *Because he has such a mellow voice, Abdul will sing the solo.* rich *ant.* harsh

melody *n.* tune, air, song, chant, theme

melt *v.* thaw, defrost, dissolve, liquefy, soften, fade *ant.* freeze

member *n.* ① fellow, associate, participant, representative ② limb, part, leg, arm

memorable *adj.* unforgettable, indelible, noticeable, striking *The maple syrup cake had such a striking flavour that everyone was still talking about it the next day.* noteworthy ▷**remarkable**

memorial *n.* remembrance, monument, memento, tribute, mausoleum

memorize *v.* learn, remember, note, learn by heart, commit to memory

memory *n.* recall, recollection *I have a faint recollection of taking my first steps.* remembrance, vestige, trace

menace *v.* threaten, intimidate, frighten, alarm ▷**bully**

mend *v.* fix, restore, correct, improve ▷**repair** *ant.* break

mental *adj.* intellectual, psychological, cerebral, rational, cognitive *ant.* physical

mention *v.* say, tell, state, name, refer to, announce, remark, disclose

mercenary ① *adj.* grasping, greedy, corrupt, ruthless, acquisitive ▷**selfish** ② *n.* soldier of fortune, freelancer, adventurer

merchandise *n.* goods, products, stock, inventory, commodities

merchant *n.* vendor, retailer, dealer, trader

merciful *adj.* humane, lenient, forgiving, compassionate, tolerant *ant.* merciless

merciless *adj.* cruel, pitiless, callous, unrelenting *There were no clouds to shade us from the unrelenting rays of the sun.* inhuman, remorseless *ant.* merciful

mercy *n.* compassion, sympathy, forgiveness, pardon, clemency, grace, charity ▷**pity** *ant.* spite

merge *v.* mix, mingle, combine, blend, fuse, weld ▷**unite**

merit ① *n.* excellence, quality, virtue, worth, calibre ▷**value** ② *v.* be worthy of, deserve, earn, warrant

merry *adj.* jolly, cheerful, gleeful, mirthful ▷**happy** *ant.* gloomy

M m M m M M m M

n. = noun

v. = verb

adj. = adjective

adv. = adverb

conj. = conjunction

prep. = preposition

ant. = antonym

hom. = homonym

▷ = cross-reference

Metals

Aluminum
Brass
Bronze
Chromium
Copper
Gold
Iron and Steel
Lead
Manganese
Mercury
Nickel
Platinum
Silver
Tin
Zinc

mesh *n.* ① net, lattice, netting, web ② snare, trap, tangle

mess *n.* ① muddle, confusion, clutter, jumble, chaos, disorder, disarray *ant.* order ② problem, difficulty, jam ▷**plight**

message *n.* communication, letter, notice, note, memo, e-mail, dispatch *The foreign affairs reporter sent a dispatch to her newspaper in Fredericton.*

messenger *n.* courier, carrier, runner, agent, bearer

meter *n.* measure, gauge *hom.* metre

method *n.* way, means, manner, technique, approach, system ▷**process**

metre *n.* rhythm, cadence, swing *hom.* meter

mettle *n.* spirit, life, fire, animation, pluck, boldness ▷**courage** *hom.* metal

middle ① *n.* centre, heart, core, interior ② *adj.* medium, average, central

midget ① *n.* dwarf, gnome, pygmy ② *adj.* little, miniature, small ▷**tiny** *ant.* giant

might *n.* strength, ability, power, force, energy, authority *hom.* mite

mighty *adj.* strong, powerful, potent, stupendous, giant, hefty *ant.* weak

mild *adj.* ① moderate, calm, gentle, bland ② easygoing, docile, tender ▷**meek** *ant.* harsh

military *adj.* martial, soldierly, warlike

mill ① *n.* grinder, factory, plant ② *v.* crush, grind, pulverize *The rock was pulverized into tiny pieces.* pound, grate

mimic *v.* copy, ape, mime, echo, imitate, impersonate, simulate

mince *v.* shred, chop, crumble, grind, hash, dice *hom.* mints

mind ① *n.* brain, intellect, thoughts, head ② *v.* obey, follow ③ *v.* guard, watch, protect ④ *v.* be careful of, watch out for, monitor *Monitor your son's behaviour while you are in the china store!*

mine ① *n.* quarry, shaft, deposit, tunnel, treasury, storehouse ② *n.* bomb, explosive ③ *v.* excavate *Some railway tunnels are excavated through solid rock.* dig out

mingle *v.* ① mix, blend, combine ▷**merge** ② socialize, rub shoulders

miniature ① *adj.* tiny, toy, dwarf, midget, minute ② *n.* model

minimum *adj.* least, smallest, lowest, slightest, minimal *ant.* maximum

minister ① *n.* pastor, vicar, priest, preacher ② *n.* ambassador, diplomat ③ *n.* secretary, cabinet member ④ *v.* serve, give aid, tend

minor ① *adj.* lesser, smaller, lower, trivial, insignificant, secondary, unimportant, petty *ant.* major ② *n.* child, youth *hom.* miner

mint ① *v.* stamp, forge, cast ② *adj.* new, perfect, untarnished *The untarnished coin didn't even have a smudge on it.* ③ *n.* candy, herb

minute ① *n.* (*min*-it) flash, instant, moment ② *adj.* (my-*nyute*) slight, tiny, small ▷**miniature** *ant.* huge

miracle *n.* marvel, wonder, phenomenon, sensation

miraculous *adj.* supernatural, astounding, wondrous, incredible, magical

mirror ① *n.* looking glass, reflector ② *v.* imitate, simulate *The chameleon changes its colour to simulate its environment.* reflect, copy, echo

misbehave *v.* disobey, do wrong, offend, be naughty, act up *ant.* obey

miscellaneous *adj.* various, varied, mixed, jumbled

mischief *n.* naughtiness, pranks, annoyance, damage, harm, trouble

mischievous *adj.* naughty, destructive, impish, playful *ant.* good

misconduct *n.* misbehaviour, wrongdoing, naughtiness, rudeness

miser *n.* scrooge, skinflint, penny-pincher, tightwad

miserable *adj.* unhappy, blue, forlorn, wretched, pitiable, desolate, suffering *ant.* cheerful

misery *n.* sorrow, grief, anguish, distress, unhappiness, gloom *ant.* happiness

misfit *n.* eccentric, oddball, nonconformist, drop-out

misfortune *n.* bad luck, hardship, evil, adversity, calamity ▷**disaster** *ant.* luck

misgiving *n.* distrust, mistrust, doubt, apprehension, anxiety ▷**qualm** *ant.* confidence

mishap *n.* misadventure, blow, accident, setback ▷**misfortune**

misjudge *v.* miscalculate, misread, underestimate, overestimate ▷**mistake**

mislay *v.* lose, misplace, miss

mislead *v.* deceive, fool, lead astray, hoodwink, take in, bluff

miss ① *v.* skip, ignore, fail, fall short of, pass over, go wide ② *v.* pine for, yearn for, lament ③ *n.* girl, young woman, damsel

missile *n.* rocket, torpedo, projectile, arrow, dart, pellet

mission *n.* task, assignment, errand, object, objective, end, aim ▷**quest**

mist *n.* moisture, dew, vapour, fog, cloud, smog, haze *hom.* missed

mistake ① *n.* error, fault, lapse, blunder, slip, oversight ② *v.* misinterpret, confuse, misunderstand, confound, misjudge

mistaken *adj.* erroneous, untrue, false, fallacious ▷**wrong** *ant.* correct

mistrust *v.* disbelieve, distrust, doubt, fear ▷**suspect** *ant.* trust

misunderstand *v.* mistake, misinterpret, take wrongly *ant.* grasp

misuse *v.* abuse, exploit, misapply, waste

mitigate *v.* moderate, ease, relieve, abate, allay, soften *ant.* aggravate

mix *v.* blend, whip, mash, fold, scramble, churn, mingle, combine, stir

mix up *v.* confuse, confound, muddle, jumble, disorder, complicate ▷**bewilder**

mixture *n.* assortment, collection, medley, jumble, blend, combination

moan *v.* wail, groan, howl, grumble, grieve, grouse

mob *n.* crowd, mass, rabble, company, throng, horde, swarm

mobile *adj.* movable, portable, flexible, changeable, transportable, migratory, wandering *ant.* immobile

mock ① *v.* mimic, imitate, jeer, laugh, ridicule ② *adj.* false, fake, sham, artificial, simulated

mode *n.* fashion, style, vogue, manner, way, format, form, setting *hom.* mowed

model *n.* pattern, original, prototype *The Avro Arrow was a prototype of a Canadian jet fighter.* replica, representation, miniature

moderate *adj.* reasonable, medium, gentle, temperate, light, mild, quiet, modest ▷**fair**

modern *adj.* new, up-to-date, stylish, recent, current, contemporary, state-of-the-art, trendy *That style is trendy now, but its popularity may not last.* *ant.* ancient

modest *adj.* humble, shy, bashful, meek, reserved, unassuming, demure, diffident *ant.* vain

modesty *n.* humility, shyness, reserve, simplicity, diffidence *ant.* vanity

modify *v.* change, alter, revise, transform, convert, redesign

moist *adj.* damp, humid, watery, clammy, dank ▷**wet** *ant.* dry

moisture *n.* damp, dampness, liquid, wetness, dew, dankness

molest *v.* ① annoy, bother, pester, tease ② pursue, attack, plague, torment, harry ▷**abuse**

M
m
M
m
m
M
m
M

n.= noun

v.= verb

adj.= adjective

adv.= adverb

conj.= conjunction

prep.= preposition

ant.= antonym

hom.= homonym

▷ = cross-reference

Money

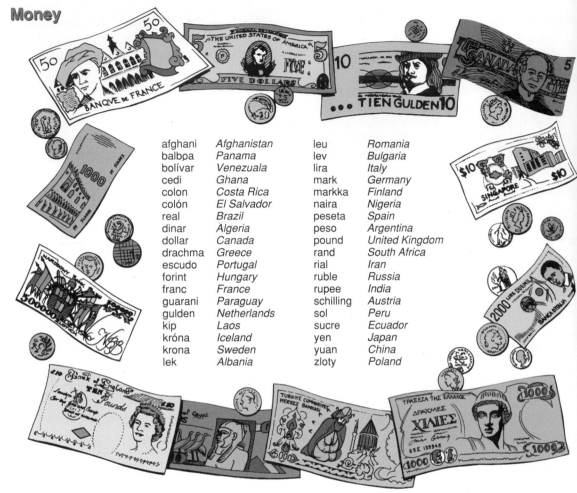

afghani	*Afghanistan*	leu	*Romania*
balboa	*Panama*	lev	*Bulgaria*
bolívar	*Venezuala*	lira	*Italy*
cedi	*Ghana*	mark	*Germany*
colon	*Costa Rica*	markka	*Finland*
colón	*El Salvador*	naira	*Nigeria*
real	*Brazil*	peseta	*Spain*
dinar	*Algeria*	peso	*Argentina*
dollar	*Canada*	pound	*United Kingdom*
drachma	*Greece*	rand	*South Africa*
escudo	*Portugal*	rial	*Iran*
forint	*Hungary*	ruble	*Russia*
franc	*France*	rupee	*India*
guarani	*Paraguay*	schilling	*Austria*
gulden	*Netherlands*	sol	*Peru*
kip	*Laos*	sucre	*Ecuador*
króna	*Iceland*	yen	*Japan*
krona	*Sweden*	yuan	*China*
lek	*Albania*	zloty	*Poland*

moment *n.* second, instant, flash, twinkling

momentous *adj.* notable, outstanding, important, significant, decisive, weighty, grave, fateful *ant.* insignificant

monarch *n.* king, queen, sovereign, ruler, emperor

money *n.* wealth, cash, legal tender, currency, funds, riches

mongrel *n.* mutt, mix, mixed breed, crossbreed, hybrid

monitor ① *n.* screen, gauge, tester, tracker, regulator, watchdog ② *v.* check, supervise, oversee

monologue *n.* lecture, oration, speech, recitation, sermon

monopolize *v.* control, take over, consume, tie up, appropriate ▷**dominate** *ant.* share

monotonous *adj.* tedious, uninteresting, dull, prosaic, repetitive, tiresome

monstrous *adj.* ① hideous, frightful, dreadful, terrible ▷**wicked** ② giant, huge

mood *n.* humour, temper, feeling, tone, air, state of mind, disposition *We all disliked his grumpy disposition.*

moody *adj.* sulky, sullen, peevish, cross, gloomy, sombre, morose, cantankerous *ant.* cheerful

mop *n.* ① sponge, swab, towel ② thatch, locks, mane

mope *v.* sulk, brood, moon, pine, grieve

moral *adj.* good, honest, ethical, virtuous, honourable, upright *ant.* immoral

morbid *adj.* gruesome, grisly, abnormal, sick, unwholesome, macabre

more ① *adj.* additional, extra, further ② *adv.* again, longer, better, moreover

morning *n.* dawn, daybreak, daylight, sunrise *ant.* evening *hom.* mourning

morose *adj.* glum, sullen, sulky, broody, taciturn *We finally persuaded our taciturn neighbour to tell us her name.* ▷**moody** *ant.* cheerful

morsel *n.* bit, bite, piece, scrap, nibble

mortal *adj.* ① human, feeble, earthly, finite ② fatal, final, deadly, severe

most ① *adj.* greatest, nearly all, highest ② *adv.* best, hardest, the highest, extremely, highly

mostly *adv.* usually, normally, as a rule, principally, chiefly, mainly

mother ① *n.* mom, ma, mommy, mama ② *v.* nurture, protect, rear, care for

motherly *adj.* maternal, caring, comforting, loving, gentle

motion *n.* ① movement, locomotion, action, passage ② proposal *I vote that we accept the proposal.* suggestion

motionless *adj.* stationary, still, immobile, stable, inert *ant.* moving

motive *n.* reason, purpose, cause, impulse

motto *n.* saying, slogan, watchword, maxim *My friend's maxim is "Always look on the bright side."* proverb

mould ① *v.* form, shape, fashion, cast, create ② *n.* pattern, form, frame, template

mouldy *adj.* mildewed, stale, musty, fusty

mound *n.* pile, heap, knoll, rise, hill, pingo

mount *v.* ascend, climb, rise, build

mourn *v.* weep, lament, deplore, regret ▷**grieve** *ant.* rejoice

mournful *adj.* sorrowful, cheerless, doleful, sombre ▷**melancholy** *ant.* joyful

mouth *n.* opening, entrance, outlet, jaws

mouthful *n.* bite, morsel, taste, tidbit

move *v.* ① march, proceed, walk, go, advance, pass, travel ② propel, drive, impel ③ propose, suggest, recommend

moving *adj.* ① touching, affecting, stirring *We were proud of our band's stirring rendition of "O Canada."* emotional ② mobile, manoeuvrable, active, travelling

much ① *adj.* abundant, considerable, ample ② *adv.* often, very, greatly, considerably ③ *n.* lots, loads, heaps, plenty

muck *n.* dirt, filth, slime, ooze, mud, scum

muddle ① *n.* confusion, clutter, jumble, daze, mix-up, disorder ② *v.* bungle, tangle, confound, botch, stumble, fumble ▷**bewilder**

muffle *v.* stifle, repress, deaden, dampen, mute, muzzle, silence

mug ① *n.* cup, beaker, tankard ② *v.* attack, beat up, rob

muggy *adj.* clammy, damp, humid, sticky, warm, dank *ant.* dry

multiply *v.* increase, spread, grow, expand, intensify, rise, gain *ant.* decrease

multitude *n.* crowd, throng, swarm, horde

munch *v.* crunch, chew, bite, nibble ▷**eat**

murder *v.* slay, assassinate, butcher, destroy, slaughter ▷**kill**

murky *adj.* foggy, cloudy, dark, gloomy, dull, misty *ant.* bright

murmur *n. & v.* whisper, mutter, mumble, drone *We heard the drone of bees in the flower garden.* sigh, gossip

muscular *adj.* brawny, athletic, burly, beefy, powerful, sturdy ▷**robust** *ant.* puny

must ① *v.* ought to, should, be obliged to, need ② *n.* duty, necessity, requirement

muster *v.* marshal, collect, assemble, rally *My teammates and I rallied our energy for one last play.* summon, gather

musty *adj.* mouldy, mildewy, rank, fusty

mute *adj.* silent, speechless, voiceless, soundless

mutilate *v.* injure, hurt, cut, damage ▷**maim**

mutiny *n. & v.* protest, revolt, riot

mutter *v.* mumble, grumble, whisper, grouse ▷**murmur**

mutual *adj.* common, reciprocal, shared ▷**joint** *ant.* one-sided

mysterious *adj.* unexplained, secret, obscure, cryptic ▷**hidden** *ant.* clear

mystery *n.* puzzle, riddle, problem, question, dilemma, secrecy

mystify *v.* confuse, puzzle, stump, bamboozle ▷**baffle** *ant.* enlighten

myth *n.* fable, legend, fabrication, fantasy, lore, fiction, invention, tradition *ant.* fact

mythical *adj.* fabulous, fabled, legendary, imaginary, traditional

M
m
M
m
M
m
M

N n

nab *v.* arrest, apprehend, seize, catch, capture, grab

nag ① *v.* pester, heckle, badger, annoy, carp, scold ② *n.* horse, mare

nail ① *n.* pin, peg, spike, tack ② *v.* hammer, fix, tack, peg

naïve *adj.* innocent, gullible *Franz was gullible and believed Clara's obvious lies.* unworldly, unsophisticated, simple, trusting, artless, natural, childlike, credulous *ant.* cunning, suave

naked *adj.* nude, bare, unclothed, undressed

name ① *n.* title, label, term, alias, pseudonym, moniker, designation ② *n.* character, reputation, distinction ③ *v.* christen, style, term, entitle, call, dub, tag, label, appoint

nap ① *v.* sleep, doze, drowse, rest, snooze, slumber ② *n.* shut-eye, forty winks, rest, snooze

narrate *v.* recount, tell, recite, relate

narrow *adj.* slender, fine, small, slim, close, tight, cramped ▷**thin** *ant.* wide

nasty *adj.* foul, offensive, unpleasant, repulsive, revolting, gross, filthy, dirty, squalid ▷**disagreeable** *ant.* pleasant

national *adj.* civil, governmental, public, general, nationwide, domestic

native *adj.* aboriginal, indigenous, local, domestic, natural

natural *adj.* frank, genuine, innate *She has an innate talent for math.* instinctive, normal, usual, wild

naturally *adv.* ① absolutely, of course ② instinctively, simply, candidly

nature *n.* ① temperament, personality, quality, essence, disposition ② the world, the outdoors, creation, the environment

naughty *adj.* mischievous, rascally, disobedient, unruly, incorrigible *Those incorrigible raccoons will never learn to stay out of our garbage.* ▷**bad** *ant.* obedient

nautical *adj.* marine, maritime, naval, sailing, seafaring

navigate *v.* sail, guide, pilot, manoeuvre, voyage, cruise

navy *n.* ships, fleet, flotilla, armada

near *adj.* close, nearby, adjacent, bordering, neighbouring *ant.* remote

nearly *adv.* about, almost, all but, approximately, roughly

neat *adj.* ① tidy, clean, orderly, trim, spruce *ant.* untidy ② skilful, clever, adroit *With an adroit move, she dribbled the ball between her opponent's legs.* ingenious

necessary *adj.* needed, essential, required, compulsory, vital, crucial *ant.* optional

need ① *v.* require, want, crave, lack, demand ② *n.* want, necessity, deprivation *hom.* knead

needless *adj.* pointless, unnecessary, useless, superfluous *Don't load your backpack with superfluous equipment.* *ant.* necessary

needy *adj.* homeless, destitute, deprived, down-and-out, ▷**poor** *ant.* well-off

negative *adj.* critical, pessimistic, unfavourable, discouraging *ant.* positive

neglect *v.* overlook, omit, forget, fail, ignore, scorn, slight, disregard *ant.* cherish

neglected *adj.* unkempt, abandoned, dilapidated, uncared for

negligent *adj.* neglectful, forgetful, slack, indifferent, derelict ▷**careless** *ant.* careful

negotiate *v.* bargain, deal, haggle, mediate, transact, arbitrate, decide, arrange

neighbourhood *n.* vicinity, surroundings, district, area, locality, block, community

neighbourly *adj.* hospitable, friendly, kind, obliging ▷**helpful**

nerve *n.* ① mettle, guts, pluck, courage ② gall, audacity, impudence

nervous *adj.* tense, edgy, jumpy, jittery, anxious, flustered *ant.* calm

nest *n.* den, burrow, refuge, resort, haunt

nestle *v.* cuddle, snuggle, huddle, nuzzle

n. = noun
v. = verb
adj. = adjective
adv. = adverb
conj. = conjunction
prep. = preposition
ant. = antonym
hom. = homonym
▷ = cross-reference

net ① *v.* catch, trap, capture, take ② *n.* mesh, lattice, web, lace ③ *adj.* clear *After subtracting his expenses, Sean had a clear profit of $15.* ultimate

neutral *adj.* ① fair, impartial, fair-minded, unbiassed, unprejudiced, even-handed *ant.* unfair ② detached, bland, indifferent ③ pale, versatile

never *adv.* not ever, at no time, not at all, under no circumstances *ant.* always

new *adj.* recent, just out, current, latest, modern, fresh, unused, original ▷**novel** *ant.* old *hom.* knew, gnu

Confusable Words

new means *unused*

knew means *understood*

news *n.* information, intelligence, account, bulletin, rumour

next *adj.* ① following, succeeding, later ② adjacent, adjoining *We could easily hear the Grade 3 class in the adjoining room.*

nibble *v.* bite, peck, gnaw, munch ▷**eat**

nice *adj.* ① pleasant, agreeable, amiable, charming, delightful, kind, acceptable *ant.* nasty ② mild, sunny, warm

niche *n.* compartment, hole, corner, recess, slot, spot

nick *v.* dent, cut, scratch, score

night *n.* dark, darkness, dusk, evening *hom.* knight

nimble *adj.* active, agile, spry, quick, lithe, skilful, deft ▷**dexterous** *ant.* clumsy

nip *v.* cut, snip, pinch, twinge, bite

noble *adj.* dignified, lofty *She will not give up her lofty ideals.* grand, stately, elevated, regal, aristocratic *ant.* base

nod *v.* ① beckon, signal, salute ② sleep, doze, nap ③ sway, bend

noise *n.* sound, din, clamour, clatter, racket, uproar, commotion, tumult, hubbub, discord, pandemonium *ant.* silence

noisy *adj.* loud, boisterous, rowdy, clamorous, turbulent, disorderly *ant.* quiet

nominate *v.* appoint, assign, elect, choose, propose, suggest

nonchalant *adj.* casual, calm, unperturbed, blasé *At first, he raved about his new bike, but now he's rather blasé about it.* cool, detached *ant.* anxious

nondescript *adj.* commonplace, colourless, dull, ordinary ▷**plain** *ant.* striking

nonsense *n.* absurdity, gibberish, garbage, drivel, balderdash *ant.* sense

Neighbourhood

N
n
N
n
n
n
N

nook *n.* compartment, hole, corner, alcove, crevice, cranny, hideout ▷**niche**

noose *n.* loop, rope, lasso, snare

normal *adj.* ① usual, common, natural, ordinary, regular, typical, general, average, standard *ant.* abnormal ② lucid, rational, sane

nose *n.* ① beak, bill, snout ② prow, bow, front, stem

nosey *adj.* curious, prying, snooping, inquisitive, intrusive

nostalgia *n.* homesickness, longing, yearning, pining, regret

notable *adj.* outstanding, great, celebrated, momentous, marked, eminent ▷**famous** *ant.* ordinary

notch *n.* ① dent, nick, score, cut, cleft, indentation ② grade, step, degree

note *n.* ① letter, message, communication, memo ② fame, renown, distinction ③ tone, pitch, key, vein

noted *adj.* great, eminent, renowned, celebrated ▷**famous** *ant.* obscure

nothing *n.* zero, null, nil, zilch, naught

notice ① *n.* announcement, ad, sign, poster ② *v.* note, detect, observe *Observing that his bike had a flat tire, Hon-Wah knew he might have to walk to school.* perceive, heed, see *ant.* ignore

Notice

Observing that his bike had a flat tire, Hon-Wah knew he might have to walk to school.

notify *v.* tell, inform, acquaint, alert, advise

notion *n.* idea, opinion, belief, view, judgment, fancy, conception *Your conception of what happened is not the same as mine.*

notorious *adj.* infamous, ill-famed, scandalous, renowned

notwithstanding *adv.* nevertheless, nonetheless, however, despite this

nourish *v.* feed, sustain, enrich, nurture, cherish, support, foster, nurse *ant.* neglect

nourishing *adj.* beneficial, nutritious, wholesome, healthful

novel ① *adj.* fresh, unusual, original, unique, unfamiliar, experimental ② *n.* fiction, story, book, blockbuster

novice *n.* beginner, learner, apprentice, pupil, trainee *ant.* expert

now *adv.* immediately, at once, currently, instantly, presently, right away, today

nude *adj.* bare, naked, unclothed, undressed, exposed

nudge *v. & n.* poke, push, prod, jog, shove, dig

nuisance *n.* annoyance, irritation, bother, pest, bore, inconvenience, pain

nullify *v.* annul, invalidate, cancel, quash ▷**abolish** *ant.* confirm

numb *adj.* dull, deadened, unfeeling, insensible, stunned, dazed *ant.* sensitive

number ① *n.* figure, digit, symbol ▷**numeral** ② *n.* amount, volume, quantity, sum, total ③ *n.* group, crowd, throng, multitude *A great multitude of people lined the streets to see the Canada Day parade.* ④ *v.* count, reckon, tally

numeral *n.* symbol, figure, character, cipher

numerous *adj.* many, several, plenty of, countless, multiple, abundant *ant.* few

nurse *v.* tend, care for, foster, support, nourish, sustain

nurture *v.* ① feed, nourish, enrich ② cherish, foster, tend, care for ▷**nourish**

nutritious *adj.* healthful, substantial, wholesome ▷**nourishing**

O o

obedient *adj.* respectful, law-abiding, obliging, docile, submissive, compliant subservient, servile, dutiful, deferential, yielding *ant.* rebellious

obey *v.* comply, conform, submit, heed, behave, follow *ant.* disobey

object ① *v.* (ob-*ject*) protest, complain, argue, oppose, disapprove *ant.* agree ② *n.* (*ob*-ject) thing, article, fact, item ③ *n.* aim, goal, end, ambition, purpose

objectionable *adj.* displeasing, distasteful, disagreeable, repugnant, unacceptable, unwanted *ant.* desirable

obligation *n.* duty, responsibility, liability, commitment *ant.* choice

oblige *v.* ① require, compel, force, make ② accommodate, please, help, humour

obliging *adj.* helpful, polite, agreeable, accommodating, courteous ▷**willing**

obliterate *v.* erase, blot out, wipe out, destroy, annihilate

oblivious *adj.* ignorant, unaware, absent-minded, heedless *ant.* aware

obnoxious *adj.* repulsive, revolting, offensive, disagreeable ▷**unpleasant** *ant.* pleasant

obscene *adj.* dirty, filthy, unclean, vile, nasty, immoral, indecent, crude, vulgar, gross *ant.* decent

obscure ① *adj.* dim, dark, unclear, hidden, confusing, indistinct ▷**vague** *ant.* clear ② *adj.* unknown, small-time, undiscovered ③ *v.* conceal, cloud, darken, cover ▷**hide** *ant.* clarify

observant *adj.* attentive, watchful, heedful ▷**alert** *ant.* inattentive

Oceans and Salt Waters

Antarctic Bay
Arctic Fiord
Atlantic Gulf
Indian Lagoon
Pacific Sound
　　Strait

observation *n.* ① notice, watch, attention, perception, study, supervision ② comment, remark, utterance, statement

observe *v.* ① note, notice, perceive, regard, supervise, study ▷**see** ② follow, abide by *I will abide by the rules, even though I don't like them.* adhere to, carry out, keep ③ honour, recognize, celebrate

obsolete *adj.* dated, outmoded *Butter churns are outmoded now.* unfashionable, out-of-date, antiquated *ant.* current

obstacle *n.* obstruction, barrier, bar, hindrance *Bad weather can be a hindrance to getting to school on time.* hitch, handicap, hurdle *ant.* advantage

obstinate *adj.* determined, unyielding, headstrong, pig headed, willful, bullheaded ▷**stubborn** *ant.* obliging

obstruct *v.* hinder, impede, block, bar, choke, prevent *ant.* help

obstruction *n.* hindrance, obstacle, barrier, snag, bar, impediment

obtain *v.* acquire, achieve, gain, receive, procure, secure *ant.* lose

obtuse *adj.* dense, thick, slow, stupid, unintelligent *ant.* bright

obvious *adj.* plain, evident, self-evident *It was self-evident to Manu, so he didn't bother looking for any proof.* explicit, apparent, distinct, unsubtle, visible ▷**clear** *ant.* hidden, obscure

occasion *n.* ① event, time, affair, episode, occurrence, instance ② cause, reason, grounds, purpose, motive

occasional *adj.* rare, infrequent, periodic, intermittent *ant.* frequent

occupant *n.* resident, tenant, inmate, inhabitant, owner, passenger, user

occupation *n.* ① profession, trade, job, activity, calling ② possession, tenancy, residence

occupied *adj.* ① busy, employed, active, involved ② settled, populated, peopled *ant.* unoccupied

occupy *v.* ① inhabit, live in, reside in, dwell in, own, possess, hold ② invade, overrun ③ employ, engage, busy, fill

O
O
O
O
O
O

occur *v.* take place, transpire, come about, result ▷**happen**

occurrence *n.* happening, circumstance, incident, occasion, affair, event

odd *adj.* ① unusual, abnormal, irregular, unique, weird, peculiar, quaint ② single, unmatched, surplus *ant.* ordinary

odious *adj.* hateful, offensive, detestable, filthy ▷**abominable** *ant.* pleasant

odour *n.* ① scent, aroma ▷**fragrance** ② stink, stench, reek

offence *n.* insult, outrage, violation, crime

offend *v.* insult, hurt, wound, outrage, displease, upset, annoy, sin *ant.* please

offensive *adj.* insulting, offending, rude, repugnant, hurtful, distasteful, evil, repulsive, vile, ugly

offer ① *v.* give, propose, present, tender *We tendered our thanks to everyone who had helped with our food drive.* attempt ② *n.* bid, tender, proposal

offering *n.* sacrifice, donation, gift, present

offhand *adj.* casual, informal, improvised, impromptu *Our teacher's impromptu decision to practise outside surprised us.*

office *n.* ① bureau, department, agency, ministry ② position, appointment, post

officer *n.* official, administrator, executive, military rank, constable, minister

official ① *adj.* authorized *The leader of our club is our only authorized spokesperson.* authentic, proper, formal *ant.* informal ② *n.* authority, executive, officeholder, bureaucrat

offspring *n.* child, children, young, family, descendant, heir, issue *ant.* ancestor

often *adv.* frequently, regularly, time after time, repeatedly, recurrently *ant.* seldom

ointment *n.* salve, cream, balm, liniment

old *adj.* ① ancient, antique, vintage, antiquated ② aged, mature, elderly, senior *ant.* young ③ crumbling, decayed, decrepit, worn-out, stale *ant.* new ④ out-of-date, old-fashioned, passé *Though most people think it is passé, it is the style I prefer.*

ominous *adj.* menacing, threatening, foreboding, sinister

omit *v.* leave out, overlook, drop, skip, ignore, disregard, neglect *ant.* include

once *adv.* earlier, formerly, previously, at one time

one ① *adj.* sole, solitary, single, lone ② *n.* unit, whole ③ *adj.* united, fused
one-sided *adj.* unfair, biassed

only ① *adj.* exclusive, unique, single, sole, lone, solitary ② *adv.* solely, barely, merely, exclusively

onset *n.* ① birth, start, beginning ② outbreak, attack, onslaught, onrush

onslaught *n.* charge, assault, attack, barrage, bombardment

ooze ① *n.* slime, muck, mire ② *v.* leak, seep, weep, flow, bleed, discharge, emit, exude

open ① *v.* uncover, unlock, unfasten, undo ② *v.* start, begin, commence ③ *adj.* uncovered, unlocked, ajar, exposed ④ *adj.* clear, unobstructed ⑤ *adj.* receptive, frank, honest, candid

opening *n.* ① aperture *Adjust the camera's aperture a little more so enough light gets in.* mouth, crevice, recess, hole ② beginning, commencement

openly *adv.* candidly, frankly, plainly, directly

operate *v.* ① function *Despite its age, the wood stove continues to function.* work, run, perform ② use, manipulate, drive ③ cut, open up

operation *n.* performance, movement, action, motion, proceeding, function

opinion *n.* belief, view, outlook, viewpoint, stance, conviction, judgment, concept

opponent *n.* rival, competitor, adversary, foe, antagonist, enemy *ant.* ally

opportune *adj.* timely *Keira was just starting her paper route, so Glen's arrival with his wagon was timely.* convenient, suitable, favourable *ant.* untimely

opportunity *n.* occasion, chance, opening, scope *Our science project will give us lots of scope for doing experiments.* moment

oppose *v.* resist, obstruct, confront, hinder, counter, contest, withstand ▷**defy** *ant.* support

n. = noun
v. = verb
adj. = adjective
adv. = adverb
conj. = conjunction
prep. = preposition
ant. = antonym
hom. = homonym
▷ = cross-reference

opposite *adj.* ① facing, fronting, obverse ② conflicting, opposing, contrary, adverse, unlike, converse *ant.* same

opposition *n.* defiance, hostility, contrast, antagonism, opponent ▷**resistance** *ant.* help

oppress *v.* crush, depress, overburden, overwhelm, subdue, harass, tyrannize

optimistic *adj.* hopeful, cheerful, confident, positive, sunny, idealistic *ant.* pessimistic

option *n.* choice, alternative, preference

optional *adj.* possible, voluntary, unforced, open *ant.* compulsory

opulent *adj.* rich, affluent, prosperous, well-to-do, luxurious, wealthy *ant.* poor

orbit *n.* ① circle, path, passage, circuit ② province, realm, territory, range, domain *Not all of the Great Lakes are within Canada's domain.*

ordeal *n.* trial, nightmare, torment, agony

order ① *n.* arrangement, pattern, sequence, calm, neatness, organization ② *n.* request, command, direction, instruction, decree ③ *n.* shipment, consignment ④ *v.* direct, instruct, command, demand, request ⑤ *v.* arrange, sort, file, classify

orderly *adj.* ① regular, methodical *She used a methodical system, beginning at A and ending at Z.* systematic, neat, tidy *ant.* untidy ② well-behaved

ordinary *adj.* common, usual, average, standard, fair, regular, commonplace, general, customary *It is customary to say thank you when you receive a gift.* *ant.* extraordinary

organization *n.* ① association, group, institute, establishment, company, outfit ② structure, arrangement, system

organize *v.* arrange, plan, order, form, structure, establish, classify

origin *n.* beginning, start, basis, foundation, root, source, birth *ant.* end

original *adj.* ① first, aboriginal, ancient, former, primary ② creative, inventive, fresh, new, novel *Noburo thought camel rides would be a novel way to raise money.* ③ authentic, real

Original

Noburo thought camel rides would be a novel way to raise money.

originate *v.* ① create, conceive, invent, found, introduce ② arise, begin, dawn ▷**start**

ornament *n.* decoration, adornment, trinket, curio, knick-knack

ornate *adj.* decorated, flowery, embellished, showy, elaborate, pretentious *ant.* plain

oust *v.* expel, eject, evict, throw out, dismiss, overthrow

outbreak *n.* flare-up, plague, rash, epidemic, rebellion, eruption

outburst *n.* eruption, explosion, fit, tantrum

outcast *n.* exile, derelict, refugee, reject

outcome *n.* effect, consequence, result, conclusion, upshot

outcry *n.* commotion, uproar, tumult, shouting, hue and cry ▷**clamour**

outdated *adj.* old, antique, old-fashioned, unfashionable, obsolete *ant.* modern

outdo *v.* surpass, excel, beat, outclass, eclipse, exceed, outshine

outfit *n.* suit, rig, equipment, gear

outing *n.* excursion, picnic, expedition, trip

outlandish *adj.* strange, eccentric, odd, quaint, bizarre *ant.* ordinary

outlaw *n.* bandit, desperado, robber

O o O o O o O o O O o O

outlet *n.* exit, way out, vent, hole, spout, channel, opening

outline ① *n.* diagram, plan, blueprint, sketch, draft, summary ② *n.* silhouette, profile, contour ③ *v.* draw, sketch, describe, draft

outlook *n.* ① lookout, view ② forecast, prospect, future ③ attitude, viewpoint

output *n.* yield, product, production, achievement, manufacture

outrage ① *n.* disgrace, injury, offence, crime, affront, atrocity ② *v.* offend, insult, shock, violate, scandalize

outrageous *adj.* ① excessive, extreme, exorbitant *Prices are reasonable here, but at the other store prices are exorbitant.* *ant.* moderate ② fantastic, unconventional, scandalous, offensive, monstrous *ant.* proper

outright ① *adj.* utter, complete, thorough, absolute, wholesale ② *adv.* at once, completely, entirely, altogether

outset *n.* first, opening, beginning, kickoff ▷**start** *ant.* end

outside ① *n.* exterior, surface, front, face, façade ② *adj.* exterior, external, outward, surface ③ *adj.* remote, slim

outsider *n.* stranger, foreigner, alien, misfit *The cygnet was a misfit among the ducklings.*

outskirts *n.* limits, bounds, boundary, suburb, perimeter, edge *ant.* centre

outspoken *adj.* frank, open, straightforward, blunt, direct, candid *ant.* shy

outstanding *adj.* ① excellent, superb, prominent, striking, pronounced, conspicuous, notable ▷**exceptional** *ant.* ordinary ② unpaid, due, owing

outward *adj.* exterior, external, outer, superficial *My sister bears a superficial resemblance to Céline Dion.* apparent

outwit *v.* outsmart, trick, foil, dupe, evade, defraud, cheat

over ① *adj.* upper, outer, superior, extra ② *prep.* above, beyond, exceeding, through ③ *adv.* above, down, again

overall ① *adj.* general, complete, inclusive, total, broad ② *adv.* by and large, on the whole

overbearing *adj.* domineering, dictatorial, haughty, pompous ▷**arrogant** *ant.* modest

overcast *adj.* cloudy, dark, murky, dull *ant.* bright

overcome *v.* overwhelm, conquer, crush, defeat, vanquish ▷**subdue**

overdo *v.* overwork, exaggerate, go too far *I didn't mind lending Jessica my thesaurus, but doing her homework was going too far!*

overdue *adj.* delayed, belated, late *ant.* early

overhaul *v.* repair, fix, inspect, examine

overhead *adv.* above, upward, aloft, on high *ant.* below

overhear *v.* listen, eavesdrop, catch

overjoyed *adj.* elated, jubilant, delighted *ant.* despondent

overlap *v.* overrun, go beyond, coincide, overlay

overlook *v.* ① excuse, forgive, pardon, condone ② ignore, neglect, miss, disregard

overpower *v.* conquer, overwhelm, crush, master, subdue, vanquish ▷**defeat**

overseer *n.* inspector, supervisor, boss, manager

oversight *n.* omission, blunder, error, fault, neglect, lapse ▷**mistake**

overtake *v.* pass, catch up with, outrun *She outran her competitors and placed first in the race.* outstrip

overthrow *v.* conquer, defeat, beat, topple, vanquish, capture ▷**overpower**

overture *n.* ① offer, proposal, invitation ② prelude, opening, introduction

overwhelm *v.* overcome, stun, shock, overpower, deluge, inundate *Canada Post is deluged with mail in December.* crush, flood

overwhelming *adj.* formidable, breathtaking, shattering, staggering, towering *ant.* insignificant

own ① *v.* have, possess, occupy, hold ② *v.* admit, confess, acknowledge *ant.* deny ③ *adj.* individual, personal, private

owner *n.* proprietor, possessor, landlord

n. = noun
v. = verb
adj. = adjective
adv. = adverb
conj. = conjunction
prep. = preposition
ant. = antonym
hom. = homonym
▷ = cross-reference

Pp

pace ① *n. & v.* step, tread, stride, walk ② *n.* speed, rate, velocity, tempo, gait

pacify *v.* appease *Perhaps giving the crying baby her blanket will appease her.* calm, quiet, tranquilize ▷**soothe** *ant.* irritate

pack ① *n.* bundle, bunch, carton, parcel ② *n.* swarm, crowd, group, band, gang ③ *v.* cram, load, fill, stuff, crowd, compress

package *n.* ① parcel, bundle, box, carton ② unit, ensemble, whole

pact *n.* contract, treaty, agreement, deal, arrangement, understanding *hom.* packed

paddle *v.* row, steer, propel, splash, wade

page *n.* sheet, leaf, paper

pageant *n.* parade, procession, spectacle, exhibition ▷**show**

pail *n.* bucket, tub, container *hom.* pale

pain ① *n.* ache, pang, throb, twinge, spasm, cramp ② *n.* misery, distress ③ *v.* hurt, sting, ache, ail ▷**distress** *hom.* pane

painful *adj.* aching, throbbing, sore, agonizing *ant.* easy

painstaking *adj.* scrupulous *Natalie kept a scrupulous record of every penny she spent.* careful, diligent, particular *ant.* careless

paint *v.* colour, draw, varnish, stain

painting *n.* illustration, picture, canvas, still life, landscape, portrait, mural, design, fresco

pair *n.* couple, brace, two, twins, twosome, duo *hom.* pare, pear

pal *n.* chum, friend, buddy, associate, sidekick, comrade *ant.* enemy

palace *n.* castle, château, mansion

pale *adj.* pallid, ashen, pasty, colourless, faint, feeble, white, dim, fair *ant.* vivid *hom.* pail

paltry *adj.* petty, mean, shabby, trifling *They paid me such a trifling amount for shovelling, but I did my best work anyway.* pitiable, trashy, shoddy

Paper

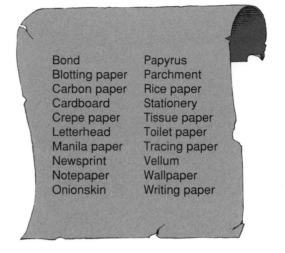

Bond	Papyrus
Blotting paper	Parchment
Carbon paper	Rice paper
Cardboard	Stationery
Crepe paper	Tissue paper
Letterhead	Toilet paper
Manila paper	Tracing paper
Newsprint	Vellum
Notepaper	Wallpaper
Onionskin	Writing paper

pamper *v.* humour, indulge, coddle, cosset, baby, spoil *ant.* neglect

pan *n.* skillet, saucepan, griddle, pot

pandemonium *n.* uproar, confusion, turmoil, bedlam *The ice storm created bedlam at the airport.* rumpus, din, chaos ▷**noise** *ant.* calm

pane *n.* panel, glass, window *hom.* pain

panel *n.* ① pane, rectangle, sheet ② jury, group, committee, forum

pang *n.* ache, twinge, throb, prick ▷**pain**

panic ① *n.* alarm, fear, terror, dread, hysteria ② *v.* spook, frighten, startle, stampede *ant.* calm

pant *v.* puff, snort, blow, gasp, huff

paper *n.* ① stationery ② document, deed, article, dossier, composition, worksheet

parade ① *n.* procession, march, display, review ▷**pageant** ② *v.* display, exhibit, flaunt, show off, strut

paralyse *v.* cripple, disable, incapacitate, deaden, stun, immobilize

paramount *adj.* leading, chief, supreme, outstanding, primary ▷**foremost** *ant.* minor

paraphernalia *n.* equipment, gear, tackle

parasite *n.* sponger, hanger-on, leech, scrounger, freeloader

parcel *n.* batch, bundle, lot, division ▷**package**

parched *adj.* arid, scorched, withered, dry, thirsty, dehydrated

P

pardon *v.* excuse, forgive, acquit, absolve, liberate, release *ant.* condemn

pare *v.* ① skin, peel, uncover, strip, scrape, shave ② decrease, cut back *hom.* pair, pear

parent *n.* father, mother, guardian

park ① *n.* garden, green, grounds, woodland ② *v.* leave, position, station

parody *n.* caricature *Some of Dennis Lee's funniest poems are caricatures of nursery rhymes.* burlesque, satire, imitation, lampoon, skit, mockery, takeoff

parsimonious *adj.* miserly, sparing, penny-pinching ▷**stingy** *ant.* generous

part ① *n.* piece, fragment, portion, scrap, share, slice, section ② *n.* character, role ③ *v.* separate, divide, detach

partial *adj.* ① imperfect, limited, part, fragmentary *When the dog had finished chewing on my knapsack, there were only fragmentary remains.* unfinished ② biassed, favourable, inclined

partially *adv.* incompletely, somewhat, in part

participate *v.* take part, share, co-operate, engage, partake

particle *n.* morsel, atom, bit, seed, crumb, grain, scrap, sliver

particular *adj.* ① choosy, fastidious, scrupulous, exacting ② special, distinct, detailed, notable

partly *adv.* in part, incompletely, to some degree, partially *ant.* totally

partner *n.* colleague, associate, ally, helper, spouse

party *n.* ① function, celebration, festival, event ② group, body, faction *A small faction of club members wants to cancel the trip.*

pass ① *v.* move, go, run, continue, proceed ② *v.* overtake, beat, exceed, surpass ③ *v.* elapse, lapse, cease, die, vanish ④ *v.* send, deliver, hand ⑤ *v.* approve, enact, ratify ⑥ *v.* succeed, ace, satisfy ⑦ *n.* way, passage, gorge, ravine, gap, notch ⑧ *n.* permit, ticket, passport, licence

passage *n.* ① corridor, pathway, alley ② journey, cruise, voyage ③ paragraph, clause, section, excerpt ④ transition

passing *adj.* casual, fleeting, hasty, temporary, brief, transitory *ant.* permanent

passion *n.* desire, warmth, excitement, zeal, devotion, rapture, love, infatuation, ardour ▷**emotion** *ant.* indifference

passionate *adj.* enthusiastic, ardent, earnest, fiery, impetuous, burning *ant.* indifferent

past ① *adj.* finished, ended, former, gone, late, previous, prior, earlier *ant.* present ② *prep.* after, exceeding, beyond ③ *n.* history, yesterday, background *hom.* passed

paste *n.* glue, cement, gum, adhesive *hom.* paced

pastime *n.* recreation, sport, fun, hobby, amusement, distraction, activity

pasture *n.* grass, field, meadow

pat *v.* tap, caress, fondle, stroke, touch

patch *v.* fix, repair, sew, darn, mend

path *n.* way, track, road, route, course, lane, trail, passage, orbit, circuit

pathetic *adj.* pitiable, sad, wretched, poor, dismal, miserable, poor, puny *The puny little runt was the skinniest in the litter.*

patience *n.* endurance *The marathon is a race that requires endurance.* perseverance, composure, calmness, restraint, fortitude, tolerance *hom.* patients

Paths and Passageways

Alley	Drive	Passage
Avenue	Highway	Path
Boulevard	Lane	Road
Freeway	Mountain pass	Street

n. = noun
v. = verb
adj. = adjective
adv. = adverb
conj. = conjunction
prep. = preposition
ant. = antonym
hom. = homonym
▷ = cross-reference

patient *adj.* forbearing, long-suffering, persevering, understanding, calm, tolerant, persistent *ant.* impatient

patriotic *adj.* loyal, public-spirited, nationalistic, flagwaving

patrol *v.* police, watch, guard, protect, tour

patronize *v.* ① support, encourage, foster, sponsor, buy from ② talk down to, condescend

pattern *n.* ① model, standard, prototype, sample ② arrangement, decoration, design, ornament, figure, form

pause ① *v.* halt, cease, wait, rest, suspend *Let's suspend our work for a moment while we have a snack.* stop, delay *ant.* continue ② *n.* lull, intermission, break, interruption *hom.* paws

pay ① *v.* reward, support, compensate, discharge, spend, invest ② *n.* income, payment, salary, wages, compensation, fee, allowance, honorarium

peace *n.* ① harmony, calm, concord, serenity, quiet, tranquillity *ant.* discord ② truce, armistice *ant.* war *hom.* piece

peaceful *adj.* serene, quiet, calm, still, restful, harmonious, tranquil *ant.* restless

peak *n.* summit, apex, top, crown, pinnacle, zenith, height

peal *v.* ring, strike, toll, knell, clang, chime, resound *hom.* peel

peculiar *adj.* ① odd, curious, unusual, uncommon, strange, funny ② unique, special, distinctive

pedestal *n.* base, stand, support

peek *n. & v.* glimpse, blink, look, peep

peel ① *v.* skin, strip, pare, flake, shell ② *n.* skin, covering, rind, coat *hom.* peal

peer ① *v.* squint, stare, scrutinize, gaze, inspect ② *n.* colleague, equal, fellow, counterpart *hom.* pier

peevish *adj.* cross, childish, ill-tempered, grumpy, testy ▷**irritable** *ant.* cheerful

peg *n.* hook, knob, pin, post, hanger

pelt ① *v.* rain, teem, pour ② *v.* throw, hurl, whip ③ *n.* skin, hide, fleece, fur

pen ① *n.* cage, coop, stall, enclosure, fold ② *v.* write, author, compose, publish

penalty *n.* fine, forfeit, punishment, price, sanction *ant.* reward

pending *adj.* waiting, unfinished, undecided, in the balance, in the works

penetrate *v.* ① pierce, perforate, stab, break, puncture, permeate *When the skunk sprayed the lynx, the smell permeated the forest.* enter ② fathom, see through, comprehend

penetrating *adj.* sharp, perceptive, discerning, shrill, stinging, biting

pennant *n.* flag, streamer, bunting, banner

penniless *adj.* destitute, needy, poverty-stricken ▷**poor** *ant.* wealthy

pensive *adj.* thoughtful, reflective, wistful, preoccupied, meditative, musing

people ① *n.* folk, persons, individuals, humans, inhabitants, subjects ② *n.* society, public, populace, masses, community, nation, citizenry ③ *v.* populate, inhabit, settle

pep *n.* energy, vigour, high spirits, punch ▷**vitality**

peppery *adj.* ① hot, piquant, sharp, spicy ② snappish, fiery *Her fiery retorts often got her into trouble.* hot-tempered, angry

perceive *v.* feel, sense, observe, notice, make out, understand, detect ▷**see**

perch ① *v.* alight, settle, sit, squat, roost, balance ② *n.* rod, rail, seat, position

perfect ① *adj.* (*per*-fect) absolute, ideal, sublime, excellent, splendid, faultless, pure, good, complete, accurate *ant.* imperfect ② *v.* (per-*fect*) improve, polish, complete, finish, fulfil, refine, sharpen, hone

perforate *v.* puncture, pierce, punch, penetrate

perform *v.* ① carry out, do, fulfil, execute *The figure skater was able to execute the most difficult jump.* accomplish ② play, act, stage, present, entertain

performer *n.* actor, player, singer, entertainer, artist

perfume *n.* scent, fragrance, essence, aroma, odour

perhaps *adv.* possibly, maybe, conceivably

peril *n.* hazard, jeopardy, menace, risk, insecurity, danger *ant.* safety

P
p
P
p
P
p
ℙ
P

period *n.* time, duration, term, interval, course, span, age, term, season, phase, stage

periodic *adj.* regular, routine, recurring, repeated, intermittent

perish *v.* die, pass away, lose one's life, wither, disintegrate, expire, shrivel

perky *adj.* bouncy, bright, cheerful, lively ▷**sprightly** *ant.* listless

permanent *adj.* endless, ageless, timeless, constant, lasting, perpetual, durable, unchangeable, fixed *ant.* temporary

permission *n.* consent, licence, approval, authorization, sanction, privilege, warrant *ant.* prohibition

permit ① *v.* (per-*mit*) let, tolerate, allow, grant, consent to, empower, enable *ant.* prohibit ② *n.* (*per*-mit) warrant, licence, pass

perpendicular *adj.* upright, erect, sheer, steep, vertical

perpetrate *v.* commit, do, inflict, perform, practise, execute, carry out

perpetual *adj.* everlasting, ceaseless, eternal, never-ending, continual ▷**endless** *ant.* fleeting

perplex *v.* mystify, baffle, bewilder, confuse, confound, flummox *ant.* enlighten

persecute *v.* harass, molest, plague, badger, torment

persevere *v.* persist, hold out, hang on, endure, continue *ant.* give up

persist *v.* remain, stand fast, abide, carry on, survive, endure, hang in ▷**persevere** *ant.* stop

persistent *adj.* tenacious, relentless, determined, enduring, stubborn, obstinate

person *n.* individual, human being, somebody, personage, character

personal *adj.* own, individual, intimate, private, special

personality *n.* ① character, disposition, nature, identity ② celebrity

perspective *n.* outlook, view, angle

persuade *v.* convince, influence, urge, win over, entice, cajole *I cajoled my mother into taking me to work with her today.* induce ▷**coax** *ant.* discourage

pert *adj.* saucy, flippant, jaunty, brash, bold, impudent, rude *ant.* shy

perturb *v.* upset, disturb, trouble, distress, unsettle, agitate ▷**concern**

peruse *v.* read, study, pore over, browse, inspect, scrutinize, examine

pervade *v.* penetrate, permeate, spread, saturate, charge, fill

perverse *adj.* obstinate, contrary, wayward, willful, disobedient, corrupt ▷**stubborn** *ant.* reasonable

pessimist *n.* defeatist, kill-joy, wet blanket, cynic *Kirpal was such a cynic that he didn't believe she would help out just to be nice.*

pessimistic *adj.* cynical, dismal, fatalistic, defeatist, gloomy, discouraging, disheartening, depressing *ant.* optimistic

pest *n.* nuisance, plague, blight, curse, vexation, bug, scourge, bother

pester *v.* nag, badger, annoy, disturb, harass ▷**bother**

pet ① *v.* fondle, caress, baby, cosset *Mary cossetted the lamb so much that it followed her everywhere she went.* cuddle, stroke ② *n.* favourite, beloved, dear ③ *adj.* endearing, cherished, dearest

petition *n.* plea, appeal, entreaty, request

petrified *adj.* ① panic-stricken, frightened, scared, terrified, frozen ② hardened, calcified

petty *adj.* paltry, cheap, insignificant, picky, trifling, minor ▷**trivial** *ant.* important

petulant *adj.* fretful, ill-tempered, displeased, irritable ▷**peevish**

phantom ① *n.* apparition, spectre, spook, ghost ② *adj.* spooky, ghostly, imaginary

phenomenal *adj.* remarkable, outstanding, marvellous, miraculous, incredible

phenomenon *n.* marvel, rarity, curiosity, sensation, spectacle, fact

philanthropic *adj.* charitable, kind, generous, humane, benevolent *ant.* selfish

philosophical *adj.* calm, logical, thoughtful, impassive, unruffled, stoical, resigned

phobia *n.* dread, fear, neurosis, horror

phrase *n.* expression, idiom, saying, utterance, figure of speech *hom.* frays

physical *adj.* material, substantial, solid, concrete, tangible, bodily

pick *v.* select, choose, decide, appoint, elect, pluck, gather

picket ① *n.* patrol, scout, sentinel, lookout, guard ② *n.* post, stake, pale, upright ③ *v.* strike, demonstrate, blockade

pickle ① *v.* cure, salt, preserve *Put the onions in brine to preserve them.* ② *n.* difficulty, predicament ③ *n.* preserve, condiment, relish, chutney

picture ① *n.* painting, portrait, illustration, drawing, image, photo, diagram ② *n.* movie, film ③ *v.* portray, imagine, represent, visualize

picturesque *adj.* scenic, attractive, quaint, artistic

piece *n.* portion, fragment, lump, morsel, share, section, particle, sliver, bit ▷**scrap** *hom.* peace

pier *n.* wharf, dock, quay, jetty *hom.* peer

pierce *v.* perforate, puncture, drill, bore ▷**penetrate**

piercing *adj.* ① loud, deafening, shrill, high, penetrating ② keen, sharp, cutting

pigment *n.* colour, dye, tint, paint, stain

pile *n. & v.* heap, mound, mass, stack, load, store, supply

pillage *v.* plunder, ravage, loot, ransack, rifle, sack, rob

pillar *n.* column, shaft, post, upright, support

pilot ① *n.* aviator, flyer ② *n.* guide, helmsman ③ *v.* drive, guide, manoeuvre ④ *adj.* experimental, test, trial

pimple *n.* acne, blemish, swelling, boil, zit

pin ① *n.* fastener, clip, brooch, peg ② *v.* fix, fasten, attach, join, tack, press

pinch ① *v.* nip, tweak, squeeze, crush ② *n.* dash, sprinkling ③ *n.* crisis, difficulty, jam

pine *v.* hanker, yearn, long, languish, sicken

pinnacle *n.* summit, top, crest, peak, apex, climax

pioneer *n.* founder, leader, trailblazer, explorer, innovator, spearhead

pious *adj.* devout, godly, holy, moral, religious, virtuous, reverent

pipe *n.* ① tube, duct, passage, hose, conduit ② whistle, flute, fife, piccolo, bagpipe

piquant *adj.* peppery, strong, flavourful, spicy, tangy, savoury, pungent

pique *v.* annoy, displease, irritate, affront, provoke, vex *hom.* peak

pirate ① *n.* corsair, buccaneer, privateer ② *n.* plagiarist ③ *v.* copy, plagiarize, steal, crib

pit *n.* ① hole, hollow, crater, quarry, mine, dent, dimple, depression ② seed, stone

pitch ① *v.* fling, throw, cast, sling, toss ② *v.* plunge, lurch, fall, drop ③ *v.* raise, set up, erect ④ *n.* angle, slope, degree ⑤ *n.* spiel, ad, plug

pitcher *n.* carafe, crock, jug, vessel

pitiless *adj.* merciless, heartless, cruel, unrelenting *ant.* merciful

pity ① *n.* mercy, compassion, charity, sympathy, tenderness ② *v.* spare, forgive, sympathize with

pivot ① *n.* axle, axis, hinge, turning point, spindle, swivel ② *v.* revolve, rotate, turn, spin, swing

placate *v.* appease, pacify, soothe, satisfy ▷**humour** *ant.* infuriate

place ① *n.* spot, locality, site, situation, point, position ② *n.* area, region, district, surroundings, venue *Is the local park a good venue for our first performance?* residence ③ *n.* position, rank, standing, status ④ *v.* set, rest, stick, lay, stand, deposit ⑤ *v.* identify

placid *adj.* peaceful, serene, mild, still, calm, motionless, unexcited ▷**quiet** *ant.* excited

plague ① *n.* epidemic, disease, contagion, pest, blight, outbreak, curse, annoyance ② *v.* persecute, pester *We were pestered by deer flies and black flies.* infest, annoy ▷**badger**

plain ① *adj.* unadorned, simple, ordinary, natural ② *adj.* obvious, clear, apparent ③ *adj.* blunt, direct, candid, forthright, straightforward ④ *adj.* homely, unattractive ⑤ *n.* prairie, plateau, tableland *hom.* plane

P
p
P
p
P
ℙ
P

Planets

The nine planets of our solar system travel round a star we call the Sun.

Mercury
Venus
Earth
Mars
Jupiter
Saturn
Uranus
Neptune
Pluto

plan ① *n.* design, chart, diagram, drawing, sketch, draft ② *n.* project, proposal, program, arrangement, scheme ③ *v.* design, prepare, chart ④ *v.* organize, schedule, program, arrange ⑤ *v.* anticipate, intend, expect

plane ① *adj.* level, even, flat, smooth ② *n.* level surface ③ *n.* aircraft *hom.* plain

plant ① *v.* seed, sow, scatter, implant ② *v.* place, set, post, station, establish ③ *n.* herb, shrub, vegetable ④ *n.* factory

plaster ① *n.* cement, mortar, paste ② *v.* spread, smear, daub, slather

plastic ① *adj.* mouldable, pliable, malleable, soft, supple ② *adj.* artificial, phony ③ *n.* credit cards

plate ① *n.* dish, platter, serving ② *n.* sheet, panel ③ *v.* laminate, cover, gild

platform *n.* stage, stand, podium, dais, rostrum *Our team was called up to the rostrum to receive our prize.* framework

plausible *adj.* believable, credible, convincing, persuasive *ant.* unlikely

play ① *v.* frisk, romp, frolic ② *v.* perform, act ③ *v.* compete, contend ④ *n.* drama, show, performance ⑤ *n.* game, amusement, recreation, make-believe

player *n.* actor, sportsman, sportswoman, artist, musician, performer, contestant

playful *adj.* frisky, frolicsome, lively, sportive *ant.* serious

plead *v.* appeal, argue, ask, implore, request, beseech, entreat, beg

pleasant *adj.* amiable, enjoyable, agreeable, comfortable ▷**charming** *ant.* unpleasant

please *v.* ① gratify, enchant, amuse, charm, satisfy, entertain, delight ② like, choose, wish, prefer, desire

pleasing *adj.* agreeable, enchanting, enjoyable, entertaining, satisfying ▷**agreeable** *ant.* offensive

pleasure *n.* delight, joy, amusement, entertainment, enjoyment

pledge ① *n.* promise, vow, oath, guarantee, commitment ② *v.* promise, vow, swear, guarantee, undertake, contract, bind, commit

plentiful *adj.* lavish, ample, profuse, bountiful, generous, rich, numerous ▷**abundant** *ant.* sparse

plenty *n.* enough, abundance, profusion, sufficiency, heap ▷**wealth** *ant.* scarcity

pliable *adj.* supple, flexible, pliant, malleable, mouldable *ant.* rigid

plight *n.* predicament, difficulty, condition, dilemma, jam

plod *v.* toil, labour, drudge, slog, trudge

plot ① *n.* scheme, plan, intrigue, strategy, ruse, conspiracy ② *n.* story line, action, structure, development ③ *n.* lot, patch, parcel ④ *v.* conspire, intrigue, scheme ⑤ *v.* chart, map, plan out, graph

pluck ① *v.* gather, pick, pull, yank, snatch ② *n.* courage, boldness, bravery

plucky *adj.* courageous, daring, heroic, spunky ▷**brave** *ant.* fearful

n.= noun
v.= verb
adj.= adjective
adv.= adverb
conj.= conjunction
prep.= preposition
ant.= antonym
hom.= homonym
▷ = cross-reference

plug ① *n.* stopper, cork ② *v.* stop, block, choke, cork, fill ③ *v.* publicize, promote, push, advertise, recommend

plum ① *n.* prize, bonus, treasure, reward ② *adj.* best, choice *Elena gave her guests the choice seats and she took the one with the worst view.* first-class

plump *adj.* stout, chubby, rotund, pudgy, buxom *ant.* skinny

plunder ① *n.* booty, loot, spoils, haul ② *v.* rob, ransack, pillage, loot, fleece

plunge *v.* dive, pitch, submerge, duck, immerse, swoop, lunge, fall, thrust

pocket *n.* pouch, bag, sac, compartment

poem *n.* rhyme, ode, sonnet, limerick, epic, lyric, ballad, verse

poetic *adj.* artistic, elegant, graceful, flowing, lyrical

poignant *adj.* moving *As I listened to the moving story, I began to cry.* touching, pathetic, heart-wrenching, piercing, intense

point ① *n.* spike, barb, prong, end, tip ② *n.* locality, place, spot ③ *n.* goal, object, aim, purpose ④ *v.* aim, direct, level, train ⑤ *v.* show, indicate, imply, hint

pointless *adj.* meaningless, senseless, silly, futile, vain ▷**absurd** *ant.* worthwhile

poised *adj.* ① confident, assured, dignified, self-possessed, composed, at ease ② hovering, balanced, ready

poison ① *n.* venom, virus, toxin, pollutant ② *v.* taint, corrupt, infect, contaminate, pollute, spike, lace

poisonous *adj.* deadly, evil, fatal, lethal, noxious, toxic, venomous

poke *v.* jab, push, nudge, jostle, ram, thrust, stab, prod, snoop, shove

pole *n.* stick, staff, stake, rod, post, bar, mast, shaft, spar

policy *n.* rules, guidelines, course, practice, procedure, plan, line

polish ① *v.* shine, wax, burnish, buff, smooth, brighten, clean ② *n.* gloss, glaze, shine ③ *n.* refinement, grace, culture, elegance

polished *adj.* ① glossy, burnished, shiny ② refined, cultivated, cultured, elegant

polite *adj.* courteous, attentive, civil, kind, refined, elegant, respectful *ant.* impolite

poll ① *n.* election, vote, count, census, ballot box ② *v.* survey, canvass, vote

pollute *v.* poison, corrupt, taint, contaminate, defile *ant.* purify

pompous *adj.* showy, self-important, affected, snobbish, stuffy, pretentious ▷**arrogant** *ant.* modest

ponder *v.* meditate, consider, reflect, deliberate, think

pool ① *n.* lagoon, pond, slough, reservoir, puddle ② *n.* accumulation, fund, reserve, kitty ③ *v.* combine, contribute, share

poor *adj.* ① destitute, penniless, miserable, homeless, needy, disadvantaged, broke *ant.* rich ② inferior, sorry, meagre, faulty, feeble, shoddy *ant.* superior

pop *v.* bang, burst, crack, explode, go off

popular *adj.* ① well-liked, favourite, accepted, fashionable ② current, common, prevailing, general

pore over *v.* scan, examine, peruse *After I had perused my report card, I let my parents look at it.* scrutinize *hom.* pour

portable *adj.* lightweight, convenient, handy, transportable, compact *ant.* awkward

Poisonous Plants

Aconite
Baneberry
Belladonna
Black nightshade
Deadly nightshade
Foxglove
Hellebore
Hemlock
Henbane
Larkspur
Nux vomica
Poison ivy

P
p
P
p
p
ℙ
P

portion *n.* piece, fragment, share, fraction, division, serving, quota *Each student receives a quota of 500 g of modelling clay for the project.* ration, bit, measure ▷**part**

portrait *n.* likeness, painting, picture, profile

portray *v.* describe, depict, represent, picture, illustrate, impersonate, act

pose ① *v.* sit, model ② *v.* disguise oneself, pretend ③ *v.* present, ask ④ *n.* position, stand, guise, stance, posture, carriage, attitude

position *n.* ① spot, situation, location, place, site ② job, post, employment ③ posture, pose, attitude ④ rank, standing, status, state ⑤ stand, view, opinion

positive *adj.* ① certain, confident *ant.* doubtful ② precise, definite, irrefutable, unmistakable, conclusive, explicit *ant.* questionable ③ encouraging, favourable, affirmative, optimistic *ant.* negative

possess *v.* have, own, hold, occupy

possessions *n.* wealth, assets, property, goods, belongings, holdings

possible *adj.* conceivable, imaginable, likely, feasible *Adrian's idea was feasible, so his mother agreed to discuss it some more.* attainable, viable, workable *ant.* impossible

possibly *adv.* perhaps, maybe, conceivably

post *n.* ① pole, stake, upright ② position, employment, job

poster *n.* placard, bill, advertisement, sign

postpone *v.* put off, defer, shelve, adjourn ▷**delay**

posture *n.* bearing, stance, attitude, pose, carriage, outlook

pot *n.* basin, bowl, pan, vessel, container, jar

potential ① *adj.* possible, eventual, probable, latent *I didn't realize I had a latent talent for languages until I first took French.* dormant, budding ② *n.* ability, talent, capacity, aptitude, power ▷**flair** ③ *n.* future, prospects, possibility, likelihood

potion *n.* elixir, medicine, mixture, tonic, brew

pouch *n.* bag, sack, purse, pocket, wallet

pounce *v.* strike, lunge, spring, swoop, fall upon ▷**attack**

pound ① *v.* beat, batter, crush, hammer ② *n.* enclosure, compound, pen

pour *v.* spout, jet, gush, spill, cascade, rain, stream, flow, rush, teem *hom.* pore

pout *v.* grimace, glower, sulk, scowl, mope *ant.* smile

poverty *n.* ① distress, need, destitution, privation ▷**want** ② scarcity, shortage *ant.* plenty, wealth

powder ① *n.* dust, sand, ash, grit ② *v.* pulverize, crunch, grind, crush, sprinkle

power *n.* ① authority, command, control, energy, force, strength, might ② ability, capacity

powerful *adj.* mighty, vigorous, forceful, potent, muscular, effective ▷**strong** *ant.* weak

practical *adj.* ① useful, effective, workable, functional, realistic ② level-headed, sensible, down-to-earth, pragmatic *ant.* impractical

practice *n.* ① performance, action, exercise, drill, training ② custom, habit, usage, policy

practise *v.* ① carry out, apply, execute, exercise, implement ② rehearse, train

praise ① *v.* honour, cheer, compliment, acclaim, applaud, glorify *ant.* criticize ② *n.* applause, flattery, tribute, approval, compliment *hom.* prays, preys

prance *v.* gambol, frolic, romp, caper, swagger

prank *n.* trick, joke, antic, lark, stunt

pray *v.* beg, beseech, entreat, implore, crave, solicit, request, adore, worship, appeal *hom.* prey

prayer *n.* petition, entreaty, worship, devotion, appeal

preach *v.* lecture, moralize, advocate, urge, proclaim

precarious *adj.* perilous, hazardous, insecure, dangerous ▷**risky** *ant.* safe

precaution *n.* forethought, safety measure, provision, care, providence, prudence

precede *v.* introduce, predate *My years at nursery school predate my years at this school.* lead, usher, go before, preface *ant.* follow

precious *adj.* invaluable, cherished, treasured, dear, favourite, beloved ▷**costly** *ant.* worthless

precise *adj.* ① definite, exact, detailed, accurate, specific *ant.* vague ② meticulous, formal, particular, strict, rigid

precisely *adv.* accurately, just so, even, exactly, correctly, literally, directly

precision *n.* exactness, accuracy, care, detail, correctness

precocious *adj.* early, advanced, fast, smart, clever *ant.* backward

predicament *n.* situation, state, condition, embarrassment, fix, bind, jam, dilemma, trouble ▷**plight**

predict *v.* foresee, foretell, prophesy, forecast, anticipate, divine

predominant *adj.* leading, main, prevailing, superior, ruling, controlling

preface *n.* introduction, foreword, prologue, prelude, preamble

prefer *v.* choose, select, desire, elect, fancy ▷**favour** *ant.* reject

prejudice ① *n.* bigotry, intolerance, bias, discrimination ② *v.* jeopardize, injure, compromise, influence, warp *Years of brainwashing had warped his judgment.* twist, distort, undermine

prejudiced *adj.* biassed, bigoted, one-sided, unfair, intolerant, narrow-minded, racist, sexist *ant.* fair

preliminary *adj.* introductory, basic, elementary, opening, initial, rough *ant.* final

premature *adj.* untimely, early, ill-timed *ant.* late

premeditated *adj.* calculated, planned, prearranged, intentional *ant.* spontaneous

premier ① *n.* prime minister, first minister, head of government ② *adj.* chief, first, leading, principal, primary

prepare *v.* arrange, adapt, provide, get ready, concoct, plan, condition, train, practise, equip, groom, cook

preposterous *adj.* absurd, ridiculous, foolish, outrageous, laughable ▷**unreasonable** *ant.* reasonable

prescribe *v.* indicate, order, propose, recommend, specify, dictate

presence *n.* occurrence, existence, appearance, bearing, attendance

present ① *n.* (*pres*-ent) gift, donation, prize, favour ② *n.* (*pres*-ent) now, today ③ *adj.* (*pres*-ent) here, on the spot, ready, current, existing, contemporary *ant.* past ④ *v.* (pre-*sent*) offer, tender, award, exhibit, propose, confer ⑤ *v.* (pre-*sent*) perform, stage, produce⑥ *v.* (pre-*sent*) introduce

presently *adv.* soon, shortly, before long

preserve *v.* protect, safeguard, conserve, shield, maintain ▷**keep** *ant.* waste

press ① *v.* bear down, depress, clamp, squeeze, compress, flatten, push ② *v.* urge, persuade, beg ③ *v.* campaign, agitate, insist ④ *n.* media, journalism

pressure *n.* ① strain, tension, stress, urgency ② weight, compression, force

prestige *n.* status, authority, glamour, power, honour, eminence

presume *v.* assume, suppose, guess, infer *I infer from your smile that you are pleased to be here.* impose, take for granted

presumptuous *adj.* arrogant, bold, audacious, insolent, brash, overconfident, rude ▷**forward** *ant.* modest

pretend *v.* make believe, simulate, sham, feign, pose, act, fake, assume, presume

pretext *n.* excuse, pretence, façade, guise, device

pretty *adj.* attractive, beautiful, comely, dainty, fair, good-looking ▷**lovely** *ant.* ugly

prevail *v.* overcome, predominate ▷**triumph** *ant.* lose

prevalent *adj.* current, common, popular, in use, accepted, existing *ant.* uncommon

prevent *v.* avert, forestall, ward off, stop, discourage, obstruct, preclude ▷**hinder**

previous *adj.* former, prior, earlier, preceding, last, past, late *ant.* latter

prey ① *n.* victim, quarry ② *v.* hunt, chase, attack, target *hom.* pray

price *n.* cost, amount, expense, payment, value, worth, charge, rate, fee

P p P p P P P

priceless *adj.* ① invaluable, precious, cherished *He was very upset when he lost his cherished rock collection.* costly ② amusing, comic, humorous, hilarious

prick *v.* jab, puncture, stab, pierce, sting

pride *n.* self-esteem, conceit, vanity *Her friends admired Janet's good marks but were unhappy about her increasing vanity.* egotism, self-importance, honour, arrogance *hom.* pried

primary *adj.* first, original, chief, essential, fundamental, cardinal, main, major

prime *adj.* ① principal, chief, basic ② best, finest, choice, excellent

primitive *adj.* ① simple, crude, early ② uncivilized, undeveloped, backward

principal ① *adj.* main, chief, head, leading, foremost ② *n.* head, leader, administrator, director, superintendent *hom.* principle

principle *n.* ① rule, ethic, idea, doctrine ② virtue, character, integrity, rectitude *ant.* wickedness *hom.* principal

Confusable Words

principal means *main*

principle means *basic idea*

print ① *v.* mark, engrave, impress, stamp, brand, publish ② *n.* impression, printing, imprint, picture, photograph

prior *adj.* previous, former, earlier, preceding

prison *n.* jail, penitentiary, dungeon, lockup

private *adj.* ① confidential, personal, secret, special, own ② solitary, secluded, remote *It took four days by boat to reach the remote island.* quiet *ant.* public

privilege *n.* advantage, perk, honour *It is an honour to be asked to speak at your school assembly.* right, authority, entitlement, prerogative

prize ① *n.* reward, premium, trophy, award ② *n.* treasure, booty, spoils, plunder ③ *adj.* best, champion, winning ④ *v.* value, appreciate, cherish *hom.* pries

probable *adj.* likely, presumable, reasonable, possible *ant.* improbable

probe *v.* ① poke, prod ② explore, examine, investigate, inquire into

problem *n.* ① puzzle, question, riddle, mystery ② difficulty, dilemma, snag, quandary, complication, predicament ③ fault, defect, bug ④ issue, matter

proceed *v.* stem, originate, advance, continue, progress, arise, flow, spring, emanate *A wonderful smell emanated from the kitchen.*

process ① *n.* procedure, operation, journey, system, method ② *v.* convert, alter, handle, refine

procession *n.* parade, march, cavalcade, file

proclaim *v.* declare, announce, advertise, publish, expound

procure *v.* acquire, win, gain, secure, obtain *ant.* lose

prod *v.* dig, goad, poke, spur, jab, nudge, incite, urge, shove, egg on

prodigious *adj.* ① miraculous, abnormal, amazing, remarkable, fabulous ▷**extraordinary** *ant.* ordinary ② huge, mighty, giant ▷**enormous** *ant.* tiny

produce ① *n.* (*pro*-duce) fruits, vegetables, yield, crop, harvest ② *v.* (pro-*duce*) yield, create, deliver, result in, manufacture, invent, develop, show

Print

Print

n.= noun

v.= verb

adj.= adjective

adv.= adverb

conj.= conjunction

prep.= preposition

ant.= antonym

hom.= homonym

▷ = cross-reference

product *n.* goods, yield, output, item, result, return, merchandise, commodity, stock

profession *n.* occupation, career, job, calling, employment

professional *adj.* skilled, efficient, experienced, expert, businesslike

proficient *adj.* competent, able, skilled, expert, efficient *ant.* incompetent

profit ① *n.* benefit, gain, advantage, use, return, dividend, bonus, royalty *ant.* loss ② *v.* gain, benefit, take advantage, reap dividends *ant.* lose *hom.* prophet

profound *adj.* deep, penetrating, intense, learned, sagacious *The leader of the band council was a sagacious old man.* insightful, unfathomable *ant.* shallow

profuse *adj.* bountiful, extravagant, exuberant, prolific, luxuriant, lush, thick ▷**lavish** *ant.* sparse

progress ① *n.* (*pro*-gress) advancement, growth, development, improvement *ant.* decline ② *v.* (pro-*gress*) advance, proceed, improve, forge ahead, travel, grow

prohibit *v.* forbid, bar, outlaw, ban, obstruct, hinder ▷**prevent** *ant.* permit

project ① *n.* (*pro*-ject) work, plan, scheme, undertaking, report, task, activity ② *v.* (pro-*ject*) propel, shoot, cast ③ *v.* jut, protrude, bulge ④ *v.* predict, anticipate

prolific *adj.* fruitful, productive, fertile

prolong *v.* lengthen, stretch, draw out, spin out, extend *ant.* shorten

prominent *adj.* ① famous, eminent, notable ② projecting, conspicuous, bulging, jutting

promise ① *n.* commitment, undertaking, pledge, oath, word, vow, pact ② *v.* pledge, assure, agree, guarantee, vow

promote *v.* ① cultivate, advance, favour, foster, enhance, boost, publicize ▷**encourage** ② dignify, elevate, upgrade, honour *ant.* degrade

prompt ① *adj.* punctual, timely, quick, swift, ready *ant.* late ② *v.* hint, remind, urge, cue ▷**inspire** *ant.* deter

prone *adj.* ① inclined, apt, liable, disposed *ant.* unlikely ② flat, prostrate, face down *ant.* upright

pronounce *v.* ① speak, utter, say, articulate ② declare, decree, proclaim, affirm

pronounced *adj.* outstanding, striking, noticeable, bold, decided ▷**distinct** *ant.* slight, inconspicuous

proof *n.* evidence, testimony, confirmation *This receipt is confirmation of your payment.* reason, sign, token

prop *n. & v.* stay, brace, truss, support

propel *v.* push, force, impel, send, power ▷**drive** *ant.* stop

proper *adj.* ① correct, right, fitting, suitable, accurate, exact ② respectable, decent, right, just, ethical *ant.* improper ③ formal, prim, strict, official

property *n.* ① land, possessions, wealth, holdings, buildings, belongings ② quality, virtue, characteristic, feature, trait, attribute

prophecy *n.* forecast, prediction, foreshadowing, oracle

prophesy *v.* predict, foretell, foresee, declare

proportion *n.* ① ratio, percentage, part, fraction ② balance, symmetry

proposal *n.* proposition, offer, outline, suggestion, submission

propose *v.* ① put forward, offer, suggest, submit ② plan, intend

proprietor *n.* owner, possessor, landlady, landlord, holder

prosaic *adj.* tedious, uninteresting, boring, dull, mundane, ordinary, everyday *ant.* interesting

prosecute *v.* ① indict, put on trial, sue ② continue, pursue, carry on, conduct

prospect *n.* ① outlook, forecast, promise, expectation, future, chance ② view, landscape, vista, aspect

prosper *v.* succeed, flourish, grow, thrive *ant.* fail

prosperous *adj.* affluent, wealthy, rich, successful, thriving, comfortable, flourishing *ant.* poor

protect *v.* defend, preserve, guard, secure, shelter, shield, screen *ant.* endanger

protest ① *v.* (pro-*test*) complain, object, dispute, challenge *ant.* accept ② *n.* (*pro*-test) objection, complaint, dissent, outcry

protracted *adj.* extended, drawn out, lengthy, prolonged, chronic *ant.* abrupt

protrude *v.* project, bulge, jut, swell *ant.* recede

proud *adj.* ① arrogant, smug, self-confident, conceited, boastful, supercilious *ant.* humble ② lofty, majestic, noble, splendid, dignified, glorious

prove *v.* show, demonstrate, attest *Fossils attest the existence of prehistoric creatures.* confirm, verify, convince, satisfy, test *ant.* refute

provide *v.* give, offer, supply, furnish, equip, contribute, afford *ant.* withhold

province *n.* area, sphere, orbit, domain, department, region, state, county

provoke *v.* prompt, incite, excite, inflame, arouse, goad, instigate, stir up ▷**aggravate** *ant.* appease

prowess *n.* ability, strength, might, bravery, skill, heroism ▷**valour**

prowl *v.* stalk, roam, slink, sneak

prudent *adj.* careful, cautious, economical, wary, discreet, shrewd, thrifty *ant.* rash

prune *v.* cut back, shorten, trim, crop

pry *v.* snoop, peek, meddle, intrude

public ① *adj.* communal, civic, popular, social, national, collective ② *n.* populace, society, nation, audience, community

publish *v.* broadcast, announce, report, declare, proclaim, reveal, distribute, circulate *Let's circulate a flyer and see if anyone claims the cat we found.* issue, bring out

pucker *v.* fold, crease, furrow, wrinkle *ant.* smooth

puff *v.* inflate, swell, blow, pant

pull *v.* haul, drag, tow, heave, gather, pluck, remove, pick, jerk, wrench, lug, strain, stretch

pump *v.* ① inflate, expand, swell, fill, inject, siphon, draw, drain ② question, interrogate

punch *v.* ① strike, beat, hit, pummel, wallop ② puncture, pierce, perforate, poke

punctual *adj.* prompt, on time, precise, timely *ant.* late

puncture *n.* hole, perforation, leak, wound

pungent *adj.* sharp, strong, piquant, spicy, aromatic, acrid *ant.* mild

punish *v.* discipline, scold, penalize, correct, chastise, reprove

puny *adj.* feeble, weak, frail, small, petty, stunted, insignificant, meagre *ant.* large

pupil *n.* student, scholar, learner, schoolchild

puppet *n.* ① doll, marionette ② pawn, figurehead

purchase ① *v.* procure, secure, obtain, get ▷**buy** *ant.* sell ② *n.* bargain, investment, acquisition

pure *adj.* ① immaculate, spotless, stainless, clear, fresh ▷**clean** *ant.* impure ② virtuous, chaste, honest, blameless ③ uniform, unmixed, genuine, authentic ④ sheer, absolute, utter

purely *adv.* simply, barely, merely, only

purge *v.* ① purify, clean, scour, cleanse ② liquidate, exterminate, kill, eliminate

purify *v.* clean, cleanse, decontaminate, wash, purge, refine

purpose *n.* aim, objective, function, intent, design, will, goal, target

purse ① *n.* handbag, pouch ② *v.* pucker, crease, compress, wrinkle

pursue *v.* ① follow, track, hound ▷**chase** ② practise, maintain, work for, seek

pursuit *n.* ① hunt, chase, quest, search ② occupation, business, practice, hobby, interest, activity, pastime

push ① *v.* shove, thrust, press, drive, propel, force, ram, jab ② *v.* coerce, urge, pressure, impel ③ *n.* advance, effort, drive, campaign ④ *v.* advocate, lobby, promote, agitate

put *v.* ① set, place, deposit, repose, lay, leave, impose ② express, propose, state ③ launch ④ apply, dab, smear

putrid *adj.* decomposed, rotten, rancid, rank, stinking, decaying *ant.* wholesome

puzzle ① *v.* baffle, confuse, mystify, perplex, confound ▷**bewilder** ② *n.* riddle, mystery, problem, dilemma, brainteaser

puzzling *adj.* baffling, curious, strange, inexplicable ▷**peculiar**

n. = noun
v. = verb
adj. = adjective
adv. = adverb
conj. = conjunction
prep. = preposition
ant. = antonym
hom. = homonym
▷ = cross-reference

Q q

quack *n.* impostor, charlatan, fake

quagmire *n.* ① bog, marsh, slough ▷**swamp** ② mess, morass

quail *v.* tremble, flinch, shrink, cower

quaint *adj.* curious, whimsical, fanciful, unusual, unique, old-fashioned

quake ① *v.* tremble, quaver, shiver, quiver, shudder, shake, vibrate ② *n.* shock, convulsion, tremor

qualification *n.* ① credential, fitness, capacity, ability, suitability ② provision, restriction, limitation, modification *They accepted the leader's report after she had made a few modifications.*

qualify *v.* ① empower, enable, fit, suit, certify, authorize, license ② distinguish, moderate, limit, restrict

quality *n.* ① nature, trait, feature, characteristic, property ② excellence, calibre, merit, worth, goodness

qualm *n.* doubt, reservation, objection, suspicion, misgiving, hesitation

quandary *n.* difficulty, spot ▷**dilemma**

quantity *n.* amount, number, volume, sum, total, extent, limit, range

quarrel ① *n.* dispute, squabble, wrangle, argument, fight, disagreement, spat, tiff *ant.* harmony ② *v.* argue, clash, fight, brawl, disagree, bicker, squabble *ant.* agree

quarry *n.* ① game, prey, object, victim, target ② mine, excavation, pit

quarter *n.* ① area, section, district, neighbourhood ② fourth quadrant

quarters *n.* lodgings, suite, rooms, billet

quaver *v.* shake, tremble, shiver, shudder, vibrate, quake

quay *n.* pier, dock, wharf, jetty *hom.* key

queasy *adj.* squeamish, sick, faint, bilious

queer *adj.* strange, odd, peculiar, unusual, unique, uncommon, eccentric

quench *v.* extinguish, slake, douse, drown out, cool, check

query ① *n.* question, doubt, objection, inquiry ② *v.* ask, inquire, question, doubt

quest *n.* chase, hunt, search, pursuit, venture

question ① *n.* query, inquiry, request, appeal, quiz, interrogation *ant.* answer ② *n.* topic, problem, issue ③ *v.* ask, inquire, interrogate, interview, quiz ④ *v. & n.* dispute, doubt, query, challenge

questionable *adj.* doubtful, uncertain, undecided, unbelievable, debatable, ambiguous *ant.* certain

queue *n.* row, line, procession, line-up *hom.* cue

quibble *v.* argue, trifle, split hairs *Split hairs about the details later, but let's try to agree on the main idea.* nit-pick, carp

quick *adj.* ① speedy, rapid, active, swift, fleet, nimble, prompt ▷**fast** ② smart, bright, clever, alert, intelligent, acute ③ sudden, abrupt *ant.* slow

quicken *v.* accelerate, speed up, rouse, stir ▷**hasten** *ant.* delay

quiet ① *adj.* silent, soundless, soft, faint, hushed *ant.* noisy, loud ② *adj.* calm, still, placid, smooth, undisturbed *ant.* hectic ③ *adj.* tame, passive *ant.* frisky ④ *adj.* shy, reserved *The reserved boy gave only the briefest answers.* ⑤ *n.* peace, rest, tranquillity, silence, calm *ant.* noise

quilt *n.* eiderdown, duvet, cover, blanket

quip *n.* joke, gag, jest, wisecrack, retort

quirk *n.* peculiarity, curiosity, eccentricity, oddity, mannerism ▷**habit**

quit *v.* ① cease, desist, stop, discontinue ② leave, resign, depart, relinquish ③ give up, surrender, abandon

quite *adv.* completely, considerably, rather, absolutely

quiver *v.* tremble, quake, shiver, shudder

quiz ① *v.* question, ask, examine, grill, test ② *n.* test, examination, contest, puzzle

quota *n.* allowance, allocation, ration, allotment, share

quotation *n.* ① extract, selection, passage ② cost, estimate, price

quote *v.* recite, state, mention, cite *To prove her point, she cited a similar example.*

R r

race ① *n.* competition, contest, match, rush ② *n.* people, folk, breed ③ *v.* rush, tear, speed, hurry, sprint, dash ④ *v.* compete

rack ① *n.* shelf, stand, frame ② *v.* distress, afflict, strain, torment, torture *hom.* wrack

racket *n.* ① uproar, noise, hubbub, disturbance, clamour, tumult, din ▷**fuss** ② fraud, scam, swindle, scheme

radiant *adj.* ① brilliant, bright, luminous, shining, glorious ② beaming, glowing, happy *ant.* dim

radiate *v.* ① gleam, sparkle, beam, shine ② emit, spread, shed, diffuse

radical *adj.* ① extreme, fanatical ② vital, essential, fundamental *Most of us have a fundamental need to be with others.* deep-seated *ant.* superficial

raffle *n.* draw, sweepstakes, lottery

rafter *n.* joist, girder, beam, support

rage ① *n.* wrath, fury, frenzy, ferocity, passion, madness ▷**anger** ② *n.* fashion, fad *Hula Hoops were a fad in the 1960s.* ③ *v.* rave, rampage, fume, storm, flare up

ragged *adj.* ① sloppy, patched, tattered, shabby, seedy, worn, torn ② jagged, barbed, rough

raid ① *n.* invasion, attack, assault, blitz, strike, sortie ② *v.* attack, invade, ransack, storm, ambush, harass, assault, plunder

rail *n.* banister, barrier, fence, railing

rain *n. & v.* deluge, drizzle, flood, shower, torrent, sprinkle, storm, downpour *hom.* reign, rein

raise *v.* ① elevate, lift, erect, jack up, boost, hoist *Hoist the flag to the top of the flagpole.* *ant.* lower ② excite, awaken, spark, arouse, promote, increase, heighten ③ cultivate, grow, breed, rear, bring up ④ collect, gather *hom.* raze

rake *v.* scrape, collect, gather, assemble

rally *v.* ① regroup, reassemble, revive, recover ② unite, join forces, mobilize ③ encourage, hearten

ram *v.* ① cram, jam, force, squeeze, stuff, wedge ② butt, shove, charge, beat, crash, drive, slam, thrust

ramble *v.* ① wander, stray, rove, stroll, roam ② chatter, digress *Stick to your point when you're speaking and don't digress so much.*

ramp *n.* gradient, slope, incline, grade

rampage ① *n.* storm, rage, riot, uproar, tumult ② *v.* rush, stampede, run wild

ramshackle *adj.* tumbledown, run-down, flimsy, rickety ▷**decrepit** *ant.* solid

rancid *adj.* sour, curdled, rank, putrid, musty

rancour *n.* spite, grudge, animosity, hatred, resentment, bitterness, hostility ▷**malice**

random *adj.* haphazard, casual, aimless, arbitrary *Have you thought this through or are you making an arbitrary decision?* accidental, chance *ant.* deliberate

range ① *n.* scope, extent, length, span, magnitude *Reduce the magnitude of your hunt from the whole park to only the playground.* distance ② *n.* habitat, domain, territory ③ *v.* wander, rove, roam, stray

rank ① *n.* grade, class, position, level, status, station ② *adj.* rotten, mouldy, foul, musty, offensive, stinking

ransack *v.* plunder, pillage, scour, loot

ransom ① *n.* release, deliverance, payoff, price ② *v.* rescue, redeem, liberate

rant *v.* rave, bluster, roar, shout, harangue

rap *v.* tap, pat, strike, knock

rape *v.* violate, abuse, assault, exploit, despoil

rapid *adj.* speedy, quick, swift ▷**fast** *ant.* slow

rapture *n.* bliss, ecstasy, delight, heaven ▷**joy** *ant.* sorrow

rare *adj.* ① unusual, uncommon, scarce, distinctive ② infrequent, occasional ③ valuable, fine, precious *ant.* common ④ underdone, lightly cooked

rascal *n.* rogue, knave, villain, scamp, scoundrel

rash ① *adj.* headstrong, impetuous, hot-headed, impulsive, hasty, foolhardy, reckless ▷**indiscreet** *ant.* cautious ② *n.* eruption, outbreak, epidemic

n.= noun
v.= verb
adj.= adjective
adv.= adverb
conj.= conjunction
prep.= preposition
ant.= antonym
hom.= homonym
▷ = cross-reference

rasp *v.* ① file, grate, scrape, grind ② irk, irritate, vex

rate ① *n.* pace, tempo, velocity, speed ② *n.* tax, charge, cost, price ③ *n.* ratio, proportion ④ *v.* appraise, assess, estimate, evaluate, regard, grade ⑤ *v.* deserve, merit

ration ① *n.* portion, share, allotment, helping ② *v.* allocate, allot, restrict, control

rational *adj.* sensible, sound, wise, intelligent, logical, reasonable, sane, calm *ant.* unreasonable

rattle *v.* ① jangle, clack, vibrate, clatter ② muddle, confuse, fluster, unnerve

ravage *v.* devastate, destroy, lay waste, desolate, wreck

rave *v.* ① rant, ramble *She rambled on for hours, but her stories helped the time pass.* babble, roar, rage, storm ② drool, gush, enthuse, swoon

ravenous *adj.* hungry, starving, famished, voracious, greedy

ravishing *adj.* beautiful, bewitching, delightful, enchanting ▷**gorgeous**

raw *adj.* ① uncooked, unrefined ② green, inexperienced, untrained ③ sensitive, painful, tender *The place where Gail grazed her arm is still a little tender.* irritated ④ cold, biting, harsh, chilly

ray *n.* beam, gleam, glimmer, stream, shaft

reach ① *v.* accomplish, gain, attain, grasp, arrive at ② *v.* stretch, extend ③ *n.* extent, grasp, distance, scope, range, expanse

react *v.* respond, retaliate, be affected

read *v.* ① peruse, pore over, study, browse, skim, examine ② understand, interpret, decode, decipher *hom.* reed

readily *adv.* easily, eagerly, freely, gladly, promptly

ready *adj.* ① prepared, alert, prompt, willing, disposed, primed *After hours of practising, I am primed to deliver my best speech ever.* ② available, convenient, handy

real *adj.* ① genuine, authentic, factual, true, valid *ant.* false ② substantial, existent, actual, tangible *The mirage was so convincing that the oasis semed tangible.* concrete *ant.* unreal *hom.* reel

Read   Reed

realistic *adj.* ① authentic, lifelike, natural ② practical *She really wanted to stay up late, but she knew it was more practical to get a good night's sleep.* down-to-earth, unromantic, pragmatic *ant.* romantic

realize *v.* ① understand, comprehend, discover, learn, grasp, conclude ② reach, attain, accomplish, fulfil

really *adv.* truly, indeed, actually, absolutely

realm *n.* area, domain, province, sphere *Tennis is outside the sphere of her interest.* region, territory, orbit, field, range

reap *v.* ① harvest, gather, glean ② obtain, realize, derive, gain

rear ① *n.* back, end, tail, behind, posterior, buttocks ② *adj.* back, hind ③ *v.* bring up, raise, breed, educate ④ *v.* loom, rise

reason ① *n.* purpose, motive, basis, cause, grounds, explanation ② *n.* wisdom, sense, logic, intellect ③ *v.* argue, conclude, deduce

reasonable *adj.* ① sensible, valid, rational *ant.* absurd ② moderate, fair, just, modest ③ inexpensive, low-priced *ant.* expensive

reassure *v.* comfort, hearten *The applause heartened the discouraged gymnast and she decided to try again.* convince ▷**encourage** *ant.* discourage

rebate *n.* refund, repayment, discount, allowance, deduction

rebel ① *v.* (re-*bel*) revolt, mutiny, disobey, resist ② *n.* (*reb*-el) revolutionary, mutineer

rebellious *adj.* defiant, disobedient, mutinous, resistant *ant.* obedient

rebuke *v.* reprimand, reproach, scold, correct, criticize, tell off *ant.* praise

recall *v.* ① recollect, remember ② cancel, retract, withdraw, countermand, call back

recede *v.* retreat, flow back, ebb, decline, shrink, subside *ant.* proceed

R
r
R
r
R
r
R

recent *adj.* new, fresh, modern, current, up-to-date, late *ant.* old

recently *adv.* lately, currently, not long ago

reception *n.* ① entertainment, function, party ② welcome, reaction, acceptance

recess *n.* ① intermission, interlude, break, pause ② alcove, socket, niche, slot, nook

recession *n.* slump, stagnation, depression, downturn *ant.* boom

recipe *n.* formula, directions, prescription

recite *v.* recount, quote, repeat, relate

reckless *adj.* careless, impetuous, irresponsible, unwary, incautious, daring, heedless, foolhardy ▷**rash** *ant.* cautious

reckon *v.* ① think, believe, surmise, guess, consider, suppose, judge, expect ② calculate, figure, count, tally *I tallied the final cost at $40 per person.*

reclaim *v.* retrieve, restore, redeem, rescue, recover, salvage

recline *v.* lounge, sprawl, lie, rest, loll, repose

recognize *v.* ① recall, recollect, remember ② identify, know, distinguish ③ admit, realize, acknowledge, accredit, reward, commend, hail

recoil *v.* ① rebound, ricochet, backfire, boomerang ② falter, flinch, shrink, quail *The kitten quailed when the large dog barked at him.*

recollect *v.* recall, recognize, place ▷**remember** *ant.* forget

recommend *v.* suggest, advise, propose, endorse, commend, approve *ant.* veto

reconcile *v.* ① reunite, make amends, come to terms, conciliate *ant.* quarrel ② resign, accept ③ settle, square, harmonize, balance, adjust

record ① *v.* (re-*cord*) write, note, register, enter, inscribe, list, log, chronicle ② *n.* (*rec*-ord) list, register, chronicle, archive *My mom searched the public archives to see when our ancestors came to Canada.* entry, account, file ③ *n.* (*rec*-ord) performance, past ④ *n.* (*rec*-ord) best (or worst) performance

recount *v.* ① (re-*count*) relate, tell, recite, describe ② (*re*-count) count again

recover *v.* ① reclaim, retrieve, repossess, retake, restore, redeem, regain, rescue ② get better, revive, improve, convalesce ▷**recuperate** *ant.* worsen

recreation *n.* sports, amusement, pastime

recruit ① *n.* trainee, beginner, apprentice ② *v.* enlist, enrol, draft, mobilize

rectify *v.* correct, repair, remedy, mend, put right, adjust, settle

recuperate *v.* get better, rally, improve, mend, convalesce *After a few weeks of convalescing at home, he'll be completely well again and will be coming back to school.* recover *ant.* worsen

recur *v.* return, reappear, come back, repeat itself, persist

redeem *v.* ① buy back, compensate for, cash in, exchange, recover ② save, liberate, free, rescue, reclaim

reduce *v.* lessen, diminish, curtail, decrease, lower, weaken, cut back, demote

reek *n.* smell, stink, fumes, stench, vapour

reel ① *v.* sway, rock, shake, stagger, falter, totter, lurch, spin ② *n.* spool, bobbin, spindle *hom.* real

refer *v.* send, pass, transfer, hand over, submit

refer to *v.* ① see, consult, check, look up ② apply to, relate to, stand for, denote, designate ③ mention, allude to, speak of

referee *n.* umpire, judge, arbitrator

reference *n.* ① allusion, mention, footnote, record ② regard, relation, respect ③ recommendation, credential, testimonial

refine *v.* clean, purify, filter, process, perfect, clarify, hone, develop, improve

refined *adj.* ① civilized, cultivated, cultured, elegant ▷**polite** *ant.* coarse ② fine, subtle, precise, delicate ③ purified, pure, clarified

reflect *v.* ① think, consider, muse, ponder, contemplate, deliberate ② mirror, copy, reproduce, echo, imitate, image ③ show, display, demonstrate

reform *v.* improve, correct, remodel, reorganize, revamp

refrain ① *v.* avoid, abstain, resist, restrain oneself, keep from ② *n.* chorus, melody, tune, slogan

refresh *v.* revive, invigorate, renew, restore, rejuvenate, energize, enliven *ant.* exhaust

refrigerate *v.* chill, cool, freeze

refuge *n.* haven, harbour, asylum, sanctuary, retreat, cover ▷**shelter**

refugee *n.* exile, fugitive, emigrant

refund *v.* repay, rebate, reimburse, pay back, return

refuse ① *v.* (re-*fuze*) decline, reject, deny, renounce, turn down *ant.* allow ② *n.* (*ref*-use) trash, garbage, rubbish, waste

refute *v.* deny, dispute, disprove, discredit, overturn *ant.* prove

regain *v.* recover, get back, retrieve, reclaim

regal *adj.* royal, majestic, noble, princely, stately, grand, impressive

regard ① *v.* admire, value, honour, respect, esteem, revere *ant.* dislike ② *v.* look at, watch, observe, gaze at ③ *n.* affection, esteem, fondness, repute, care, concern *ant.* contempt ④ *v.* view, consider, judge, think of

regardless *adv.* despite this, nevertheless, notwithstanding, anyhow, anyway, in any case

region *n.* area, district, zone, territory, locality, province, country

register ① *n.* list, roll, roster, record, archives ② *v.* enter, record, post, enrol, sign on ③ *v.* dawn on, sink in ④ *v.* show, indicate

regret ① *v.* repent of, lament, grieve, rue, deplore, mourn ② *v.* apologize, be sorry ③ *n.* remorse, sorrow, grief, disappointment, unhappiness ④ *n.* apology

regular *adj.* ① usual, ordinary, normal, customary, typical *ant.* unusual ② constant, orderly, steady, unchanging *ant.* variable ③ symmetrical *ant.* irregular

regulate *v.* ① control, manage, govern, restrict ② adjust, monitor, correct

regulation *n.* ① rule, law, ordinance, by-law ② order, control, management

rehearse *v.* practise, prepare, repeat, drill, recite, recount

reign ① *n.* rule, power, control, sway, regime, government ② *v.* govern, rule, dominate, hold sway *hom.* rain, rein

rein *v. & n.* bridle, hold, check *Check your applause until the performance is over.* harness, control *hom.* rain, reign

reinforce *v.* support, strengthen, toughen, bolster, back up, follow up *ant.* weaken

reject ① *v.* (re-*ject*) discard, get rid of, throw out, decline, refuse, repel, deny, expel, spurn ② *n.* (*re*-ject) castoff, scrap, discard

rejoice *v.* celebrate, revel, glory, exult, cheer, triumph, delight *ant.* lament, grieve

relapse ① *v.* lapse, regress, revert *He said a few words in Dutch and then reverted to English.* backslide, slip back ② *n.* setback, repetition, recurrence

relate *v.* ① describe, recount, tell, mention, detail ② identify, empathize ③ link, connect, associate

related *adj.* associated, affiliated, allied, akin, connected, linked, similar, *ant.* different

relative ① *n.* relation, kin, kinsman, kinswoman, sibling ② *adj.* comparative, approximate, variable

relax *v.* ① rest, pause, repose, unwind ② loosen, slacken *Don't slacken your pace near the end of the race.* weaken, ease up, reduce, diminish *ant.* tighten

relaxed *adj.* composed, cool, easygoing, loose, mellow, laid-back, informal ▷**casual** *ant.* tense

release *v.* let go, loose, liberate, acquit, discharge, rid ▷**free** *ant.* detain, capture

relent *v.* relax, soften, yield, ease up, give in, back down, take pity, subside

relentless *adj.* ① unmerciful, remorseless, grim, pitiless ▷**cruel** *ant.* gentle, lenient ② constant, persistent, continual, ceaseless

relevant *adj.* applicable, pertinent, to the point *ant.* irrelevant

reliable *adj.* dependable, trustworthy, responsible, honest, faithful, dutiful, steadfast ▷**sound** *ant.* unreliable

relief *n.* ① aid, assistance, support, help ② comfort, ease

relieve *v.* ① support, comfort, lighten, rest, ease, aid, reassure ② excuse, release

religious *adj.* pious, devout, holy, spiritual, devotional, inspirational, scrupulous

relinquish v. renounce, let go, waive *It's not my skipping rope anymore, so I waive all rights to it.* disclaim, give up, abdicate, yield ▷**abandon** *ant.* retain

relish ① v. enjoy, like, savour, delight in ▷**appreciate** *ant.* loathe ② n. flavour, savour, tang, gusto, zest, appetite

reluctant adj. hesitant, unwilling, disinclined, squeamish *ant.* willing

rely on v. depend on, count on, believe in

remain v. ① stay, linger, loiter, dwell, wait, rest *ant.* leave ② continue, persist, last, endure *ant.* die, perish

remainder n. remnant, residue, balance

remark ① v. state, mention, quip, comment, observe ▷**say** ② n. statement, observation, comment, quip, crack, slur ③ v. notice, perceive, note ▷**see**

remarkable adj. unusual, rare, surprising, prominent, exceptional ▷**extraordinary**

remedy ① n. cure, medicine, treatment ② n. relief, solution, corrective ③ v. relieve, correct, rectify

remember v. recollect, recognize, think back, retain ▷**recall** *ant.* forget

remind v. cue, prompt

remit v. ① relax, abate, slacken ② defer, postpone, put off ③ pardon, forgive ④ pay, square, settle up

remnant n. residue, remains, rest, scrap, leftover, balance, end ▷**remainder**

remorse n. regret, pity, contrition, sorrow

remote adj. ① distant, far, isolated, secluded *ant.* near ② slight, slim, negligible

remove v. take away, withdraw, drop, cut, eliminate, get rid of, carry off, extract, excise, move, clear away *ant.* retain

render v. ① give, present, surrender, deliver ② represent, interpret *Can you help me interpret the meaning of this confusing poem?* translate, play, execute, perform ③ make, cause to become

renew v. ① restore, renovate, recondition, modernize ② extend, continue, prolong

renounce v. disown, disclaim, give up, repudiate, forsake, abdicate, abandon *ant.* retain

renowned adj. eminent, noted, famed, notable, celebrated ▷**famous** *ant.* obscure

rent v. lease, let, charter

repair ① v. fix, patch, mend, restore, renew, improve, correct, remedy, rectify *If you change this 't' to an 'l', you'll rectify your spelling mistake.* ② n. restoration, adjustment, maintenance

repay v. ① refund, reimburse, pay, compensate, reward ② avenge, take revenge on, punish, retaliate against

repeal v. revoke, abolish, reverse, lift, annul, cancel *ant.* establish

repeat v. duplicate, renew, echo, rehearse, practise, reiterate *If I reiterate it yet again, I'll have said it five times!*

repel v. ① repulse, reject, push back, ward off, resist, parry ② disgust, revolt, nauseate *ant.* attract

repellent adj. distasteful, hateful, offensive ▷**repulsive** *ant.* attractive

replace v. ① substitute for, fill in for, succeed, supersede ② restore, reinstate, put back

replenish v. fill, refill, restock, top up *ant.* empty, exhaust

replica n. copy, likeness, duplicate, facsimile, reconstruction

reply ① v. answer, respond, retort, rejoin, acknowledge ② n. answer, response, acknowledgment, reaction, retort

report ① n. document, story, statement, account, message, communication ② n. noise, explosion, bang ③ v. tell, reveal, expose, describe, communicate, disclose

repose ① v. rest, lie, sleep, recline ② n. peace, quiet, tranquillity, rest, sleep

represent v. ① illustrate, show, set forth, depict, picture, portray ② denote, signify, symbolize, mean, embody ③ speak for

representative ① n. agent, delegate, envoy, deputy ② adj. typical ③ adj. symbolic, descriptive

repress v. suppress, stifle, smother, muffle, restrain, bottle up, squelch, strangle

reprimand ① v. criticize, blame, rebuke, chide ② n. reproach, scolding, disapproval, criticism, rebuke *ant.* praise

reproach *v.* scold, reprove, reprimand, blame, criticize, rebuke *ant.* compliment

reproduce *v.* ① copy, duplicate, imitate, simulate, repeat ② breed, multiply

reprove *v.* reproach, reprimand, criticize ▷**rebuke** *ant.* praise

repudiate *v.* renounce, disown, disavow, disclaim, deny, reject *ant.* acknowledge

repugnant *adj.* offensive, unattractive, disagreeable ▷**repulsive** *ant.* pleasant

repulse *v.* ① repel, rebuff, drive back, reject ▷**spurn** ② offend, disgust *ant.* attract

repulsive *adj.* obnoxious, disgusting, offensive ▷**repugnant** *ant.* attractive

reputation *n.* standing, position, honour, fame, character, name

request ① *v.* demand, beg, solicit, appeal ② *n.* demand, appeal, petition, entreaty, invitation

require *v.* ① need, want, crave ② demand, insist, command

required *adj.* ① supposed, expected, obliged ② obligatory, compulsory, mandatory

rescue ① *v.* save, free, set free, release, liberate *ant.* capture ② *v.* recover, restore, salvage ③ *n.* liberation, deliverance, salvation *The Canadian Coast Guard was the salvation of the shipwrecked crew.*

research *v.* examine, explore, investigate, inquire into, read up on, study

resemble *v.* look like, mirror, take after, be like *ant.* differ

resent *v.* begrudge, dislike, take exception to *ant.* like

resentful *adj.* offended, bitter, huffy, angry, spiteful, piqued ▷**jealous** *ant.* content

Rescue

reserve ① *v.* hoard, retain, withhold ▷**keep** ② *v.* book, hold, speak for, set aside ③ *n.* modesty, shyness, restraint, control ④ *n.* supply, backlog, stock, hoard

reservoir *n.* tank, pool, container

reside *v.* live, occupy, inhabit, stay, dwell

residence *n.* home, habitation, dwelling

resign *v.* retire, abdicate, step down, give notice, abandon, relinquish ▷**quit**
  resign oneself *v.* accept, be reconciled, yield, give in, submit *ant.* resist

resist *v.* ① oppose, defy, fight, confront, withstand, challenge, hold off *ant.* submit ② refrain from, keep from ▷**thwart**

resistance *n.* opposition, defiance, defence, obstruction, hindrance *ant.* welcome

resolute *adj.* determined, resolved, obstinate, stubborn, set, unwavering, firm, faithful, decisive, dogged *Instead of quitting when the going got tough, the dogged climbers kept on climbing.* *ant.* weak, cowardly

resolve ① *v.* determine, settle, decide ② *v.* clear up, unravel, explain, disentangle ③ *n.* resolution, purpose, will, decision

resort *n.* ① alternative, chance, course, recourse ② spa, hotel, holiday centre

resourceful *adj.* clever, ingenious, inventive, quick-witted

respect ① *n.* esteem, honour, regard, repute, dignity, admiration ② *v.* esteem, honour, revere, admire, appreciate, venerate

respectable *adj.* decent, admirable, honest, honourable, acceptable *ant.* disreputable

respectful *adj.* courteous, polite, dutiful, deferential *ant.* rude

respond *v.* answer, reply, retort, react *ant.* question

responsible *adj.* ① accountable, liable, guilty, at fault ② capable, dependable, sensible ▷**reliable** *ant.* unreliable

rest ① *n.* break, pause, interval, spell ② *n.* repose, relaxation, leisure, relief, sleep, nap, peace, tranquillity ③ *n.* remainder, balance, residue ④ *v.* repose, settle, sleep, relax, laze, nap *hom.* wrest

R
r
R
r
R
r
R

restful adj. peaceful, quiet, calm, tranquil *A week in the tranquil atmosphere of Lake Vernon refreshed our family.* relaxing, soothing ant. hectic

restless adj. uneasy, edgy, unsettled, agitated, nervous, fretful ant. calm

restore v. ① replace, reinstate, return ② refurbish, recondition *This chesterfield looks like new, but it's the one we bought second-hand and reconditioned.* rebuild, renovate

restrain v. rein in, prevent, hold back, curb, inhibit, subdue, control, check ant. excite

restrict v. confine, limit, cramp, handicap ▷**regulate** ant. free

result ① n. effect, consequence, outcome, end, answer ant. cause ② v. follow, ensue, turn out, issue

result in v. produce, lead to, trigger

resume v. renew, recommence, recover, start again, continue ant. interrupt

retain v. ① hold, withhold, detain ▷**keep** ant. relinquish ② employ, hire

retaliate v. avenge, reciprocate, fight back, repay, retort ant. forgive

retire v. ① retreat, go back, adjourn ▷**withdraw** ant. advance ② resign, relinquish, abdicate

retort ① n. reply, answer, riposte, rejoinder ② v. answer, reply, return

retract v. deny, take back, disavow, revoke, repudiate, recant ant. maintain

retreat ① v. back up, escape, flee, recede, retire, shrink ▷**withdraw** ant. advance ② n. sanctuary, shelter, den, haven ③ n. withdrawal, evacuation

retrieve v. recover, regain, rescue, redeem ▷**salvage** ant. lose

return ① v. rejoin, recur, reappear, retreat ② v. restore, replace ③ v. repay, refund ④ n. recurrence, reappearance

reveal v. show, expose, display, uncover, disclose, divulge, unveil ant. hide

revel ① v. celebrate, frolic, luxuriate *Luxuriate in the warmth now, because tomorrow it's going to be freezing.* ② n. celebration, gala, party, spree

revenge n. vengeance, reprisal, retaliation

revenue n. income, receipts, earnings

revere v. honour, esteem, regard, adore, venerate, respect ant. despise

reverse ① v. cancel, overrule, repeal, revoke, rescind ② v. exchange, switch, invert ③ adj. opposite, backward, contrary

review ① v. examine, survey, study, analyse, reconsider ② n. inspection, examination ③ n. critique, commentary hom. revue

revise v. edit, amend, improve, rewrite, alter

revive v. awaken, recover, refresh, restore, invigorate, renew, resurrect, rally

revoke v. abolish, cancel, annul, reverse, withdraw, lift, repeal

revolt ① v. rebel, mutiny, riot ② v. nauseate, sicken, disgust, offend ③ n. rebellion, uprising, revolution

revolting adj. obnoxious, repulsive, disgusting, ▷**repugnant** ant. pleasant

revolve v. rotate, spin, turn, gyrate

reward ① n. award, prize, payment, benefit, bonus, profit ant. penalty ② v. compensate, pay, remunerate ant. punish

rhyme n. verse, poem, ditty, limerick

rhythm n. beat, pulse, throb, tempo, time, stroke, cycle

rich adj. ① wealthy, prosperous, affluent, opulent *We admired the opulent interior of Casa Loma.* ant. poor ② fertile, fruitful, productive ant. barren ③ lavish, profuse, extravagant, abundant ④ delicious, sweet, luscious ⑤ mellow, full, vivid, deep

riddle ① n. puzzle, mystery, problem, enigma ② v. puncture, pierce, perforate

ride ① v. travel, drive, journey ② n. journey, trip, drive, excursion, spin, lift

ridge n. ① bump, strip ② highland, chain, range *A range of hills could be seen in the distance.* rise, esker, moraine, hogback

ridicule ① n. scorn, derision, sarcasm, mockery ② v. mock, tease, taunt, insult, sneer, jeer, deride, scoff

ridiculous adj. laughable, absurd, foolish, nonsensical *The fable may seem nonsensical, but it actually has a deep meaning.* preposterous ▷**silly** ant. sensible

n. = noun
v. = verb
adj. = adjective
adv. = adverb
conj. = conjunction
prep. = preposition
ant. = antonym
hom. = homonym
▷ = cross-reference

Rivers and Waterways

Brook
Canal
Channel
Creek
Lake
Pool
Pond
Mere
River
Slough
Spring
Strait
Stream
Waterfall

rifle ① *v.* loot, rob, plunder, ransack, strip ② *n.* gun, musket, firearm

rift *n.* ① crack, split, cleft, fissure, breach ② disagreement, clash, break, tension

right ① *adj.* correct, proper, true, accurate, precise, exact *ant.* wrong ② *adj.* honest, fair, just ③ *adj.* suitable, appropriate *ant.* improper ④ *n.* honesty, truth, justice ⑤ *n.* privilege, claim *hom.* rite, write

Confusable Words

right means *correct*

write means *put on paper*

righteous *adj.* honourable, upright, ethical

rigid *adj.* ① stiff, firm, inflexible ② strict, stern, narrow, intolerant *ant.* flexible

rigorous *adj.* stern, severe, strict, accurate

rim *n.* border, margin, edge, side, fringe, verge, brink

ring ① *n.* circle, band, hoop, loop ② *n.* gang, band, clan ③ *n.* chime, tinkle ④ *v.* chime, sound, toll, peal, jingle, strike *hom.* wring

riot ① *n.* uproar, clash, brawl, struggle, tumult *ant.* calm ② *v.* revolt, rebel, brawl, rampage

ripe *adj.* mature, developed, aged, seasoned, adult, mellow, ready *ant.* raw, immature

rise ① *v.* stand, mount, bob up, ascend *ant.* fall ② *v.* grow, increase, escalate, soar *ant.* decrease ③ *v.* wake, arise, get up *ant.* sleep ④ *n.* ascent, advance, increase *ant.* decrease

risk ① *v.* chance, dare, hazard, gamble, wager, venture ② *n.* adventure, peril, danger, gamble, jeopardy *ant.* safety

risky *adj.* dangerous, chancy, perilous, tricky, uncertain *ant.* safe

rite *n.* ceremony, custom, ritual, practice *hom.* right

rival ① *adj.* opposing, competing, vying, conflicting ② *n.* opponent, adversary, competitor, foe *ant.* partner

river *n.* stream, waterway, brook, torrent *Before the rains came, this torrent was only a trickle.*

road *n.* street, avenue, drive, lane, alley, highway, route, way *hom.* rode, rowed

roam *v.* wander, rove, stroll, ramble, range

roar *v.* bellow, shout, bawl, yell, blare, cry

rob *v.* loot, plunder, thieve, fleece, deprive, pilfer, cheat, defraud

robber *n.* bandit, thief, crook, brigand

robust *adj.* strong, healthy, sturdy, muscular, flourishing ▷**vigorous** *ant.* delicate, fragile

rock ① *n.* stone, boulder, pebble, crag, reef ② *v.* sway, swing, wobble, totter, reel, shake, toss ③ *v.* soothe, quiet, still, lull

rod *n.* baton, stick, pole, staff, cane, stave

role *n.* ① character, part, position ② task, duty, function *My function at the restaurant is to clear the tables. hom.* roll

roll ① *n.* record, register, list ② *n.* spool, scroll, reel ③ *n.* bun, kaiser, loaf ④ *n.* spin, somersault, flip ⑤ *v.* revolve, rotate, turn ⑥ *v.* lurch, reel, pitch, ⑦ *v.* smooth, level, press ⑧ *v.* wrap, bind *hom.* role

romance *n.* ① love story, novel, love affair ② adventure, excitement, fantasy, glamour

romantic *adj.* ① amorous, starry-eyed, passionate, tender ② sentimental, sensitive ③ fictional, imaginative, glamorous, fanciful *Your plans need to be a little more down-to-earth and a little less fanciful.* unrealistic *ant.* realistic

R r R r R r R

romp *v.* play, leap, skip, frolic, caper

roof *n.* ceiling, covering, cover, canopy, shelter

room *n.* ① apartment, chamber, suite, cell, hall, salon ② scope, space, capacity

root *n.* ① rootlet, tuber, radicle ② origin, source, cause, reason, heart, seed, centre, basis, element *hom.* route

rope *n.* cable, cord, line, lasso

rosy *adj.* ① cheerful, encouraging, hopeful, optimistic ② pink, ruddy, red, flushed, bloodshot

rot *v.* crumble, decay, moulder, decompose, deteriorate, perish

rotate *v.* revolve, turn, spin, pivot, gyrate

rotten *adj.* ① decayed, decomposed, rancid, foul, stinking, putrid, rank ② dishonest, corrupt, bad, deplorable, despicable, nasty, vicious

rough *adj.* ① craggy, coarse, shaggy, broken, uneven, wrinkled, bumpy ② rude, impolite, discourteous, crude, harsh, gruff, brusque ③ stormy, turbulent *hom.* ruff

round ① *adj.* curved, circular, spherical, globular, cylindrical ② *adj.* plump, rotund ③ *n.* circuit, beat, hand, routine, sequence, run

rouse *v.* ① wake, arouse, excite, disturb ② provoke, anger, stir up, incite *ant.* calm

route *n.* road, course, path, track, way, direction *hom.* root

routine *n.* habit, practice *After being a page in the House of Commons for two months, Jake was familiar with all the parliamentary practices.* round, grind, method, formula

rove *v.* roam, wander, stroll, drift, stray, ramble, range, tramp

row ① *n.* (*ro*) string, line, queue, rank, column ② *v.* paddle, scull *hom.* roe ③ *n.* (rhymes with *now*) fight, squabble, quarrel, dispute, brawl *ant.* harmony

rowdy *adj.* unruly, boisterous, rambunctious, riotous, disorderly *ant.* quiet

royal *adj.* sovereign, princely, stately, majestic, noble, regal

rub *v.* stroke, brush, scrub, wipe, polish

rubbish *n.* garbage, trash, waste, refuse, debris, junk

rude *adj.* impolite, bad-mannered, insolent, curt, vulgar, crude, gruff, coarse, boorish *ant.* polite

ruffle *v.* ① crumple, rumple, crease ② fluster, worry, excite, agitate, annoy, upset

rugged *adj.* ① hardy, robust, strong, hearty, sturdy, tough ② rough, craggy, harsh, stormy

ruin *v.* ① demolish, wreck, damage, smash, spoil, destroy, deface ② bankrupt, impoverish, overwhelm

rule ① *v.* control, govern, command, manage, direct, dominate ② *v.* decide, determine, judge ③ *n.* law, regulation, statute, decree

ruler *n.* lord, sovereign, king, queen, monarch, governor, chief, head, prime minister, premier

rumble *v.* roar, thunder, boom, roll, crash

rumour *n.* hearsay, report, gossip, scandal

run ① *v.* sprint, jog, race, rush, dash, dart, speed, hurry ② *v.* leak, flow, ooze ③ *v.* operate, drive, work, manage, function ④ *v.* escape, flee, abscond, bolt *He left us angry and hungry when he bolted with our snack money!* *ant.* stay ⑤ *n.* race, sprint, dash, rush

rural *adj.* country, rustic, pastoral

rush *v. & n.* dash, scramble, stampede, rampage, scurry, gush *ant.* lag

rust *v.* corrode, eat away, stain, deteriorate, oxidize

rustic *adj.* rural, pastoral, country, homey, simple, natural

rustle *n. & v.* crackle, crinkle, swish, murmur, whisper

rut *n.* ① groove, furrow, track, channel, score ② routine, habit

ruthless *adj.* cruel, savage, harsh, ferocious, pitiless, unscrupulous *ant.* merciful

n. = noun
v. = verb
adj. = adjective
adv. = adverb
conj. = conjunction
prep. = preposition
ant. = antonym
hom. = homonym
▷ = cross-reference

S s

sack ① *n.* bag, pouch, pack ② *v.* rob, plunder, pillage, loot, ravage *hom.* sac

sacred *adj.* holy, blessed, hallowed, spiritual, consecrated, revered, protected

sacrifice ① *n.* victim, offering ② *n.* cost, loss, expense, self-denial ③ *v.* give up, forfeit, relinquish, forego, lay down, offer up

sad *adj.* ① sorrowful, melancholy, unhappy, mournful, woeful, gloomy, upset, blue ▷**sorry** *ant.* happy ② poor, wretched, miserable *ant.* splendid

sadden *v.* grieve, distress, dismay, dishearten, depress *ant.* cheer

safe ① *adj.* protected, guarded, sheltered, secure *ant.* dangerous ② *adj.* reliable, sure *ant.* risky ③ *n.* vault, coffer, strongbox

safety *n.* shelter, security, sanctuary, protection, refuge *ant.* danger

sag *v.* bend, curve, bow, decline, flag, slump, slouch, wilt ▷**droop**

sage ① *adj.* wise, sensible, shrewd, sagacious *ant.* foolish ② *n.* pundit, scholar, savant, philosopher *ant.* fool

sail *v.* cruise, voyage, navigate, float, skim, glide, coast, pilot, steer *hom.* sale

sailor *n.* seaman, seafarer, mariner, navigator, seadog, yachtsman, yachtswoman

salary *n.* pay, earnings, wages, income, fee, emolument

sale *n.* auction, transaction *Lots of people showed interest in her crafts, but Gerda did not complete a single transaction.* selling, trade, disposal *hom.* sail

salute ① *v.* greet, welcome, hail, honour ② *n.* greeting, welcome, acknowledgment, tribute

salvage *v.* save, conserve, rescue, restore, reclaim ▷**recover** *ant.* abandon

same *adj.* identical, duplicate, alike, similar, equal, consistent *Rob's bedtime routine is consistent every night.*

sample ① *n.* specimen, example, model, pattern, taste, swatch ② *v.* inspect, try, taste, experience, test

sanction *v.* permit, allow, authorize, approve

sanctuary *n.* retreat, shelter, shrine, asylum, haven, cover, preserve, refuge

sane *adj.* rational, reasonable, lucid, coherent, logical, well-balanced ▷**sensible** *ant.* insane

sap *v.* bleed, drain, exhaust, reduce, weaken, deplete, diminish *ant.* refresh

sarcastic *adj.* biting, cutting, sardonic, cynical, acerbic, ironic, cutting, jeering, mocking, scornful, caustic

satire *n.* caricature, sarcasm, burlesque, ridicule, parody, lampoon, humour

satisfaction *n.* ① contentment, delight, gratification ② compensation

satisfy *v.* gratify *Visiting the cockpit helped gratify her desire to learn more about airplanes.* fulfil, appease, suit, please, convince, meet *ant.* disappoint

saturate *v.* soak, steep, drench, souse, wet, water-log *The old raft was so water-logged that it wouldn't float.* permeate

savage ① *adj.* barbaric, wild, uncivilized, ferocious, brutal, violent, fierce, cold-blooded *ant.* tame ② *n.* brute, barbarian

save *v.* ① liberate, set free, rescue, protect, deliver, salvage, guard ② keep, reserve, collect, hoard, put aside *ant.* spend

savoury *adj.* appetizing, flavourful, luscious, mouth-watering, delicious *ant.* tasteless

Sacred Books

Apocrypha
Bhagavad-Gita
Bible
Book of Mormon
Granth
Koran
Talmud
Torah
Tripitaka
Upanishad
Veda

say *v.* speak, utter, state, pronounce, convey, tell, assert, declare, remark, comment, communicate, announce, indicate

saying *n.* proverb, statement, adage, idiom, maxim, aphorism, epigram, slogan, axiom

scale ① *n.* measure, balance, spectrum, ratio ② *n.* crust, plate, flake ③ *n.* clef, key, mode ④ *v.* climb, ascend, clamber up

scamper *v.* hurry, run, scurry, hasten, dart, scoot, flit, skip

scan *v.* examine, gaze at, scrutinize, pore over, browse, peruse, survey ▷**check**

scandal *n.* disgrace, outrage, offence, infamy, rumour, discredit *ant.* honour

scanty *adj.* meagre, insufficient, sparse, inadequate, poor, sparing, skimpy, measly *ant.* abundant

scar ① *n.* blemish, mark, stigma, wound ② *v.* brand, damage, disfigure

scarce *adj.* rare, infrequent, short, tight, scanty, uncommon, in demand, insufficient, lacking, occasional *ant.* common

scarcity *n.* shortage, lack, insufficiency, dearth, rarity, infrequency *ant.* plenty

scare *v.* frighten, startle, shock, alarm, terrify, dismay *ant.* reassure

scatter *v.* spread, sprinkle, disperse, strew, broadcast, sow, dispel *Your optimistic words have dispelled my doubts.* disband, separate, flee ▷**shower** *ant.* gather

scene *n.* sight, spectacle, vision, panorama, landscape, setting, locale *hom.* seen

scent ① *n.* aroma, tang, fragrance, odour, perfume, essence ▷**smell** ② *v.* detect, sniff *hom.* cent, sent

sceptical *adj.* unbelieving, incredulous *We were incredulous when we heard her story, but she convinced us it was true.* doubtful, cynical ▷**dubious** *ant.* naïve

schedule *n.* timetable, program, catalogue

scheme *n.* plot, plan, project, design, proposal, idea

scholar *n.* ① pupil, student, schoolchild, learner ② intellectual *Dr. John Polanyi is a Canadian intellectual who won the 1986 Nobel Prize for Chemistry.* savant, academic, sage, philosopher

scholarly *adj.* learned, educated, literate, intellectual, studious *ant.* illiterate

scoff *v.* sneer, mock, deride, jeer, ridicule

scold *v.* rebuke, reprove, criticize, find fault, reprimand, admonish, blame, chide ▷**nag** *ant.* praise

scoop ① *v.* bail, ladle, spoon, excavate, dig, gouge, hollow ② *n.* information, details, inside story, latest

scope *n.* extent, breadth, compass, range, latitude, field, opportunity

scorch *v.* sear, burn, singe, blister, shrivel

score *v.* ① cut, mark, scratch, slash ② register, record, win, grade, mark, earn

scorn ① *n.* mockery, disdain, ridicule, disregard, contempt, disrespect ② *v.* despise, mock, spurn, slight

scoundrel *n.* rascal, thief, rogue, vagabond ▷**villain**

scour *v.* ① cleanse, scrub, purge, scrape ② search, ransack, rake, comb

scourge ① *v.* beat, whip, thrash ② *n.* curse, evil, misfortune, plague *ant.* blessing

scowl *v.* & *n.* frown, glower, grimace, glare *ant.* smile

scramble ① *v.* clamber, climb ② *v.* jostle, struggle, push, hurry, rush, compete ③ *v.* mix up, confuse, jumble ④ *n.* turmoil, bustle, confusion, disorder *ant.* order

scrap ① *n.* piece, morsel, bit, portion, fragment, grain, particle, crumb ② *v.* abandon, discard, junk, demolish *ant.* preserve

scrape ① *v.* scratch, graze, file, grate, scour, scrub, scratch ② *n.* predicament, fix, difficulty, trouble

scratch *v.* & *n.* wound, cut, mark, score, nick, scrape

scream *v.* & *n.* screech, cry, shriek, howl

screen ① *n.* partition, divider, blind, filter, guard, canopy, shade, protection ② *v.* protect, hide, conceal, veil, shade, censor, filter, sift, test, examine

scribble *v.* write, scrawl, scratch, doodle, jot

script *n.* handwriting, manuscript, text, words, libretto, screenplay

scrub *v.* scour, brush, mop, cleanse

n. = noun
v. = verb
adj. = adjective
adv. = adverb
conj. = conjunction
prep. = preposition
ant. = antonym
hom. = homonym
▷ = cross-reference

scruffy *adj.* messy, dirty, sloppy, unkempt, untidy, slovenly ▷**shabby** *ant.* neat

scrumptious *adj.* mouth-watering, delicious, appetizing, exquisite

scrupulous *adj.* particular, painstaking *Her painstaking record did not miss one detail.* rigorous, conscientious, careful *ant.* careless

scrutinize *v.* examine, inspect, peruse, study

scuffle *v. & n.* tussle, skirmish, fight, struggle, squabble, wrestle

scum *n.* foam, froth, skin, film, crust

scuttle *v.* ① scramble, scamper, scoot, hurry ② destroy, smash, wreck

seal ① *n.* signet, stamp ② *n.* cork, closure ③ *v.* stick, close, stop, secure *ant.* open ④ *v.* fix, settle

seam *n.* ① ridge, scar, lode, furrow, joint ② stitching, tuck *hom.* seem

search ① *v.* seek, quest, hunt, scour, explore, examine, investigate, probe ② *n.* probe, exploration, investigation, quest, pursuit, hunt, chase

season ① *n.* period, time, stage, phase, term ② *v.* accustom, acclimatize *Benjamin, who immigrated from Israel, is now an acclimatized Canadian.* mature ③ *v.* flavour, spice, salt, temper, moderate

seat ① *n.* bench, chair, stool, sofa, couch, throne, bottom, base, centre ② *n.* site, headquarters, ③ *v.* accommodate, locate, place, set, establish, base

secret *adj.* mysterious, hidden, concealed, obscure, private, personal, confidential

section *n.* division, group, department, slice, segment, portion, part, piece, fraction

secure ① *adj.* safe, protected, guarded ② *adj.* confident, certain, sure, stable, tight, sound ③ *v.* fasten, protect, close, lock, attach, tie *ant.* unfasten ④ *v.* get, take, acquire, procure, obtain *ant.* lose

sedate *adj.* staid, sober, demure, earnest, dignified, grave ▷**calm** *ant.* wild

see *v.* ① glimpse, witness, sight, observe, spy, notice, examine, watch, note ② understand, comprehend, know, appreciate, experience ③ regard, view, consider *hom.* sea

seedy *adj.* shabby, squalid, poor, grubby, unkempt, slovenly ▷**scruffy** *ant.* smart

seek *v.* ① look, search, inquire, hunt, investigate, pursue, follow, trail, track ② endeavour, strive, attempt, try

seethe *v.* simmer, fizz, bubble, boil, foam

seize *v.* snatch, clutch, arrest, catch, grab, confiscate ▷**grasp** *ant.* abandon

seldom *adv.* rarely, infrequently, hardly, scarcely *ant.* often

select ① *adj.* choice, preferred, fine, prime, exclusive, favourite, best *ant.* common ② *v.* choose, opt for, pick out, single out, prefer

selfish *adj.* greedy, self-centred, narrow, cheap, miserly, thoughtless, careless, inconsiderate, egotistical ▷**stingy** *ant.* generous

sell *v.* vend, market, retail, trade, peddle, barter, hawk *ant.* buy

send *v.* transmit, dispatch, forward, mail, direct, ship, convey *ant.* keep

sensation *n.* ① feeling, perception, impression, awareness, sensitivity ② stir, excitement, commotion, scandal, uproar

sensational *adj.* exceptional, scandalous, lurid, marvellous, exciting ▷**dramatic** *ant.* ordinary

sense ① *n.* sensation, impression, feeling ② *n.* understanding, intuition, prudence, discretion, logic, point, wisdom, judgment, meaning ③ *v.* feel, detect, notice, suspect

senseless *adj.* silly, meaningless, pointless, absurd, unwise, mindless, unconscious ▷**foolish** *ant.* sensible

sensible *adj.* ① wise, intelligent, astute, shrewd, sage ② reasonable, rational, sound ③ conscious, aware, mindful *ant.* senseless

sensitive *adj.* ① susceptible, vulnerable, responsive, acute, impressionable *Anne is an impressionable child; she feels things deeply and never forgets them.* ② touchy, thin-skinned, irritable, tender, moody, temperamental, testy, emotional

sentence *n.* ① phrase, clause ② judgment, decision, condemnation, punishment

sentimental *adj.* romantic, tender, emotional

S

separate ① *adj.* disconnected, apart, detached, isolated, distinct *ant.* united ② *v.* detach, part, divide, break, disconnect, sever, free *ant.* unite

sequel *n.* continuation, consequence, result, outcome

serene *adj.* tranquil, calm, peaceful, undisturbed, clear *ant.* violent

series *n.* sequence, progression, succession, run, string, chain, cycle, course

serious *adj.* grave, earnest, solemn, thoughtful, severe, grim, critical, staid, sober, intent *ant.* frivolous

serve *v.* attend, assist, aid, oblige, help, officiate, act, satisfy, wait on

service *n.* ① aid, help, assistance, attendance, employment, favour, duty ② ceremony, rite

set ① *n.* group, pack, outfit, series, collection, bunch ② *n.* setting, scene ③ *v.* settle, deposit, place, seat, locate, lay, position ④ *v.* stiffen, congeal, harden ⑤ *v.* adjust, regulate, establish ⑥ *adj.* decided, resolved, determined, fixed, firm, unchanging

setback *n.* defeat, delay, problem, snag, reverse, holdup *ant.* progress

settle *v.* ① establish, determine, arrange, fix ② pay, clear ③ populate, colonize, inhabit ④ ensconce, install ⑤ calm, quiet, pacify

several *adj.* various, numerous, sundry
I guessed the answer to the riddle from the sundry hints of my classmates.
separate, assorted, some, many *ant.* few

severe *adj.* strict, rigid, unkind, hard, bleak, austere, unyielding ▷**stern** *ant.* lenient

sew *v.* stitch, tack, baste, fasten, mend, darn *hom.* sow

shabby *adj.* torn, ragged, mean, shoddy, worn, threadbare, mangy, scruffy, tacky, squalid ▷**scruffy** *ant.* neat

shack *n.* hut, cabin, shanty, shed, hovel

shackle *v. & n.* manacle, handcuff, chain, rope, fetter, bind, bond

shade *n.* ① shadow, gloom, darkness, dusk ② blind, awning, screen ③ colour, tint, hue, tone ④ trace, hint, tinge, whisper

shadow ① *n.* shade, silhouette, image, suggestion, trace ② *v.* follow, stalk, tail

shady *adj.* ① shadowy, shaded, sheltered, dark *ant.* sunny ② crooked, disreputable, suspicious, doubtful *ant.* honest

shaft *n.* ① beam, ray, arrow ② hilt, rod, handle, shank ③ mine, pit, well, tunnel

shaggy *adj.* hairy, unkempt, rough, dishevelled

shake *v.* ① tremble, throb, shudder, quake, quiver, jolt, jar, vibrate, rock, shiver ② agitate, unsettle, shock, upset

shallow *adj.* ① not deep ② trivial, empty, silly, superficial *ant.* profound

sham *adj.* false, imitation, counterfeit, forged, fake, artificial ▷**bogus** *ant.* genuine

Ships and Boats

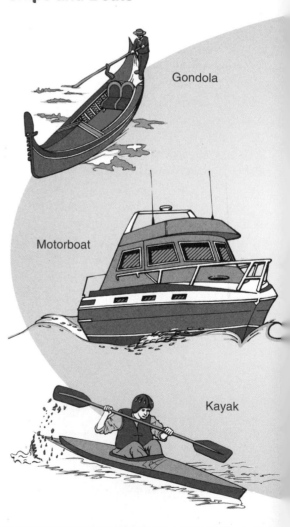

Gondola

Motorboat

Kayak

shame *n. & v.* dishonour, discredit
▷**disgrace, humiliate**

shameful *adj.* disgraceful, scandalous,
outrageous, deplorable, degrading
ant. honourable

shape ① *n.* form, structure, outline, pattern,
design, figure, silhouette ② *v.* form,
fashion, mould, create, sculpt

share ① *v.* allot, divide, co-operate,
participate, distribute ② *n.* part, allotment,
serving, quota, helping, portion, allowance

sharp *adj.* ① acute, keen, pointed, piercing,
honed ② clear, distinct, clean-cut,
unmistakable ③ painful, severe, intense,
agonizing, gnawing ④ pungent, acrid, acid
⑤ alert, shrewd, astute ▷**clever**

shatter *v.* destroy, wreck, fracture, ruin
▷**smash**

shave *v.* shear, crop, slice, shred, graze,
trim, scrape

shear *v.* fleece, strip, deprive, shave
hom. sheer

shed ① *n.* hut, barn, lean-to, shanty
② *v.* cast off, slough off *Slough off your
bad spirits and cheer up.* moult, slip
③ *v.*cast, radiate, emit, throw

sheer *adj.* ① absolute, simple, pure, utter,
unmixed ② transparent, filmy, thin, gauzy
③ steep, abrupt, perpendicular *The
perpendicular cliff rose straight up in
front of her like a wall.* *hom.* shear

shell *n.* pod, case, husk, hull, shuck, crust

Ferry

Catamaran

Canoe

Liner

S

shelter ① *n.* roof, sanctuary, safety, home, retreat, cover, haven, asylum ② *v.* shield, cover, protect, screen, hide, defend, harbour *ant.* expose

shield *n. & v.* guard, screen, safeguard ▷**shelter**

shift ① *v.* alter, move, change, displace, turn, remove, disturb ② *n.* turn, spell, stint

shifty *adj.* untrustworthy, devious, treacherous, dishonest, underhanded ▷**wily** *ant.* honest

shine *v. & n.* glow, gleam, glitter, sparkle, flash, polish, shimmer

ship ① *n.* boat, barge, craft, vessel ② *v.* export, send, transport

shirk *v.* dodge, avoid, shun, evade, slack off

shiver *v.* quaver, quiver, shake, shudder ▷**tremble**

shock ① *n.* blow, jolt, impact ② *n.* scare, start, fright ③ *v.* stupefy, daze, stun, electrify ④ *v.* astonish, surprise, appal, offend, outrage

shocking *adj.* scandalous, awful, frightful, terrible, outrageous ▷**horrible** *ant.* agreeable

shoot ① *v.* fire, discharge, bombard, propel ② *n.* bud, sprout, runner, sprig *hom.* chute

shop ① *n.* store, boutique, business, stall ② *v.* buy, stock up, browse, hunt

shore *n.* beach, coast, strand, waterfront, seaside

short *adj.* ① brief, concise, condensed *ant.* long ② insufficient, scanty, deficient, incomplete ③ rude, terse, abrupt, curt, bad-tempered ④ little, small, puny, squat, diminutive, tiny *ant.* tall

shortcoming *n.* defect, fault, flaw, inadequacy, disadvantage ▷**weakness**

shorten *v.* cut, crop, abbreviate, lessen, condense, summarize, reduce *ant.* lengthen

shortly *adj.* presently, soon, before long, directly

shout *n. & v.* cry, scream, roar, shriek, cheer, whoop, bellow, yell, call, bawl

shove *v.* push, jostle, prod, elbow, move, propel, poke, ram *ant.* pull

show ① *v.* display, parade, exhibit, flaunt, reveal, present, uncover, expose *ant.* hide ② *v.* prove, testify, indicate ③ *v.* explain, teach, instruct, demonstrate ④ *n.* exhibition, display, exposition, play, entertainment, performance, spectacle

shower ① *v.* scatter, spray, sprinkle, rain, lavish ② *n.* sprinkling, cloudburst, rain ③ *n.* barrage, volley, discharge

shred ① *n.* bit, particle, piece, scrap, fragment ② *v.* tear, rip, strip

shrewd *adj.* profound, deep, discerning, astute, sharp, knowing, canny ▷**wise** *ant.* obtuse

shriek *n. & v.* screech, scream, cry, hoot, squeal ▷**shout**

shrill *adj.* treble, high-pitched, screeching, piercing

shrink *v.* ① contract, dwindle, shrivel, wither, decrease, reduce, shorten, diminish ② flinch, cringe, recoil, withdraw

shrivel *v.* wither, waste away, wrinkle, decrease, pucker, parch ▷**wilt**

shudder *v.* shake, quake, tremble ▷**quiver**

shuffle *v.* ① mix, jumble, rearrange, scramble ② shamble, drag, scrape

shun *v.* avoid, boycott, ignore, spurn, snub *ant.* accept

shut *v.* fasten, close, secure, slam, bar, latch, lock, seal *ant.* open

shy ① *adj.* bashful, diffident, timid, wary, shrinking, modest, reserved, coy *ant.* bold ② *v.* flinch, quail, recoil, balk

sick *adj.* ① ill, diseased, unhealthy, ailing, unwell, nauseous, queasy ② tired, weary, fed up, bored, disgusted ③ twisted, perverted

side *n.* ① border, edge, flank, margin, half, slope, bank, wing, face ② party, group, team, faction ③ aspect, view *hom.* sighed

sift *v.* strain, filter, separate, screen

sigh *v.* murmur, exhale, wheeze, breathe, moan

sight ① *n.* spectacle, scene, view, eyesore, mirage ② *n.* seeing, perception, vision ③ *v.* behold, glimpse, observe *hom.* cite, site

sign ① *n.* symbol, emblem, mark, omen, token, signal ② *n.* hint, trace, symptom ③ *n.* notice, poster, bill, placard ④ *v.* endorse, autograph, inscribe, initial

signal ① *n.* beacon *The lighthouse beacon at Peggy's Cove warns ships away from the rocky coastline.* sign, cue, flag, indicator ② *adj.* distinguished, impressive, outstanding, noticeable

significant *adj.* symbolic, meaningful, momentous, memorable, major, weighty, important *ant.* unimportant

signify *v.* denote, indicate, stand for, imply, count ▷**mean**

silence *n.* quiet, hush, peace, tranquillity, still, stillness *ant.* noise

silent *adj.* ① hushed, noiseless, soundless, still, calm, mute, quiet *ant.* noisy ② unexpressed, unsaid, unspoken, implicit, understood

silly *adj.* absurd, senseless, stupid, childish, idiotic, ridiculous, absurd, inane ▷**foolish** *ant.* wise

similar *adj.* resembling, alike, equal, like, corresponding, akin, harmonious, common ▷**related** *ant.* different

simple *adj.* ① elementary, plain, ordinary, effortless, clear, uncomplicated ▷**easy** *ant.* intricate ② trusting, open, naïve

simply *adv.* ① merely, purely, absolutely, solely, only ② easily, directly, plainly

sin ① *n.* misdeed, wrong, vice, evil, crime, wickedness ② *v.* err, offend, trespass, stray, do wrong, violate

since ① *conj.* because, as, considering that, for ② *prep.* subsequent to, after

sincere *adj.* unaffected, frank, open, honest, candid, real, truthful ▷**genuine** *ant.* insincere, dishonest

sing *v.* warble, yodel, croon, chant, carol, hum, chirp

singe *v.* scorch, burn, scald, sear, char

singer *n.* vocalist, minstrel, songster, chorister, crooner, troubadour

single *adj.* ① one, only, sole, solitary, lone, individual, unique ② unwed, unmarried, unattached

Singers

Alto
Baritone
Bass
Basso profundo
Cantor
Chorister
Contrabass
Contralto
Countertenor
Mezzo-soprano
Prima donna
Soprano
Tenor
Treble
Vocalist

singular *adj.* odd, peculiar, curious, surprising, rare, eccentric ▷**unusual** *ant.* ordinary

sinister *adj.* menacing, threatening, ominous ▷**evil** *ant.* harmless

sink ① *v.* drop, dip, descend, decline, plunge, submerge, collapse ▷**fall** *ant.* rise ② *n.* basin, drain

sit *v.* perch, seat, squat, roost, rest, settle

site *n.* spot, plot, location, place, lot, premises, position, scene, situation *hom.* cite, sight

situation *n.* ① position, location, place, site, whereabouts, bearing ② predicament, plight, state of affairs, condition, circumstances, case, context

size *n.* dimensions, proportions, measurements, magnitude, bulk, volume, mass, amount, weight *hom.* sighs

sketch ① *n.* drawing, picture, cartoon ② *n.* draft, blueprint, outline ③ *n.* skit, act ④ *v.* draw, portray, describe, outline, delineate, illustrate, depict

skilful *adj.* able, adept, adroit, dexterous, expert, competent, deft, handy ▷**clever** *ant.* clumsy

skill *n.* ability, aptitude, expertise, knack, facility ▷**talent**

skim *v.* brush, touch, graze, float, glide, fly, glance, browse

skimp *v.* stint, scrimp, economize, scrape

S
S
S
S
S

skin

skin *n.* peel, rind, hide, husk, pelt, fur, coat, crust, epidermis, film, scum

skinny *adj.* thin, lean, scraggy, weedy, slender, gaunt *ant.* fat

skip *v.* ① jump, hop, dance, leap, frisk ② pass over, miss, disregard, omit

skirmish *n. & v.* scuffle, fight, scrap, brush

skirt ① *n.* clothing, kilt ② *n.* border, hem, edge, margin ③ *v.* border, flank, evade, avoid, bypass, detour, sidestep

skulk *v.* lurk, hide, cower, slink, sneak

slab *n.* board, stone, block, piece, chunk

slack *adj.* ① limp, flabby, loose, relaxed *ant.* tight ② lazy, sluggish ▷**idle** *ant.* busy

slander *v.* smear, insult, malign, accuse, abuse, defame ▷**libel** *ant.* praise

slant *v. & n.* incline, angle, list, pitch ▷**slope**

slap *v.* smack, whack, strike, hit, spank

slash *v. & n.* cut, slit, gash, hack, rip

slaughter *v.* slay, butcher, massacre ▷**kill**

slave ① *n.* serf, vassal, drudge, captive, pawn ② *v.* drudge, toil, labour, grind

slavery *n.* captivity, bondage, enslavement, serfdom, drudgery *ant.* liberty

slay *v.* murder, massacre ▷**kill** *hom.* sleigh

sleek *adj.* shiny, slick, glossy, polished

sleep *v. & n.* snooze, doze, drowse, slumber

slender *adj.* narrow, thin, fine, slight, meagre, scanty, remote ▷**slim**

slice ① *v.* shred, shave, cut, gash, divide ② *n.* piece, segment, slab, section

slick *adj.* ① shiny, smooth, slippery ▷**sleek** ② clever, suave, plausible *The story was plausible but not quite convincing.* polished, shrewd, glib

slide *v.* slip, slither, glide, skim, skate, coast, drift, skid

slight ① *adj.* delicate, tender, petite, dainty ▷**slender** ② *adj.* small, little, puny, meagre, trifling, trivial *ant.* significant ③ *n. & v.* snub, insult, affront

slim *adj.* ① trim, slight, thin, svelte ▷**slender** *ant.* fat ② remote, insignificant, small

slime *n.* mire, ooze, mud, filth

sling ① *v.* hurl, toss, throw, hang, swing ② *n.* loop, bandage, strap, support

slink *v.* prowl, creep, sneak ▷**skulk**

slip ① *v.* slide, slither, glide, skid ② *v.* fall, fail, blunder, trip, stumble, drop ③ *n.* blunder, error, mistake

slippery *adj.* ① smooth, glassy, slick ② cunning, untrustworthy, tricky, sharp, evasive, elusive ▷**shifty** *ant.* honest

slit *v.* gash, cut, rip ▷**slash**

slogan *n.* motto, watchword, war cry, catch phrase

slope ① *n.* slant, grade, gradient, incline, ascent, descent, rise, pitch, angle ② *v.* lean, incline, descend, ascend, slant, list, tilt

sloppy *adj.* ① careless, slipshod, inattentive, neglectful, thoughtless ② messy, slovenly, unkempt, dirty, untidy, disordered

slot *n.* ① recess, opening, niche, groove ② place, position

slow ① *adj.* inactive, late, slack, leisurely, gradual ▷**sluggish** *ant.* fast ② *v.* slacken, lose speed, relax, delay *ant.* accelerate *hom.* sloe

sluggish *adj.* slothful, lazy, inactive, languid, indolent, lifeless, slow, lethargic *ant.* brisk

slumber *v.* snooze, doze, snore ▷**sleep**

sly *adj.* cunning, tricky, furtive, sneaky, shrewd, sharp, devious, artful ▷**wily** *ant.* frank

smack *v.* slap, strike, spank ▷**hit**

small *adj.* ① minute, tiny, slight, puny, miniature, short, diminutive *ant.* large ② trivial, petty, feeble, paltry, inferior, minor, unimportant, measly

smart ① *adj.* alert, bright, sharp, shrewd, clever, brilliant ▷**intelligent** *ant.* stupid ② *adj.* elegant, neat, stylish, fashionable, trendy, dressy *ant.* seedy ③ *v.* sting, burn, tingle ▷**ache**

smash *v.* break, hit, destroy, wreck, demolish, defeat, crush, shatter

smear *v.* plaster, coat, daub, apply, cover, spread, smudge

smell *n.* aroma, fragrance, scent, perfume, stink, stench, odour, tang, bouquet, whiff

smile *v.* grin, smirk, beam ▷**laugh** *ant.* frown

smoke ① *n.* vapour, fumes, gas ② *v.* reek, whiff, smoulder

n.= noun
v.= verb
adj.= adjective
adv.= adverb
conj.= conjunction
prep.= preposition
ant.= antonym
hom.= homonym
▷ = cross-reference

smooth ① *adj.* level, even, flat, plain ② *adj.* polished, slippery, glassy, sleek *ant.* rough ③ *v.* iron, flatten, level, press, plane, polish, even *ant.* pucker

smother *v.* choke, throttle, stifle, restrain, repress, overwhelm

smudge *n.* & *v.* mark, smear, blur, stain

smug *adj.* self-satisfied, content, complacent, conceited, self-righteous

snack *n.* lunch, morsel, bite, meal

snag *n.* catch, complication, drawback, hitch

snap *v.* ① break, crack, pop ② nip, bite, bark, retort, snatch

snare ① *v.* trap, catch, seize, net ② *n.* trap, noose, pitfall, lure

snatch *v.* seize, grab, clutch, grip, whisk, pluck, grasp, snap

sneak ① *v.* slink, prowl, creep, lurk ▷**skulk** ② *n.* wretch, coward, informer, rat

sneer *v.* jeer, scoff, scorn, ridicule, taunt, deride, snicker, despise, mock

sniff *v.* smell, breathe in, inhale, scent

snivel *v.* weep, cry, sob, sniffle, whimper

snobbish *adj.* condescending, snooty, lofty, patronizing, stuck-up, elitist

snoop *v.* pry, eavesdrop, spy, peek, sneak, poke, meddle, interfere

snooze *v.* doze, nap, slumber ▷**sleep**

snub *v.* slight, slur, spurn, rebuff, shun, ignore, insult, cold-shoulder

snug *adj.* ① cosy, sheltered, secure, safe ▷**comfortable** ② close-fitting, tight, neat

so *adv.* accordingly, thus, therefore, likewise *hom.* sew, sow

soak *v.* steep, wet, douse, saturate, drench, immerse, swamp

soar *v.* glide, fly, rise, ascend, climb, tower *hom.* sore

sob *v.* lament, cry, sigh ▷**weep**

sober *adj.* calm, composed, serious, sombre, temperate, grave, realistic *ant.* frivolous

sociable *adj.* companionable, friendly, genial, chatty, affable *ant.* withdrawn

social *adj.* ① civic, public ② convivial, friendly, gregarious, neighbourly ▷**sociable**

soft *adj.* ① pliable, plastic, flexible, supple, fluffy, silky, fleecy *ant.* hard ② kind, gentle, mild, lenient ▷**tender** *ant.* harsh ③ low, faint, quiet *ant.* loud

soften *v.* ① thaw, melt, dissolve *ant.* solidify ② moderate, diminish, blunt, mellow, weaken, mollify

soil ① *n.* earth, dirt, mould, clay ② *v.* foul, dirty, sully, taint

sole *adj.* only, single, lone, one *hom.* soul

solemn *adj.* grave, stern, grim, sombre, reverential, stately, sedate ▷**serious** *ant.* frivolous

solid *adj.* ① steady, stable, sturdy, sound, sure, dependable ② dense, compact, hard, firm *ant.* soft

solidify *v.* congeal, harden, clot, cake, freeze, set, gel *ant.* soften

solitary *adj.* alone, lonely, remote, separate, only, single, sole

solution *n.* ① blend, mixture, brew, fluid ② answer, explanation, key

solve *v.* unravel *Here is a clue that may help us unravel the mystery.* clear up, untangle, work out, decode, resolve ▷**explain**

sombre *adj.* dark, serious, solemn, grim, gloomy, grave, dark, depressing *ant.* cheerful

some *adj.* any, more or less, about, several, various, certain *hom.* sum

sometimes *adv.* at times, from time to time, occasionally

song *n.* air, tune, jingle, lullaby, melody, carol, ballad, ode, ditty

soon *adv.* shortly, before long, presently

soothe *v.* mollify, quiet, console, pacify *Reading him a story might pacify your angry baby brother.* ease, lull, comfort, calm *ant.* irritate

sordid *adj.* seamy, miserable, dirty, sleazy, tawdry, contemptible, vile, squalid ▷**base**

sore ① *adj.* painful, tender, aching, inflamed ② *adj.* miffed, annoyed, upset, grieved ③ *n.* wound, cut, blister, infection, ulcer, boil *hom.* soar

sorrow *n.* grief, woe, remorse, anguish, heartbreak, regret *ant.* joy, happiness

S

sorrowful *adj.* sad, doleful, mournful, dejected *ant.* joyful

sorry *adj.* ① remorseful, ashamed, apologetic *ant.* brash ② pained, grieved, hurt, distressed *ant.* glad ③ miserable, wretched, mean, poor, shabby, filthy *ant.* excellent

sort ① *n.* kind, type, variety, order, class, species ② *v.* sift, arrange, catalogue, classify, order, group

soul *n.* spirit, passion, mind, vitality, fire, essence, heart, human being *hom.* sole

sound ① *n.* noise, din, tone, racket *ant.* silence ② *v.* blare, blast, blow ③ *adj.* well, hearty, fit, whole, perfect ▷**healthy** *ant.* unhealthy ④ *adj.* firm, stable, solid ⑤ *adj.* true correct, reasonable

sour *adj.* ① tart, rancid, bitter, acid, sharp, curdled, green *ant.* sweet ② morose, glum, sullen, peevish, broody ▷**harsh** *ant.* genial

source *n.* origin, spring, cause, beginning, root, fountain

souvenir *n.* token, memento, keepsake, reminder, remembrance, trophy

sow *v.* plant, seed, scatter, strew, spread *hom.* sew, so

space *n.* ① extent, expanse, capacity, room, area, gap, opening, distance ② universe, heavens, cosmos

spacious *adj.* roomy, extensive, open, broad, wide *ant.* narrow

span ① *n.* stretch, reach, extent, length, period, term ② *v.* cross, bridge, link, connect, traverse, cover

spare ① *adj.* extra, reserve, surplus, supplemental ② *adj.* bare, meagre, poor, thin, scanty ▷**sparse** ③ *v.* afford, give, do without ④ *v.* save ⑤ *v.* forgive, pardon, excuse

sparkle *v. & n.* glitter, glow, gleam, glint, twinkle, shine, glimmer, shimmer

sparse *adj.* scanty, thin, scattered ▷**meagre** *ant.* dense

speak *v.* utter, pronounce, lecture, express, articulate, enunciate, tell, declare, chat, converse, consult, confer

spear *n.* pike, javelin, lance

special *adj.* ① distinct, different, unique, rare, individual, particular ② memorable, extraordinary, wonderful *ant.* ordinary

species *n.* breed, kind, sort, class, family

specific *adj.* definite, exact, precise ▷**special**

specimen *n.* ① sample, example, type, model ② character, type

speck *n.* dot, spot, particle, bit

spectacle *n.* sight, scene, display, pageant, presentation ▷**exhibition**

spectacular *adj.* wonderful, fabulous, sensational, dramatic, flamboyant ▷**marvellous**

spectator *n.* witness, observer, onlooker

speech *n.* ① language, pronunciation, dialect, tongue *Corin translated the message into the tongue of the Calormen.* ② lecture, talk, address

speed *n.* velocity, rapidity, dispatch *Time is short; this message must be delivered with dispatch.* pace, swiftness, haste, tempo

speedy *adj.* swift, rapid, fleet, quick, lively ▷**fast** *ant.* slow

spell ① *n.* magic, charm, power ② *n.* period, term, space, time ③ *v.* write, decipher

spend *v.* ① expend, lay out, lavish, pay, disburse ② use, pass, while away, put in

sphere *n.* ① globe, ball, orb, planet ② range, realm, orbit, domain, field, province

spice *n.* seasoning, flavouring, zest, relish, savour

Spices

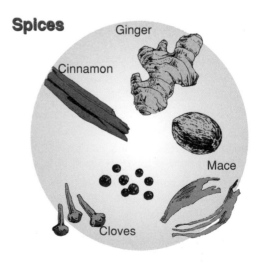

Ginger

Cinnamon

Mace

Cloves

n. = noun

v. = verb

adj. = adjective

adv. = adverb

conj. = conjunction

prep. = preposition

ant. = antonym

hom. = homonym

▷ = cross-reference

spill *v.* pour, stream, gush, overflow, spurt, upset, drop, overturn, shed, fall, sprawl

spin *v.* revolve, rotate, turn, whirl, twist, twirl, swirl

spirit *n.* ① essence, heart, nature, character, soul ② vigour, energy, morale, courage ③ phantom, spectre, ghost, spook, apparition ④ mood, tone, attitude

spiritual *adj.* ① religious, divine, unworldly, holy ② pure, immaterial

spite ① *n.* malice, rancour, hostility, hatred, venom, pique ② *v.* hurt, annoy, offend, irritate

spiteful *adj.* vicious, malicious, vindictive, malevolent ▷**hostile** *ant.* kind

splash *v.* wet, spatter, shower, sprinkle, dash, douse, soak, wash, spray

splendid *adj.* grand, brilliant, sumptuous, showy, glorious, majestic, stately, excellent, marvellous ▷**magnificent** *ant.* ordinary

splendour *n.* glory, pageantry, brilliance, show, magnificence, pomp

split *v.* ① slice, cut, burst *If you stuff that backpack any fuller, you'll burst the seams!* crack, tear, splinter, cleave ② share, divide

spoil *v.* ① deface, disfigure, botch, ruin, mar ② rot, sour, decay ③ pamper, indulge

spoiled *adj.* decayed, rotten, bad, rancid

spontaneous *adj.* natural, impulsive, free, instinctive, unplanned, voluntary

spoof *n.* takeoff, roast, parody, satire

sport ① *n.* game, amusement, fun, athletics, recreation ② *v.* play, frolic, gambol, romp

spot ① *n.* dot, speck, mark, stain, blemish ② *v.* see, observe, find, notice, recognize, distinguish, spy

spotless *adj.* pure, clean, unstained, faultless, perfect, immaculate

sprawl *v.* recline, stretch, lie, spread ▷**lounge**

spray *v.* sprinkle, squirt, splash, shower

spread *v.* ① scatter, set out, sow, circulate, distribute ② unfold, extend, stretch, expand, open ③ smear, daub, slather

sprightly *adj.* lively, cheerful, agile, vigorous, energetic, vivacious ▷**brisk** *ant.* sluggish

spur *v.* arouse, drive, urge, incite, encourage, provoke, motivate

spurn *v.* reject, scorn, disdain, disregard, decline ▷**snub** *ant.* accept

spurt *v.* jet, stream, squirt, emerge, gush

spy ① *n.* agent, detective, observer, snoop, scout, informer, sleuth ② *v.* see, glimpse, pry, peek, spot, observe, investigate, watch

squabble *n.* & *v.* quarrel, clash, fight, wrangle ▷**dispute**

squad *n.* group, company, troop, force, band, team

squall ① *n.* blast, gust, storm, tempest ② *v.* squawk, scream, bawl, howl

squander *v.* waste, fritter, misspend, lavish

squash *v.* ① mash, crush, squelch, flatten ② quell, suppress, humiliate

squat *v.* crouch, sit, roost, perch

squeal *v.* squawk, squeak, yelp, grunt, cry

squeeze *v.* ① compress, press, constrict, force, pinch, squish ② clasp, cuddle, hug

squirm *v.* wriggle, fidget, twist, wiggle, writhe

squirt *v.* spray, splash ▷**spurt**

stab ① *v.* cut, jab, puncture, wound, pierce, knife ② *n.* pang, thrust, jab ③ *n.* crack, try

stable ① *adj.* firm, fixed, steady, solid, constant, dependable, lasting, predictable *ant.* unstable ② *n.* barn, shed, stall

stack ① *n.* pile, tower, bundle, sheaf, heap ② *v.* arrange, pile, load, layer

staff *n.* ① team, workers, force, personnel, crew ② stick, cane, pole, rod

stage ① *n.* platform, scaffold, podium, arena, theatre, playhouse ② *n.* step, degree, position, point, period ③ *v.* perform, produce, present, plan, arrange, set up

stagger *v.* ① reel, totter, waver, lurch ② boggle, dumfound, floor

stagnant *adj.* ① motionless, standing, still, ② inert, sluggish, inactive, dead *ant.* vital

staid *adj.* serious, steady, earnest, sober, demure, grave ▷**sedate** *ant.* frivolous *hom.* stayed

stain ① *n.* blemish, blur, spot, blot, smudge ② *n.* disgrace, shame, stigma ③ *v.* tarnish, sully, defile, blemish, soil, blot

stake ① *n.* stick, stave, spike ▷**post** ② *n.* bet, claim, wager, involvement, interest *hom.* steak

S

stale *adj.* ① musty, old, tasteless, faded, dry, flat ② trite, hackneyed *ant.* fresh

stalk *v.* hunt, pursue, shadow, tail, track

stall ① *v.* delay, hedge, obstruct, hamper, balk, play for time *ant.* advance ② *n.* compartment, booth, stand, bay

stamina *n.* endurance, vitality, strength, power, energy *ant.* weakness

stammer *v.* stutter, falter, hesitate, stumble

stamp ① *v.* print, imprint, mark, impress, engrave ② *v.* stomp, tramp ③ *n.* impression, mark, print, brand ④ *n.* kind, sort, type, class ⑤ *n.* seal, sticker

stand ① *n.* easel, counter, table, booth ▷**stall** ② *v.* set, lean, put, locate, place ③ *v.* tolerate, abide, endure, bear ④ *v.* get up, rise *ant.* sit

standard ① *adj.* normal, regular, uniform, routine ② *n.* pattern, criterion, norm, benchmark, model ③ *n.* flag, banner, pennant

staple *adj.* ① main, principal, important, leading, chief ② stock, regular

stare *v.* gaze, gape, look, peer, gawk, glare, regard *hom.* stair

stark *adj.* severe, plain, downright, bare, absolute, empty, bleak

start ① *v.* commence, begin, found, initiate, launch, introduce ② *v.* depart, set out, leave ③ *v.* jump, wince, flinch ④ *n.* beginning, commencement *The torch-lighting ceremony is the official commencement of the Olympics.* outset ⑤ *n.* origin, cause, root ⑥ *n.* shock, scare

startle *v.* frighten, alarm, scare, surprise, jolt, shock, spook ▷**start**

state ① *n.* condition, situation, position, shape, plight ② *n.* country, commonwealth, nation, land ③ *v.* tell, declare, assert, express, utter ▷**speak** ④ *n.* tizzy, flap

stately *adj.* imposing, grand, dignified ▷**magnificent** *ant.* humble

statement *n.* ① declaration, utterance, remark, assertion, expression, report ② bill, account, invoice

station ① *n.* post, spot, position, depot, terminal ② *v.* park, place, position, establish, post, assign

stationary *adj.* still, unmoving, motionless, standing, fixed, *ant.* mobile *hom.* stationery

stationery *n.* paper, envelopes, cards, letterhead *hom.* stationary

Confusable Words

stationary means *not moving*

stationery means *writing paper*

statue *n.* carving, bust, figure, effigy, monument, sculpture

staunch *adj.* constant, faithful, reliable, firm, stalwart, sure ▷**loyal** *ant.* unfaithful

stay ① *v.* endure, last, remain, dwell, linger, wait, pause, visit, lodge ② *n.* visit, stopover

steady ① *adj.* firm, fixed, established, constant, consistent, regular ▷**stable** ② *v.* brace, stabilize, balance, secure, support

steal *v.* ① filch, thieve, pilfer ▷**rob** ② slink, tiptoe, creep ▷**prowl** *hom.* steel

stealthy *adj.* furtive, sneaky, sly, skulking, underhanded, silent, unseen *ant.* open

steep *adj.* sheer, sharp, abrupt, precipitous

steer *v.* guide, direct, pilot, control, navigate, conduct, manoeuvre

stem ① *n.* stalk, shoot, stock, trunk ② *v.* arise, derive, originate, flow ③ *v.* check, restrain

step ① *n.* pace, tread, stride, gait, walk ② *n.* stair, tread, rung ③ *n.* stage, phase, degree, notch ④ *n.* measure, action ⑤ *v.* walk, skip, trip, pace, dance *hom.* steppe

sterile *adj.* ① barren, unfertile, lifeless ② sanitary, disinfected, antiseptic

stern *adj.* strict, severe, harsh, austere ▷**grim** *ant.* mild

stew *v.* ① cook, simmer, boil, steam ② worry, fuss, brood

stick ① *n.* stave, pole, rod, cane, staff, club, bar, shaft ② *v.* adhere, cling, cleave, glue, paste, seal, attach ③ *v.* insert, extend, deposit

sticky *adj.* ① gluey, gummy, adhesive, gooey, tacky ② humid, muggy

stiff *adj.* ① inflexible, firm, unyielding, unbending, rigid *ant.* flexible ② strict, severe, stern *ant.* lenient ③ formal, stilted, prim *ant.* relaxed

n. = noun
v. = verb
adj. = adjective
adv. = adverb
conj. = conjunction
prep. = preposition
ant. = antonym
hom. = homonym
▷ = cross-reference

stifle *v.* suffocate, throttle, gag, muzzle, choke, suppress, muffle ▷**smother**

stigma *n.* ① blot, blur, scar, stain ▷**blemish** ② disgrace, dishonour, shame

still ① *adj.* fixed, motionless, static ② *adj.* calm, quiet, serene, tranquil, placid, peaceful *ant.* upset, restless ③ *adj.* mute, quiet, hushed, noiseless, silent *ant.* loud ④ *v.* quiet, hush, silence, quell ▷**calm**

stimulate *v.* inspire, provoke, motivate, arouse, encourage ▷**excite** *ant.* discourage

sting *v.* prick, wound, pain, hurt, injure, bite, burn, smart, irritate

stingy *adj.* cheap, miserly, tight-fisted, selfish, mean ▷**tight** *ant.* generous

stink *n.* smell, reek, stench

stint ① *n.* job, task, chore ② *n.* turn, spell, share, quota

stir ① *v.* inspire, arouse, spur, agitate ▷**stimulate** ② *v.* whisk, churn, mix, blend ③ *v.* excite, agitate, disturb *ant.* calm ④ *n.* disturbance, flurry, fuss, uproar ⑤ *v.* move, budge

stock ① *n.* hoard *He kept a private hoard of candies in his desk.* reserve, supply, inventory, repertoire ② *v.* provide, supply, equip, fill, deal in

stocky *adj.* chunky, sturdy, pudgy, stout, beefy, squat, thickset ▷**burly** *ant.* slender

stodgy *adj.* dull, heavy, tedious, boring

stoop *v.* bend, crouch, kneel, bow

stop ① *v.* cease, desist, end, terminate, halt, finish, quit, arrest, discontinue, check *ant.* start ② *v.* prevent, prohibit, restrain, ban ③ *n.* halt, end, check, cessation ④ *v.* plug, fill in

store ① *v.* keep, stow, stock, reserve, hoard, save *ant.* use ② *n.* stock, supply, reserve ③ *n.* warehouse, emporium, outlet ▷**shop**

storey *n.* floor, landing, level

storm ① *n.* blizzard, tempest, gale, cyclone, hurricane, tornado, squall, downpour *ant.* calm ② *n.* turmoil, upheaval, outburst, barrage ③ *v.* rage, rant, fume, attack, assault, raid

story *n.* ① yarn, tale, narrative, fiction, fable, account, anecdote ② untruth, lie, fib

stout *adj.* ① sturdy, solid, thick, robust ▷**strong** *ant.* flimsy ② fat, corpulent ▷**plump** *ant.* thin ③ brave, resolute, firm ▷**courageous** *ant.* timid

straight *adj.* ① undeviating *She didn't turn right or left, but kept an undeviating course.* unswerving, direct ② frank, honourable, candid, truthful, fair ▷**honest** *ant.* crooked

straightforward *adj.* open, outspoken, direct, frank, plain *ant.* devious

strain ① *n.* tension, fatigue, exertion, effort ▷**stress** *ant.* rest ② *n.* melody, tune, air ③ *v.* struggle, labour, toil *ant.* relax ④ *v.* wrench, injure ⑤ *v.* filter, sift, separate

strait *n.* channel, sound, narrows *hom.* straight

strait-laced *adj.* prim, prudish, strict

strand *n.* hair, fibre, tress, lock

stranded *adj.* marooned, abandoned

strange *adj.* ① unusual, extraordinary, curious, bizarre ▷**odd** *ant.* ordinary ② foreign, alien, unfamiliar

stranger *n.* outsider, foreigner, visitor, newcomer, alien *ant.* friend

strangle *v.* choke, throttle, constrict, repress

strap *n.* belt, harness, thong, leash

stray *v.* wander, deviate, depart, rove, roam, meander, digress

streak *n.* smear, stripe, band, line, bar, strip

stream ① *n.* current, flow, torrent, brook, creek ② *v.* flow, gush, spill, pour

strength *n.* ① power, force, might ▷**energy** ② concentration, intensity ③ solidity, stability, sturdiness *ant.* weakness

Storey

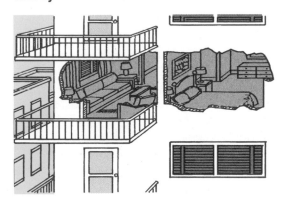

strenuous *adj.* ① tiring, laborious, arduous, ② determined, vigorous ▷**earnest**

stress ① *n.* tension, force, effort, pressure, anxiety ▷**strain** ② *n.* accent, emphasis, weight, force ③ *v.* emphasize, accentuate *Accentuate the positive and minimize the negative.* highlight, underline

stretch *v.* ① expand, reach, lengthen, elongate, increase ▷**extend** *ant.* shorten ② tighten, pull, strain ③ exaggerate

strict *adj.* ① severe, rigorous, rigid, austere, harsh, stiff, demanding, inflexible, stern *ant.* lenient ② exact, rigorous, thorough, accurate ▷**precise** *ant.* inaccurate

stride *n. & v.* walk, step, tread, march, tramp, tromp, pace

strife *n.* struggle, quarrelling, friction, dissension, conflict *ant.* peace

strike ① *v.* hit, pound, punch, beat, collide, knock ▷**thump** ② *v.* discover, arrive at ③ *v.* delete, omit, cancel ④ *v.* attack, invade ⑤ *n.* assault, attack ⑥ *n.* walkout, boycott

striking *adj.* eye-catching, remarkable, noticeable ▷**extraordinary** *ant.* dull

strip ① *v.* take off, peel, remove, uncover, deprive ② *n.* ribbon, piece, length, band

stripe *n.* streak, band, bar, chevron, line

strive *v.* seek, aim, contend, struggle, labour, endeavour ▷**try** *ant.* neglect

stroke ① *n.* seizure, fit, convulsion ② *v.* pat, rub, caress, smooth, comfort

stroll *v. & n.* walk, promenade, saunter, tramp, ramble

strong *adj.* ① powerful, vigorous, hardy, muscular, athletic, sturdy ▷**robust** *ant.* weak ② potent, hot, spicy, intense ▷**pungent** ③ enthusiastic, ardent, vehement

structure *n.* ① construction, organization, composition ② building, edifice

Structure

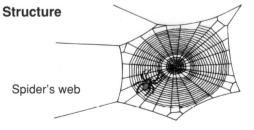

Spider's web

struggle ① *v.* endeavour, labour, battle, wrestle, strive, toil, fight, oppose *ant.* yield ② *n.* conflict, battle, quarrel, contest ▷**fight** ③ *n.* strain, trouble, effort, hardship

strut *v.* parade, prance, swagger, flounce

stubborn *adj.* ① dogged, persistent, tenacious, resolute, persevering ② willful, pig-headed, headstrong, uncompromising, persistent ▷**obstinate** *ant.* flexible

studious *adj.* scholarly, attentive, bookish, diligent ▷**industrious**

study ① *v.* read, peruse, scrutinize, examine, investigate, research, learn ② *n.* learning, analysis, examination, thought, contemplation, research ③ *n.* den, office

stuff ① *v.* fill, congest, pack, crowd, jam ② *n.* matter, substance, material, goods

stumble *v.* stagger, fall, muddle, err ▷**trip**

stump ① *v.* perplex, mystify, confuse ▷**baffle** ② *n.* stub, tip, log, root

stun *v.* knock out, overpower, stupefy, dumfound, paralyse ▷**shock**

stunt *n.* deed, feat, achievement, act, performance, trick ▷**exploit**

stupefy *v.* daze, muddle, bewilder, astonish, paralyse, flabbergast ▷**stun**

stupid *adj.* ① silly, ridiculous, inane ▷**foolish** ② simple, dense, thick, idiotic *ant.* clever

sturdy *adj.* rugged, stalwart, tough, robust, firm, strong, durable ▷**hardy** *ant.* weak

stutter *v.* stumble, falter ▷**stammer**

style *n.* ① vogue, fashion ② way, method, technique, mode, manner, form ③ taste, flair, elegance *hom.* stile

suave *adj.* sophisticated, elegant, polite, pleasant, smooth, urbane, polished, refined

subdue *v.* suppress, soften, tame, moderate, mellow, overpower, defeat ▷**repress**

subject ① *n.* (*sub*-ject) matter, topic, theme, content ② *n.* (*sub*-ject) subordinate, citizen, dependant ③ *adj.* (*sub*-ject) dependent, subordinate ④ *adj.* (*sub*-ject) liable, prone, susceptible ⑤ *v.* (*sub*-*ject*) rule over, subdue, subjugate, enslave, expose

submerge *v.* plunge, immerse, sink, dip

submissive *adj.* yielding, servile, meek, passive ▷**obedient** *ant.* obstinate, defiant

n. = noun
v. = verb
adj. = adjective
adv. = adverb
conj. = conjunction
prep. = preposition
ant. = antonym
hom. = homonym
▷ = cross-reference

submit *v.* ① yield, give in, accede, surrender, succumb, defer ② offer, tender, propose

subordinate *adj.* junior, minor, subject, dependent, secondary, inferior *ant.* superior

subscribe *v.* sign, enrol, register, agree, assent, contribute

subsequent *adj.* later, following, succeeding, after, further *ant.* previous

subside *v.* decline, decrease, diminish, wane *He's read hundreds of books on lizards, but his interest in them hasn't waned.* recede, ebb, lapse, ease ▷**abate**

substance *n.* ① matter, object, stuff, material ② essence, thrust, meaning ▷**gist**

substantial *adj.* ① strong, sturdy, firm ② real, physical ③ serious, worthwhile, solid ④ ample, considerable, sizable

substitute ① *n. & adj.* alternative, backup, replacement, stand-in, makeshift ② *v.* swap, change, replace, fill in, exchange, switch

subtle *adj.* ① fine, delicate ② unobvious, hidden, elusive, faint ③ shrewd, clever, crafty, perceptive

subtract *v.* deduct, take away, remove, eliminate, withdraw *ant.* add

succeed *v.* ① flourish, prosper, thrive, manage, triumph *ant.* fail ② follow, inherit, replace, ensue *ant.* precede

success *n.* prosperity, triumph, victory, achievement, luck *ant.* failure

successful *adj.* victorious, prosperous, flourishing, thriving, lucky *ant.* unlucky

sudden *adj.* unexpected, abrupt, impulsive, rapid, surprising, unforeseen *ant.* gradual

suffer *v.* experience, bear, endure, sustain

sufficient *adj.* adequate, ample, plenty, satisfactory, enough *ant.* insufficient

suffocate *v.* smother, choke, strangle ▷**stifle**

suggest *v.* recommend, advise, submit, hint, intimate, propose, indicate

suit ① *v.* fulfil, gratify, please, suffice, qualify, satisfy, serve, fit ② *n.* ensemble, outfit, costume ③ *n.* action, lawsuit

suitable *adj.* apt, convenient, eligible, appropriate, correct, proper *ant.* unsuitable

sulk *v.* pout, grouch, brood, mope, fret, scowl, frown

sulky *adj.* glum, morose, moody, brooding ▷**sullen** *ant.* genial

sullen *adj.* gloomy, heavy, dismal, cheerless, glum, dark, sombre ▷**sulky** *ant.* cheerful

sum *n.* amount, total, figure *hom.* some

summary *n.* synopsis, précis, abstract, outline

summit *n.* peak, pinnacle, top, apex, zenith, acme, culmination, height *ant.* bottom

summon *v.* call, beckon, command, invite, muster, assemble *ant.* dismiss

sumptuous *adj.* rich, costly, gorgeous, splendid, magnificent ▷**lavish**

sunny *adj.* bright, cheerful, light, clear, cloudless ▷**radiant** *ant.* gloomy

superb *adj.* magnificent, outstanding, excellent, best ▷**grand** *ant.* poor

superficial *adj.* slight, external, shallow, skin-deep *ant.* profound, radical

superfluous *adj.* excess, non-essential, extra, spare, redundant, unnecessary, surplus *ant.* essential

superior *adj.* ① better, greater, higher, best ▷**excellent** ② senior, elder *ant.* subordinate

supersede *v.* succeed, replace, displace

supervise *v.* boss, oversee, monitor, control, manage, run, administer, handle, direct

supple *adj.* lithe, pliable, flexible, bending

supplement ① *n.* addition, complement *This apple is the perfect complement to your lunch.* sequel, postscript, attachment ② *v.* complement, round out, add to

supply ① *v.* give, provide, furnish, yield, contribute *ant.* withhold ② *n.* store, hoard, reserve, stock

support ① *v.* help, maintain, sustain, bear, favour ▷**uphold** *ant.* oppose ② *v.* hold up, prop, strut, brace ③ *v.* confirm, reinforce *Reinforce your argument with examples.* substantiate ④ *n.* base, foundation, framework, prop ⑤ *n.* help, aid, assistance, encouragement *ant.* opposition

suppose *v.* assume, presume, believe, imagine, imply, guess ▷**reckon**

suppress *v.* restrain, extinguish, stop, crush, quash, censor, quell ▷**repress** *ant.* incite

supreme *adj.* dominant, highest, greatest, maximum, ultimate, ideal *ant.* average

sure *adj.* ① certain, positive, definite, proven, clear, unfailing ② secure, dependable, safe, tested, faithful, reliable, *ant.* uncertain

surface *n.* ① area, expanse, stretch ② face, outside, exterior, covering, façade, veneer

surge ① *v.* swell, rise, heave, rush, flow, ② *n.* rush, swell, spurt, wave

surly *adj.* morose, cross, testy, touchy, crusty, curt, bad-tempered ▷**sullen**

surmise *v.* guess, speculate, gather, suspect ▷**presume** *ant.* know

surpass *v.* eclipse, beat, outstrip, excel, exceed, pass, top ▷**outdo**

surplus *n.* excess, remainder, balance, residue, overabundance, glut *ant.* lack

surprise ① *v.* startle, astonish, amaze, confound, stun, daze ▷**astound** ② *n.* amazement, astonishment, wonder

surrender *v.* quit, give up, yield, submit, abandon, collapse ▷**relinquish**

surround *v.* enclose, encircle, encompass

survey ① *v.* (sur-*vey*) examine, overlook, scan, scrutinize, study ② *n.* (*sur*-vey) overview, analysis, study, questionnaire

survive *v.* exist, continue, outlast, persist

susceptible *adj.* sensitive, impressionable, subject, prone, vulnerable

suspect ① *v.* (sus-*pect*) disbelieve, distrust, doubt, ② *v.* (sus-*pect*) believe, imagine, think ③ *adj.* (*sus*-pect) questionable, dubious

suspend *v.* ① interrupt, delay, adjourn, postpone, arrest ▷**stop** *ant.* continue ② swing, dangle ▷**hang** *ant.* drop

suspense *n.* anticipation *Parents and friends waited with great anticipation for the school concert to begin.* waiting, uncertainty, tension

suspicious *adj.* incredulous, sceptical, doubtful, suspecting, distrustful *ant.* naïve

sustain *v.* ① support, bear, uphold, keep up, maintain ② nourish, feed

swallow ① *v.* absorb, consume, eat, engulf, devour, drink ▷**gulp** ② *v.* believe, accept ③ *n.* mouthful, gulp

swamp ① *n.* bog, marsh, muskeg, wetland, morass, quagmire ② *v.* submerge, submerse, overflow, deluge ▷**drench**

swap *v.* exchange, switch, trade, barter

swarm ① *n.* throng, horde, multitude ② *v.* teem, abound, mass, crowd, cluster

sway ① *v.* swing, rock, totter, reel, wave ▷**waver** ② *v.* influence, affect ③ *n.* rule, authority, control ▷**influence**

swear *v.* ① vow, assert, pledge, promise, affirm, attest ② curse, cuss, blaspheme

sweat *v.* perspire, ooze, exude, boil, swelter

sweep *v.* brush, clear

sweet *adj.* ① sugary, syrupy, luscious *ant.* sour ② melodic, tuneful, musical, mellow *ant.* harsh ③ gentle, tender, mild, lovable, adorable *ant.* unpleasant ④ fragrant, pure, clean, fresh, wholesome, aromatic *ant.* putrid

swell *v.* expand, distend, inflate, bulge, increase, dilate ▷**enlarge** *ant.* shrink

swerve *v.* veer, deviate, skid, lurch

swift *adj.* prompt, rapid, quick ▷**fast** *ant.* slow

swim *v.* bathe, wade, paddle, float, glide

swindle ① *n.* scam, fraud, blackmail, racket ② *v.* rip off, defraud, fleece ▷**cheat**

swing ① *v.* hang, suspend, dangle, turn ② *v.* waver, vacillate *Once you've made your decision, don't start to vacillate back and forth again.* reel, sway ③ *n.* tempo, time, rhythm

switch ① *v.* replace, change, exchange, alter, trade, substitute, swap ② *n.* lever, pedal, control

swivel *v.* pivot, spin, rotate, revolve, turn

swoop *v.* pounce, descend, plummet, plunge

sword *n.* sabre, rapier, blade, foil, cutlass, steel *hom.* soared

symbol *n.* character, figure, numeral, letter, sign, token, emblem, badge *hom.* cymbal

sympathetic *adj.* thoughtful, understanding, kind, affectionate, friendly, compassionate *ant.* hostile

synopsis *n.* outline, summary, résumé, digest, review, abstract, brief

system *n.* ① method, setup, plan, order, scheme, arrangement, philosophy ② whole, network, organization

n. = noun
v. = verb
adj. = adjective
adv. = adverb
conj. = conjunction
prep. = preposition
ant. = antonym
hom. = homonym
▷ = cross-reference

T t

table *n.* ① stand, desk, bench, counter, stall ② list, catalogue, chart, schedule, index ③ slab, tablet,

tackle ① *n.* outfit, gear, rig, harness ② *v.* intercept, seize, attack ③ *v.* deal with, assume, undertake, approach, wade into

tact *n.* diplomacy, judgment, sensitivity, discretion *hom.* tacked

tactful *adj.* diplomatic, subtle *The hint was so subtle, she almost missed it.* prudent, sensitive, delicate ▷**discreet** *ant.* tactless

tactics *n.* strategy, method, procedure, manoeuvre, campaign

tactless *adj.* inconsiderate, undiplomatic, insensitive, impolite ▷**blunt** *ant.* tactful

tag *n.* label, ticket, slip, sticker

taint *v.* contaminate, infect, pollute, stain, soil, tarnish, sully ▷**defile** *ant.* purify

take *v.* ① grasp, grab, seize, snatch, capture, steal, borrow, remove *ant.* return ② receive, accept, adopt *ant.* give ③ carry, convey, lead, conduct ④ choose, select, opt for

tale *n.* story, fable, anecdote, yarn, narrative, legend, myth, parable *hom.* tail

talent *n.* knack, gift, ability, aptitude, flair, art, craft, skill, genius

talk ① *v.* speak, chat, discuss, confer *The principal regularly confers with the staff about school issues.* converse, gossip ② *n.* speech, conversation, discussion, dialogue, negotiation, lecture, discourse

tall *adj.* high, towering, elevated, lofty, giant, gangly, lanky *ant.* short

tame ① *adj.* domesticated, housebroken, gentle, mild, obedient, docile *ant.* savage ② *adj.* dull, bland, safe, predictable ③ *v.* domesticate, train, discipline

tamper *v.* meddle, interfere, tinker, fiddle, mess around

tangible *adj.* concrete, solid, substantial, real, material, physical, palpable

tangle *n.* & *v.* twist, muddle, jumble, knot

tantalize *v.* tease, taunt, excite, torment

tantrum *n.* rage, fit, hysterics, temper

tap ① *v.* pat, hit, knock, rap, strike ② *n.* faucet, spout, nozzle ③ *n.* knock, rap

taper *v.* narrow, decline, wane, dwindle, decrease, lessen *ant.* spread *hom.* tapir

target *n.* goal, aim, end, ambition, objective

tariff *n.* tax, rate, toll, duty, levy, price

tarnish *v.* stain, sully, spot, darken, blemish, blacken, injure

tart ① *adj.* acid, sour, sharp, tangy ② *n.* pie, pastry, flan, quiche

task *n.* job, chore, assignment, undertaking, duty, mission

taste ① *n.* bite, mouthful, sample ② *n.* flavour, savour, tang, zest ③ *n.* fondness, inclination, discernment *His choice of reading material shows a lack of discernment.* appreciation ④ *v.* try, sip, sample, detect, experience, know

tasteful *adj.* graceful, elegant, smart ▷**refined** *ant.* tasteless

tasteless *adj.* ① bland, mild, plain, flavourless, insipid ② gaudy, tacky, coarse, inelegant ▷**vulgar** *ant.* tasteful

tasty *adj.* appetizing, savoury, flavourful, piquant ▷**delicious** *ant.* tasteless

taunt *v.* ridicule, scoff at, bait, reproach, rebuke, jibe ▷**sneer** *ant.* compliment

taut *adj.* tense, tight, stretched, snug ▷**rigid** *ant.* relaxed *hom.* taught

tax ① *n.* levy, duty, toll, tariff, burden ② *v.* load, oppress, charge *hom.* tacks

teach *v.* instruct, educate, tutor, coach, guide, train, drill, inform, show *ant.* learn

teacher *n.* educator, instructor, professor, tutor, trainer, coach, lecturer, guide

Tame

T t T t T t T

n. = noun

v. = verb

adj. = adjective

adv. = adverb

conj. = conjunction

prep. = preposition

ant. = antonym

hom. = homonym

▷ = cross-reference

team *n.* group, gang, band, crew, company, party, side, faction *hom.* teem

tear *v.* ① rip, tatter, shred, rend, cut, gash, snatch ② hurry, run, dash, rush, sprint, bolt *hom.* tare

tearful *adj.* weepy, crying, sobbing, sad

tease *v.* mock, pester, taunt, rib, heckle, annoy, irritate, badger, harass, vex, provoke ▷**tantalize** *ant.* soothe *hom.* teas, tees

tedious *adj.* uninteresting, boring, wearisome, tiresome, irksome, exhausting ▷**dull** *ant.* interesting

tell *v.* ① inform, notify, advise ② relate, describe, recount, disclose, speak, state, indicate, communicate ③ distinguish, discern, discover

temper ① *n.* anger, annoyance, passion, fury, rage, cool, fuse ② *n.* temperament, disposition, nature, character, humour, mood ③ *v.* moderate, soften, weaken, strengthen, mix, balance

temporary *adj.* interim, passing, fleeting, momentary, makeshift *ant.* permanent

tempt *v.* entice, invite, attract, persuade ▷**lure** *ant.* deter

tenacious *adj.* stubborn, firm, obstinate, unwavering *ant.* weak

tend *v.* ① lean, incline, slant, bend, verge *ant.* deviate ② care for, manage, serve, guard, nurse, cultivate, nurture, attend, watch *ant.* neglect

tendency *n.* disposition, leaning, trend, inclination, bent, *ant.* horror

tender ① *adj.* delicate, soft ▷**fragile** ② *adj.* mild, kind, sympathetic, loving, compassionate ▷**gentle** ③ *adj.* raw, painful, sore, sensitive ④ *v.* offer *Before anyone had to ask, Charlotte offered her help.* present, volunteer, bid

tense *adj.* ① nervous, edgy, uneasy, anxious, stressed, worried *ant.* relaxed ② rigid, stretched, tight, strained, taut

tension *n.* strain, stress, worry, pressure, suspense *ant.* rest

term ① *n.* expression, word, phrase ② *n.* time, season, span, stretch, period, duration ③ *v.* name, entitle, call, dub

terminate *v.* stop, end, quit, cease, close, conclude ▷**finish** *ant.* begin

terrible *adj.* appalling, fearful, dreadful, hideous ▷**horrible** *ant.* wonderful

terrify *v.* panic, alarm, petrify, appal ▷**frighten** *ant.* calm

territory *n.* domain, area, expanse, dominion, land, terrain, property ▷**country**

terror *n.* horror, fear, alarm, panic, dismay ▷**fright**

test ① *n.* exam, quiz, trial, check, criterion, experiment ② *v.* examine, quiz, try out, check, analyse, question, evaluate

text *n.* book, manual, content, wording, passage, print, copy

thanks *n.* gratitude, appreciation, credit *Everyone gave her credit for rescuing the boy from the icy lake.* recognition

thaw *v.* melt, liquefy, soften *ant.* freeze

theft *n.* robbery, burglary, looting, piracy, shoplifting, plagiarism, fraud, larceny

Confusable Words

their means *belonging to them*
there means *in that place*
they're means *they are*

theme *n.* subject, topic, motif, tune

theory *n.* idea, concept, premise, hypothesis, supposition, speculation, explanation

therefore *adv.* thus, then, hence, consequently, accordingly

thick *adj.* dense, solid, bulky, compact, heavy, wide, crowded, deep *ant.* thin

thief *n.* crook, robber, burglar, bandit, pirate, shoplifter, pickpocket

thin *adj.* ① slender, slim, skinny, lean, slight, spare, spindly *ant.* fat ② sheer, fine, delicate, flimsy ③ narrow ④ watery, diluted, unsubstantial ⑤ sparse, scattered, meagre *ant.* thick

thing *n.* ① article, object, substance, item, device, gadget, entity ② event, deed, act

think *v.* ① ponder, wonder, contemplate, mull ▷**reflect** ② believe, suppose, suspect, conclude, imagine, presume, conceive, surmise ▷**reckon**

thirsty *adj.* parched, dry, craving, burning

thorough *adj.* ① absolute, complete, outright, utter ② detailed, exhaustive, intensive, careful *ant.* incomplete

though *conj.* although, however, albeit, notwithstanding that

thought *n.* idea, notion, reflection, consideration, study, concept, opinion, feeling, reasoning

thoughtful *adj.* ① reflective, pensive, studious, contemplative ② considerate, kind, attentive, careful *ant.* thoughtless

thoughtless *adj.* careless, rash, impulsive, unthinking, inconsiderate, heedless, inattentive ▷**indiscreet** *ant.* thoughtful

thrash *v.* ① beat *Each wave beat mercilessly against the rocks.* whip, flog, lash ② toss, turn, flail

thread *n.* yarn, fibre, strand, filament

threaten *v.* ① intimidate, bully, torment, terrorize, menace ▷**endanger** ② loom, impend, warn, forebode

thrifty *adj.* frugal, economical, saving, sparing, careful *ant.* wasteful

thrilling *adj.* exciting, gripping, stimulating

Thrash

Each wave beat mercilessly against the rocks.

thrive *v.* prosper, flourish, grow, bloom, boom, succeed *ant.* wane

throb ① *n.* rhythm, pulse, beat, palpitation ② *v.* beat, pulsate, thrum, vibrate, palpitate

throng *n.* multitude, mob, horde

throttle *v.* choke, smother, gag, suppress ▷**strangle**

Confusable Words

through means *in, over, by, during*

threw means *tossed*

throw *v.* fling, toss, pitch, shoot, cast, thrust, chuck, hurl, project, propel, roll, knock *ant.* catch *hom.* throe

thrust *v. & n.* push, poke, ram, jab, prod, drive, force, stab

thug *n.* bully, gangster, mugger, bandit, hoodlum, assassin

thump *v & n* beat, hit, knock, bang, wallop

thus *adv.* so, therefore, accordingly, hence, consequently

thwart *v.* hinder, obstruct, frustrate, block, foil, baffle *ant.* assist

ticket *n.* ① pass, label, card, coupon, token, tag ② key, secret, route, passport

tickle *v.* ① caress, stroke, brush, titillate, itch, tease, tingle ② please, amuse, delight

tide *n.* current, drift, ebb, flow, stream *hom.* tied

tidy *adj.* ① neat, well-kept, orderly, trim, shipshape ② substantial, considerable sizable

tie ① *v.* join, secure *Be sure to secure the gate so the dogs can't get out.* unite, link, knot, bind, relate ▷**fasten** ② *n.* cravat, necktie, bow tie ③ *n.* bond, connection ④ *n.* draw, stalemate

tight *adj.* ① fast, tense, secure ▷**taut** *ant.* loose ② cramped, close, compact ③ miserly, penny-pinching, cheap ▷**stingy** *ant.* generous

tighten *v.* strain, tense, narrow, stiffen, constrict, secure ▷**squeeze** *ant.* loosen

till ① *prep.* until, up to ② *v.* plough, cultivate, turn, hoe ③ *n.* cash register, money box

tilt *v. & n.* slant, slope, incline, lean, list, tip, lurch

time *n.* ① period, duration, term, span, interval, interlude, season, age, era ② metre, step, tempo, rhythm *hom.* thyme

timid *adj.* bashful, unassertive, afraid, fearful, diffident ▷**shy** *ant.* bold

tinge *v. & n.* colour, tint, shade, stain

tingle *v.* sting, smart, prickle, vibrate, tickle, thrill

tinkle *v.* jingle, jangle, ring, clink

tint *n. & v.* dye, tinge, shade, tone, colour

tiny *adj.* small, puny, miniature, diminutive ▷**little** *ant.* huge

tip ① *n.* peak, point, apex, extremity ▷**top** ② *n.* gratuity, gift, bonus, reward ③ *n.* clue, information, hint, cue ④ *v.* lean, tilt, incline ▷**slope** ⑤ overturn

tire *v.* exhaust, fatigue, weary, tax, strain, bore, weaken, flag

title *n.* ① name, term, denomination, designation ② possession, claim, right, ownership ③ publication

Titles

Admiral	Lama
Ambassador	Lieutenant
Archbishop	Madame, Sir
Baron, Baroness	Maharajah, Maharani
Begum, Shah	Major
Brigadier	Mandarin
Cardinal	Marchioness, Marquis
Chancellor	Margrave
Colonel	Marshal
Commodore	Master, Mistress
Constable	Mayor
Countess, Count	Mikado
Czar, Czarina	Mogul
Dame	Monsignor
Deacon	Pasha
Dean	Pope
Don, Doña	Princess, Prince
Duchess, Duke	Professor
Earl, Countess	Queen, King
Emir	Rabbi
Empress, Emperor	Regent
General	Senator
Governor	Sergeant
Graf, Gräfin	Sheik
Infanta	Sheriff
Kaiser	Shogun
Khan	Sultan, Sultana
Knight	Taoiseach
Lady, Lord	Viceroy, Vicereine
Laird	Viscount, Viscountess

Professor

n. = noun
v. = verb
adj. = adjective
adv. = adverb
conj. = conjunction
prep. = preposition
ant. = antonym
hom. = homonym
▷ = cross-reference

toast *v.* ① drink to, salute, pay tribute to, hail, compliment ② brown, roast, grill, broil, bake

together *adv.* jointly, unitedly, collectively, simultaneously, concurrently

toil *v. & n.* struggle, labour, grind ▷**work** *ant.* rest

token *n.* memento *I hope you will think of me when you wear this small memento of my friendship.* keepsake, sign, symbol

tolerable *adj.* bearable, endurable, acceptable, passable *ant.* unbearable

tolerant *adj.* indulgent *Her parents are a little too indulgent where bedtime is concerned.* liberal, open-minded ▷**lenient** *ant.* intolerant

tolerate *v.* accept, permit, allow, endure, abide ▷**bear** *ant.* forbid

toll ① *v.* ring, chime, clang, strike, knell ② *n.* charge, duty, tax, levy, fee, cost

tone *n.* ① note, pitch, sound, timbre ② emphasis, accent, inflection, intonation ③ temper, air, manner, attitude ④ colour, hue, shade, tint, cast

too *adv.* ① also, as well ② extremely, excessively, unduly

tool *n.* ① implement, appliance, device, gadget, utensil, machine, means ② pawn, puppet, dupe, stooge

top ① *n.* summit, pinnacle, peak, crest, tip, crown, apex *ant.* bottom ② *n.* lid, cover, cap, stopper ③ *adj.* highest, topmost, best, uppermost, excellent, maximum

topic *n.* theme, motif, question ▷**subject**

topical *adj.* ① up-to-date, current, contemporary, popular ② thematic

topple *v.* collapse, totter, surrender, upset, overthrow, overturn ▷**fall**

torment *v. & n.* pain, distress, plague ▷**torture** *ant.* comfort

torrent *n.* flood, stream, cascade, waterfall, cataract *ant.* trickle

torture ① *n.* agony, pain, anguish ② *v.* rack, oppress, persecute ▷**torment**

toss *v.* fling, pitch, heave, hurl, cast ▷**throw**

total ① *n.* whole, sum, amount, aggregate ② *v.* add, calculate, equal, work out to ③ *adj.* complete, entire, full

totally *adv.* completely, absolutely, entirely, utterly *ant.* partially

touch ① *v.* feel, fondle, handle, stroke, pat, caress, rub, brush, graze ② *v.* affect, concern ③ *v.* contact, move, stir, adjoin *Our home is in Lloydminster, where Alberta and Saskatchewan adjoin.* meet, border ④ *n.* feeling, palpation ⑤ *n.* hint, trace, shade

touchy *adj.* grumpy, testy, sensitive, prickly ▷**moody** *ant.* genial

tough *adj.* ① strong, rugged, sturdy, hardy, vigorous, durable, firm ② difficult, demanding, arduous

tour *n.* trip, journey, excursion, voyage, ride, visit, course, circuit

tournament *n.* contest, championship, competition, joust, match

tow *v.* haul, drag, tug, lug, pull *hom.* toe

tower ① *v.* soar, rise, loom ② *n.* turret, spire, belfry, skyscraper

toy ① *n.* trinket, novelty, doll, game, plaything ② *v.* trifle, play, flirt, tinker, fiddle, twiddle

Toys

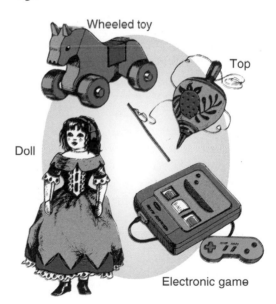

Wheeled toy

Top

Doll

Electronic game

T *t* **T** *t* **T** *t* **T**

trace ① *v.* trail, track, follow, pursue, find, hunt down ② *v.* sketch, draw, copy, etch ③ *n.* drop, speck, hint

track *v.* monitor, plot, follow, trail, pursue ▷**trace**

tract *n.* area, expanse, extent, plot *hom.* tracked

trade ① *v.* barter, exchange, swap, change, buy, sell, deal ② *n.* occupation, livelihood, business ③ *n.* commerce, traffic

tradition *n.* custom, convention, practice, habit, usage, heritage, lore

traffic *n.* ① transport, vehicles, movement ② business, commerce, dealing, trade

tragedy *n.* catastrophe, disaster, adversity ▷**calamity** *ant.* success

tragic *adj.* disastrous, catastrophic, calamitous, wretched ▷**deplorable**

trail *n.* track, scent, path, wake, traces

train ① *v.* teach, educate, instruct, drill, school, tutor, coach, discipline ② *n.* chain, procession, series

traitor *n.* betrayer, rebel, mutineer, renegade, deserter, turncoat, dissident

tramp ① *n.* vagabond, wanderer, vagrant, hobo, beggar ② *v.* roam, rove, trudge, hike, slog, march, stomp, plod

trample *v.* stamp, stomp, tramp, tread, flatten ▷**crush**

tranquil *adj.* peaceful, placid, serene, restful ▷**calm** *ant.* restless

transaction *n.* deal, dealing, negotiation, agreement, bargain, business, sale

transfer *v.* move, displace, change, convert, switch, pass

transmit *v.* radio, forward, relay *I probably won't see Paul until tomorrow, so would you please relay this information to him today?* broadcast, communicate, pass ▷**send** *ant.* accept

transparent *adj.* clear, lucid, crystal, sheer, filmy, see-through, self-evident, obvious

transport *v.* carry, convey, conduct, transfer, bear, haul, deliver, move

trap ① *v.* catch, capture, entrap, net, ensnare ② *n.* snare, decoy, lure, pitfall, noose, ambush

trash *n.* garbage, junk, waste, rubble, debris ▷**rubbish** *ant.* prize

travel *v.* & *n.* trek, voyage, cruise ▷**journey**

treacherous *adj.* traitorous *The traitorous crew abandoned the ship and its captain.* unfaithful, deceptive, disloyal, perilous, unsafe *ant.* faithful, safe

tread ① *v.* step, walk, tramp, march, go ② *n.* stride, gait, step, footstep, footfall

treason *n.* treachery, betrayal, disloyalty, sedition

treasure ① *n.* fortune, riches, wealth, hoard ② *v.* appreciate, esteem, cherish ▷**value**

treat ① *v.* deal with, handle, regard, use, serve ② *v.* entertain, amuse, regale, take out, pay for ③ *v.* nurse, doctor, attend to, medicate ④ *n.* pleasure, celebration, gift, goody, reward

treaty *n.* agreement, accord, pact, charter, covenant, alliance, understanding

tremble *v.* quake, quaver, shudder ▷**shake**

tremendous *adj.* ① immense, enormous, giant ▷**huge** ② terrible, dreadful, awful, fearful

tremor *n.* earthquake, quiver, shake, flutter, ripple, vibration ▷**quake**

trench *n.* ditch, moat, trough, gully, gutter

trend *n.* ① tendency, movement, direction ② fashion, style, fad

trespass ① *v.* infringe *I'll move away as I don't want to infringe on your private workspace.* overstep, intrude, break in, offend ② *n.* offence, sin, crime, violation

trial *n.* ① test, experiment ② ordeal, affliction, suffering, hardship ③ effort, attempt, endeavour ④ hearing, lawsuit

tribe *n.* ① clan, family group ② people, gang

tribute *n.* testimonial, salute, ovation, praise, compliment

trick ① *n.* fraud, deception, con, hoax, swindle, ruse ② *n.* joke, gag, caper, prank ③ *n.* magic, illusion, feat, stunt ④ *v.* deceive, defraud, fool, bluff, outwit, cheat, dupe

trickle *v.* leak, ooze, seep, drip, drop, dribble

trifling *adj.* petty, worthless, slight, unimportant, paltry ▷**trivial** *ant.* important

trim ① *v.* prune, clip, shorten, crop ② *v.* decorate, adorn, ornament ③ *adj.* tidy, neat, orderly, sleek *ant.* scruffy

trip ① *n.* journey, outing, visit, voyage, excursion, jaunt ▷**tour** ② *v.* stumble, fall, slip, skip, falter, stagger

triumph *n.* victory, achievement, conquest ▷**success** *ant.* defeat

trivial *adj.* common, unimportant, petty, little, ordinary, minor, trifling, trite ▷**insignificant** *ant.* important

troop *n.* band, gang, group, pack, team, unit, company, squad, assembly *hom.* troupe

trophy *n.* prize, award, cup, souvenir

trot *v.* jog, canter, scamper, lope

trouble ① *n.* disturbance, distress, hardship, calamity, misfortune ▷**misery** ② *n.* difficulty, annoyance, inconvenience ③ *v.* bother, disturb, upset, worry ▷**distress**

true *adj.* ① accurate, precise, factual, correct *ant.* inaccurate ② faithful, loyal, constant, honest, reliable ③ pure, real, actual ▷**genuine** *ant.* fake

trunk *n.* ① chest, case, box ② nose, snout, proboscis ③ body, torso, stem, stalk

trust ① *n.* faith, confidence, belief, reliance, assurance ② *v.* believe, confide in, credit, rely on *ant.* doubt *hom.* trussed

trustworthy *adj.* dependable, credible, honourable, faithful ▷**reliable** *ant.* unreliable

truth *n.* reality, honesty, certainty, veracity, accuracy ▷**fact** *ant.* falsehood

truthful *adj.* open, sincere, candid, straight, forthright, frank, reliable ▷**honest** *ant.* dishonest

try ① *v.* endeavour, attempt, aspire ▷**strive** ② *v.* sample, taste, experience, examine, test *ant.* decline ③ *n.* trial, attempt, effort, crack, stab, shot

tub *n.* basin, bowl, pot, container, vat

tube *n.* pipe, spout, duct, hose, shaft

tuck *v.* insert, stuff, fold, pack, hide

tug *v.* drag, tow, haul, schlep ▷**pull** *ant.* push

tumble *v.* drop, descend, trip, topple, stumble, collapse ▷**plunge**

tumult *n.* noise, racket, uproar, disturbance, disorder *ant.* peace

tune *n.* melody, theme, air, strain ▷**song**

tunnel *n.* subway, shaft, passage, gallery

turn ① *v.* spin, revolve, whirl, swivel ▷**rotate** ② *v.* bend, curve, reverse, flip ▷**twist** ③ *v.* change, alter, divert ▷**convert** ④ *v.* deviate, stray, wander ⑤ *v.* aim, direct ⑥ *v.* spoil, sour ⑦ *n.* stint *After a short stint of lifting the heavy crates, I had to rest.* tour, watch, spell, chance, move ⑧ *n.* rotation, cycle, gyration, twist, movement, revolution *hom.* tern

twinge *n.* stab, pang, spasm, gripe ▷**ache**

twinkle *v.* glitter, gleam, glisten, glimmer, blink, flash ▷**sparkle**

twist *v.* ① bend, curve, turn, wring ② warp, contort, writhe ③ wind, coil, twine

twitch *v.* jerk, jump, jiggle, blink, flutter

Confusable Words

two	means *one more than one*
to	means *toward*
too	means *also, more than necessary*

type ① *n.* kind, sort, character, description, class, group ② *n.* prototype, model, pattern ③ *v.* keyboard, input, enter

typical *adj.* characteristic, representative, symbolic, regular, stock, classic, common, distinctive *ant.* unusual

tyrant *n.* despot, autocrat, dictator, martinet

U u

ugly *adj.* unattractive, homely, plain, unsightly, ungainly, repulsive, ghastly, hideous, horrid, nasty *ant.* beautiful

ultimate *adj.* furthest, farthest, extreme, eventual, supreme, last, maximum, final

umpire *n.* referee, judge, mediator

unabashed *adj.* unconcerned, composed, brazen, shameless ▷**bold** *ant.* discouraged

unable *adj.* unfit, incapable, helpless, powerless *ant.* able

unaccustomed *adj.* inexperienced, unfamiliar, unacquainted, strange

unaffected *adj.* natural, sincere, true, artless, simple ▷**genuine** *ant.* insincere

unafraid *adj.* courageous, brave, intrepid, dauntless ▷**fearless** *ant.* afraid

unanimous *adj.* concurrent, in agreement, universal, common, unqualified *Don's excellent field trip suggestion had the unqualified approval of the class.* ▷**united**

unassuming *adj.* reserved, quiet, simple, modest, diffident ▷**humble** *ant.* forward

unattached *adj.* single, free, loose ▷**separate** *ant.* united

unavoidable *adj.* inevitable, irresistible, certain, sure, necessary *ant.* unlikely

unaware *adj.* ignorant, unheeding, forgetful, unknowing ▷**oblivious** *ant.* aware

unbalanced *adj.* ① top-heavy, lopsided, uneven ② insane, unhinged, crazy, eccentric, deranged, irrational

unbearable *adj.* painful, trying, intolerable, impossible, unendurable, unacceptable ▷**outrageous** *ant.* tolerable

unbiassed *adj.* impartial, fair, just ▷**neutral** *ant.* prejudiced

uncanny *adj.* weird, unearthly, creepy, eerie, mysterious, extraordinary ▷**strange**

uncertain *adj.* dubious, vague, indefinite, questionable, debatable ▷**doubtful** *ant.* certain

uncivilized *adj.* primitive, barbaric, coarse, gross, rude, wild ▷**vulgar** *ant.* refined

uncomfortable *adj.* awkward, embarrassed, cramped, self-conscious, distressing, uneasy *ant.* comfortable

uncommon *adj.* rare, scarce, infrequent, extraordinary ▷**unusual** *ant.* common

unconscious *adj.* ① ignorant, oblivious ▷**unaware** ② insensible, senseless, stunned, dazed, comatose *ant.* conscious

unconventional *adj.* unusual, strange, unorthodox, peculiar, individualistic, noncomformist ▷**eccentric** *ant.* regular

uncouth *adj.* crude, boorish, ill-mannered, vulgar, unrefined ▷**coarse** *ant.* polite

uncover *v.* expose, discover, show, divulge, bare, unwrap, betray ▷**reveal** *ant.* conceal

under *prep.* less than, lower than, subject to, underneath, below, beneath

undergo *v.* submit to, tolerate, sustain, suffer, experience ▷**bear**

underground *adj.* ① secret, clandestine, hidden, subversive ② subterranean

underhand *adj.* stealthy, undercover, shifty, deceitful, sneaky ▷**dishonest** *ant.* honest

underneath *prep.* beneath, under, below *ant.* above

underrate *v.* undervalue, understate, disparage *My jealous competitor disparaged my efforts, and was very surprised when I won the ribbon.* misjudge *ant.* exaggerate

understand *v.* grasp, take in, figure out, catch, comprehend, fathom, follow, appreciate, sympathize, gather ▷**realize** *ant.* misunderstand

undertake *v.* attempt, commence, contract, embark on, start, assume ▷**tackle**

undesirable *adj.* objectionable, distasteful, unwelcome ▷**unpleasant** *ant.* desirable

undignified *adj.* improper, inelegant, clumsy, unseemly ▷**foolish** *ant.* graceful

undo *v.* unfasten, disentangle, unravel, open, loose, loosen, untie, cancel *ant.* fasten

uneasy *adj.* uncomfortable, restless, self-conscious, edgy, anxious, awkward *ant.* calm

unemployed *adj.* unoccupied, jobless, out of work, idle

uneven *adj.* irregular, rough, bumpy, lopsided, unequal, unbalanced, unsteady, inconsistent *ant.* even

unexpected *adj.* abrupt, unplanned, chance, surprising ▷**sudden** *ant.* usual

unfair *adj.* prejudiced, one-sided, partial, unjust, discriminatory *ant.* fair

unfaithful *adj.* fickle, faithless, untrue, false, disloyal, traitorous *ant.* faithful

unfamiliar *adj.* alien, new, unknown *It is an adventure to travel in unknown territory.* unacquainted, bizarre ▷**strange** *ant.* familiar

unfasten *v.* release, open, unlatch, untie, unhitch, unbuckle ▷**undo** *ant.* fasten

unfinished *adj.* incomplete, imperfect, crude, rough *ant.* complete

unfit *adj.* unqualified, unsuitable, incapablc, inappropriate, inadequate, incompetent *ant.* suitable

unfold *v.* open, expand, develop, explain, be revealed, unravel, spread out *ant.* conceal

unforeseen *adj.* surprising, sudden, accidental ▷**unexpected** *ant.* probable

unforgettable *adj.* memorable, impressive, noteworthy, exceptional

unfortunate *adj.* deplorable, lamentable, adverse, unhappy, hapless, inappropriate ▷**unlucky** *ant.* fortunate

unfriendly *adj.* antagonistic, surly, cold, aloof, antisocial, distant ▷**hostile** *ant.* friendly

ungrateful *adj.* thankless, unappreciative, ungracious, ill-mannered *ant.* grateful

unhappiness *n.* sadness, misery, gloom, discontent, disappointment, depression

unhappy *adj.* miserable, morose *My friend Tom was morose for weeks after he found out I was moving away.* melancholy, gloomy, blue, dismal, doleful, wretched, forlorn ▷**sad** *ant.* happy

unhealthy *adj.* ① sick, ill, diseased *ant.* healthy ② harmful, unwholesome

uniform ① *n.* costume, dress, outfit ② *adj.* unvarying, steady, unchanging, level, even, consistent *ant.* uneven

unimportant *adj.* insignificant, trivial, little, puny ▷**petty** *ant.* important

Uniform

unintentional *adj.* inadvertent, involuntary, unplanned, unwitting, accidental *ant.* deliberate

union *n.* ① alliance, association, league, club, organization, society ② agreement, accord, harmony ③ fusion, blend, compound, junction

unique *adj.* rare, special, original, single, sole, exceptional, exclusive *ant.* common

unit *n.* entity, whole, individual

unite *v.* join, combine, merge, blend, fuse, rally, bond *ant.* separate

united *adj.* ① joined, combined, undivided ② in agreement, harmonious ▷**unanimous**

unity *n.* union, harmony, accord, agreement, solidarity *ant.* discord

universal *adj.* global, planetary, cosmic, worldwide *Canada's physical beauty has worldwide appeal.* general, all-embracing

unjust *adj.* oppressive, unfair, prejudiced, biassed ▷**wrong** *ant.* just

unkind *adj.* inhuman, heartless, brutal, callous ▷**mean** *ant.* kind

unknown *adj.* hidden, obscure, alien, undiscovered, dark *ant.* familiar

unlike *adj.* unrelated, dissimilar, distinct, contrasting ▷**different** *ant.* similar

unlikely *adj.* rare, improbable, doubtful ▷**dubious** *ant.* likely

unlucky *adj.* unfortunate, luckless, ill-fated, unhappy, hapless *As night fell, the hapless campers realized they'd forgotten their tent.* jinxed, disappointing *ant.* lucky

unnatural *adj.* ① artificial, synthetic, phony, affected ② abnormal, strange, mysterious

U

unnecessary *adj.* non-essential, excess, superfluous, useless, irrelevant ▷**needless**

unoccupied *adj.* ① uninhabited, unreserved, deserted, empty ▷**vacant** ② unemployed, spare, free, unengaged ▷**idle** *ant.* occupied

unpleasant *adj.* disagreeable, displeasing, objectionable, bad ▷**offensive** *ant.* pleasant

unpopular *adj.* obnoxious, detested, shunned, unfashionable, disliked *ant.* popular

unqualified *adj.* ① unable, incompetent, inadequate ▷**unfit** ② complete, thorough, absolute, unconditional, utter

unreal *adj.* imaginary, fictional, artificial, false, fanciful *ant.* real

unreasonable *adj.* ① extravagant, extreme, excessive *ant.* moderate ② far-fetched, absurd, illogical, foolish, outrageous

unreliable *adj.* untrustworthy, undependable, irresponsible ▷**fickle** *ant.* reliable

unrest *n.* ① disquiet, rebellion, storm, turmoil ② anxiety, distress, worry, restlessness, unease *ant.* peace

unrestricted *adj.* unrestrained, unlimited, open, free, unhindered *ant.* limited

unripe *adj.* green, immature, callow, unseasoned, unready *ant.* ripe

unrivalled *adj.* inimitable *More than anything, she admired his inimitable style of dancing.* unequalled, matchless, peerless, unique *ant.* ordinary

unruly *adj.* disorderly, troublesome, unmanageable, wild, disobedient, defiant ▷**rowdy** *ant.* orderly

unselfish *adj.* generous, liberal, charitable, hospitable, selfless ▷**kind** *ant.* selfish

unstable *adj.* ① unsteady, shaky, rickety, wobbly ② fickle, volatile, unbalanced, insecure *ant.* stable

unsuitable *adj.* unqualified, ineligible, unfit, inappropriate *ant.* suitable

untidy *adj.* bedraggled, disorderly, muddled, messy, chaotic, disorganized, scruffy, slovenly *ant.* tidy

untie *v.* unfasten, unravel, free, release ▷**undo**

until *prep.* till, as far as, up to

untimely *adj.* inopportune, ill-timed, premature, early, inconvenient

unusual *adj.* strange, queer, exceptional, quaint, curious, unique, different, rare, remarkable, atypical ▷**odd** *ant.* normal

unwilling *adj.* averse, slow, grudging, opposed, hesitant ▷**reluctant** *ant.* willing

upheaval *n.* disturbance, disruption, turmoil, shake-up, revolution

uphold *v.* sustain, keep up, endorse ▷**support**

upper *adj.* higher, superior, more elevated, uppermost *ant.* lower

upright *adj.* ① standing, perpendicular, erect, vertical *ant.* flat ② honourable, ethical, virtuous, honest *ant.* dishonest

uproar *n.* noise, clamour, tumult, turmoil, hue and cry ▷**disorder**

upset ① *v.* bother, perturb *It perturbed me that she still hadn't arrived after I'd waited for an hour.* unsettle, annoy, disturb, irritate, offend, distress ② *v.* overthrow, overturn, topple, capsize ③ *adj.* disturbed, angry, worried, agitated, perturbed, indignant, distraught

urge ① *v.* goad, plead with, spur, beseech, beg, push, press, coax, prompt, insist ② *n.* desire, compulsion, itch ▷**impulse**

urgent *adj.* critical, pressing, vital, burning

use ① *v.* (yooz) employ, practise, apply, exploit, utilize, operate ② *v.* (yooz) consume, exhaust, deplete, expend ③ *n.* (yoos) usage, benefit, application, utility, exercise, function

useful *adj.* worthwhile, sound, applicable, valuable, constructive, practical, beneficial, helpful, handy *ant.* useless

useless *adj.* ① hopeless, futile ② pointless, valueless, frivolous ▷**worthless** *ant.* useful

usual *adj.* common, general, habitual, familiar, regular, customary, conventional, ordinary ▷**normal** *ant.* extraordinary

utilize *v.* employ, apply, exploit, exercise

utmost *adj.* extreme, supreme, greatest, ultimate, last, furthest

utter ① *adj.* thorough, absolute, complete ② *v.* declare, pronounce, speak, voice

utterly *adv.* thoroughly, completely, entirely, fully, wholly

---

n. = noun
v. = verb
adj. = adjective
adv. = adverb
conj. = conjunction
prep. = preposition
ant. = antonym
hom. = homonym
▷ = cross-reference

V v

vacant *adj.* empty, unoccupied, blank *ant.* occupied

vacation *n.* holiday, rest, recess, intermission, break

vague *adj.* indefinite, imprecise, inexact, uncertain, ambiguous, approximate *If you can't remember exactly, just give me an approximate idea of what happened.* unclear, faint ▷**obscure** *ant.* certain

vain *adj.* ① conceited, self-absorbed, egotistical ▷**proud** *ant.* modest ② fruitless, useless ▷**futile** *hom.* vane, vein

valiant *adj.* gallant, daring, courageous, heroic, stout, worthy ▷**brave** *ant.* cowardly

valid *adj.* genuine, legitimate, reasonable, sound, official, proper

valley *n.* gorge, dale, glen, ravine, basin, vale

valour *n.* courage, fortitude, heroism, gallantry, bravery *ant.* cowardice

valuable *adj.* ① costly, precious, priceless, expensive *ant.* worthless ② worthwhile, helpful, useful, beneficial *The long, hot prairie summers are beneficial for growing wheat.* worthy

value ① *n.* worth, benefit, merit, importance ② *n.* price, rate ③ *v.* appreciate, esteem, prize, treasure, admire ④ *v.* appraise, assess, rate, estimate

vandalize *v.* damage, trash, deface, ruin, destroy, wreck, sabotage

vanish *v.* disappear, fade away, dissolve, depart, evaporate *ant.* appear

vanity *n.* pride, conceit, ego, egotism *ant.* modesty

vanquish *v.* conquer, defeat, overcome, subdue ▷**beat**

vapour *n.* steam, fog, mist, fumes, smoke

variable *adj.* changeable, fickle, capricious, wavering, uneven, unpredictable, fitful, erratic, volatile *ant.* constant

varied *adj.* various, diverse, miscellaneous, mixed, assorted *ant.* uniform

variety *n.* ① assortment, diversity, array, mixture, medley *The medley of songs included many of my favourites.* ② sort, type, kind, class, category, species, breed, brand

various *adj.* mixed, different, many, diverse, miscellaneous, assorted ▷**varied**

vary *v.* differ, alter, change, diversify, diverge, deviate

vase *n.* jug, jar, urn

vast *adj.* great, enormous, extensive, huge, wide, unmeasurable, giant ▷**immense** *ant.* narrow

vault ① *n.* safe, grave, mausoleum, cellar, crypt, dungeon ② *v.* jump, clear, bound, leap, hurdle, spring

veer *v.* swerve, skid, turn, tack, deviate, change

vehement *adj.* heated, fiery, passionate, forceful, violent, intense ▷**strong** *ant.* indifferent

vehicle *n.* ① car, automobile, conveyance, carriage, cart, transportation ② agency, means

veil ① *n.* cloak, cover, curtain ② *v.* hide, conceal, shade, screen, wrap, cover *ant.* expose *hom.* vale

Vehicles

Ambulance
Automobile
Bicycle
Bulldozer
Bus
Cab
Car
Cart
Chariot
Coach
Fire engine
Hearse
Jeep
Limousine
Motorcycle
Rickshaw
Sedan
Ski-Doo
Sled
Stagecoach

Streetcar
Subway
Surrey
Tank
Toboggan
Tractor
Train
Trap
Travois

Tricycle
Trolley bus
Truck
Wagon

V

vein *n.* ① seam, strain, streak, stripe, thread, course ② tone, mood, style *hom.* vain, vane

velocity *n.* rate, pace, tempo ▷**speed**

vengeance *n.* reprisal, retaliation, revenge

venomous *adj.* ① poisonous, toxic ② spiteful, malicious, hostile, malevolent ▷**vindictive**

vent ① *v.* discharge, exhaust, release ② *v.* voice, express, utter, air ③ *n.* aperture, duct, opening, outlet

ventilate *v.* air, aerate, cool, fan

venture ① *n.* enterprise, undertaking, endeavour, adventure, project ② *v.* chance, bet, hazard, gamble, presume ▷**risk**

verbal *adj.* stated, said, expressed, spoken, unwritten, oral *He used a tape recorder to preserve their oral legends.* told, literal *ant.* written

verdict *n.* decision, judgment, finding, conclusion, opinion, sentence

verge ① *n.* border, brink, edge, boundary, threshold ② *v.* incline, tend, border, adjoin

verify *v.* confirm, ascertain, authenticate, prove, corroborate *The note from her doctor corroborated her claim to being sick.* *ant.* contradict

versatile *adj.* adaptable, variable, adjustable, handy, multi-purpose, flexible

version *n.* story, account, variation, type, interpretation, adaptation

vertical *adj.* upright, erect, perpendicular, sheer, steep *ant.* flat

very ① *adv.* extremely, exceedingly, greatly, intensely, absolutely ② *adj.* exact, same, true, actual, sheer

vessel *n.* ① bowl, pot, canister, container, basin, jar, receptacle ② craft, ship, boat

vestige *n.* remains, remnant *My gerbil chewed my homework and this page is the only remnant of it.* hint, glimmer, residue, trace

veteran ① *n.* master, old hand, expert, pro *ant.* novice ② *adj.* experienced, practised, adept, skilled, seasoned *ant.* inexperienced

veto ① *v.* ban, reject, prohibit, stop, forbid, decline, deny, disallow, refuse, overturn ② *n.* embargo, prohibition, disapproval

vibrate *v.* shake, quiver, oscillate, throb, shudder, resonate, pulse ▷**tremble**

vice *n.* evil, failing, fault, corruption, immorality ▷**sin** *ant.* virtue

vicinity *n.* area, neighbourhood, locality, environs, surroundings

vicious *adj.* cruel, ruthless, savage, evil, violent, immoral ▷**wicked** *ant.* virtuous

victim *n.* sufferer, scapegoat, casualty, martyr, prey, pawn, dupe, quarry

victor *n.* winner, conqueror, champion

victory *n.* success, triumph, achievement

view ① *n.* landscape, sight, panorama, spectacle, scene, vista, outlook ② *n.* impression, belief, theory, opinion, perspective ③ *v.* watch, see, witness, scan, survey, inspect, examine, regard

vigilant *adj.* attentive, wary, alert, on guard ▷**watchful** *ant.* lax

vigorous *adj.* forceful, energetic, powerful, dynamic, lively, peppy, zealous, active ▷**strong** *ant.* weak

vigour *n.* energy, vim, stamina, enthusiasm, intensity, vitality, drive, spirit ▷**strength**

vile *adj.* low, wretched, contemptible, nasty, miserable, evil, filthy, foul, offensive ▷**despicable** *ant.* noble

villain *n.* scoundrel, criminal, culprit, outlaw, felon, rascal, rogue *ant.* hero

vim *n.* stamina, zip, strength, spirit, energy ▷**vigour**

vindicate *v.* confirm, support, defend, establish, uphold ▷**justify** *ant.* accuse

vindictive *adj.* vengeful, unforgiving, spiteful ▷**malicious** *ant.* merciful

violate *v.* ① disobey, dishonour, defy, resist, infringe, break, transgress *ant.* obey ② abuse, defile, outrage, desecrate, profane

violent *adj.* furious, rabid, vehement, unruly, forcible, raging, wild, turbulent *ant.* calm

virtually *adv.* almost, nearly, practically

virtue *n.* goodness, honesty, purity, decency, character, merit ▷**quality** *ant.* vice

virtuous *adj.* chaste, innocent, honourable, moral ▷**righteous** *ant.* wicked

visible *adj.* perceptible, discernible, apparent, exposed, obvious, noticeable

n. = noun
v. = verb
adj. = adjective
adv. = adverb
conj. = conjunction
prep. = preposition
ant. = antonym
hom. = homonym
▷ = cross-reference

vision n. ① eyesight, seeing, eyes
② revelation, foresight, imagination
③ apparition, spectre, ghost, mirage, dream

visit ① n. call, sojourn, stay, excursion
② v. call, tour, sojourn, drop in, stay

visitor n. guest, company, tourist, caller

vital adj. ① essential, indispensible,
▷**necessary** ② vibrant, dynamic, lively,
vivacious, energetic, vigorous

vitality n. stamina, animation, spirit, force,
vigour, dynamism ▷**strength**

vivacious adj. lively, spirited, animated,
exuberant ▷**sprightly** ant. languid

vivid adj. ① clear, bright ▷**brilliant**
② vigorous, strong, eloquent, colourful,
graphic ant. dull

vocal adj. ① spoken, verbal, voiced,
articulate, eloquent, outspoken ② strident,
vociferous ant. quiet

vogue n. style, fashion, mode, popularity

voice ① n. speech, words, articulation,
utterance ② n. say, choice, influence, vote
③ v. utter, express, verbalize

void ① adj. bare, barren, empty
② adj. invalid, cancelled, useless
③ n. cavity, chasm, space, nothingness,
emptiness, hole, gap

volatile adj. changeable, fickle, unstable,
unpredictable, capricious, elusive

volume n. ① bulk, capacity, mass, quantity,
extent, dimension, amount ② loudness,
amplitude ③ book, publication, edition

voluntary adj. deliberate, willing, free,
optional, intended, spontaneous, unforced
ant. compulsory

vote ① n. ballot, election, poll, referendum
② v. ballot, opt, choose, elect, select

vow ① v. promise, swear, assure, pledge,
undertake ② n. oath, pledge, promise

voyage n. trip, journey, cruise, passage

vulgar adj. common, coarse, crude,
indelicate, rude, tasteless, uncouth
ant. elegant

vulnerable adj. unprotected, unguarded,
exposed, defenceless, insecure, susceptible
ant. safe

W w

wad n. bundle, chunk, mass, plug, lump

waddle v. wobble, totter, shuffle, toddle

wag v. waggle, shake, wiggle, twitch

wage ① n. pay, salary, earnings, fee
② v. carry out, undertake *We are not
prepared to undertake another major
battle.* conduct, pursue

wager ① v. gamble, bet, speculate, chance,
hazard, stake ② n. pledge, stake, gamble

wagon n. cart, truck, van, trolley

wail ① v. weep, bawl, howl, lament, grieve,
mourn ▷**cry** ant. rejoice ② n. cry, moan,
howl, whine

wait v. await, pause, remain, lag, dawdle,
delay, stop ▷**linger** hom. weight

wait on v. serve, attend

waive v. relinquish, forego, disclaim
▷**renounce** hom. wave

wakeful adj. ① restless, awake ② alert,
vigilant, watchful

waken v. awaken, stimulate, excite ▷**rouse**

walk ① v. advance, march, step, progress,
move ② n. stroll, hike, promenade, march,
stride ▷**ramble** ant. run

wand n. baton, stick, sceptre, rod, mace

wander v. ① meander, roam, stroll, ramble,
saunter ② swerve, stray, deviate, digress

wane v. fade, subside, droop, decline,
decrease, lessen, ebb *By the time it was her
turn to perform, her nervousness had
ebbed away.* sink ant. grow

want ① v. desire, crave, need, require, wish,
long for, hope, covet, fancy ② n. hardship,
need, necessity, demand ③ n. absence,
poverty, deficiency ▷**scarcity** ant. plenty

war n. hostilities, fighting, bloodshed,
conflict, battle, struggle, strife, combat
ant. peace

wardrobe n. outfit, clothes, apparel

warm ① adj. tepid, mild, lukewarm,
sunny ② adj. sympathetic, friendly,
approachable, kindhearted ▷**cordial**
③ v. heat, cheer, bask

warn *v.* alert, caution, alarm, forewarn, admonish, advise, apprise *hom.* worn

warning *n.* caution, alarm, tip, admonition

warp *v.* contort, bend, twist, kink, deform, distort, bias, corrupt

warrant ① *n.* order, reason, justification, licence, authorization ② *v.* guarantee, certify, justify, authorize, license, call for

wary *adj.* cautious, shy, careful, watchful, heedful *Be heedful of traffic when crossing the street.* ▷**suspicious** *ant.* rash

wash ① *v.* launder, scrub, rinse, cleanse, wet ② *n.* laundry, washing, clothes

waste ① *n.* misuse, loss ② *n.* sewage, garbage, rubbish, debris, trash ③ *v.* squander, misspend, lavish, fritter ④ *v.* wither, decay, shrivel, perish *hom.* waist

wasteful *adj.* lavish, prodigal, spendthrift ▷**extravagant** *ant.* economical

watch ① *v.* view, gaze at, witness, regard ② *v.* note, observe, guard, spy on, oversee, mind, attend *ant.* ignore ③ *n.* timepiece ④ *n.* guard, sentry, surveillance, vigil

watchful *adj.* attentive, observant, vigilant *The vigilant babysitter watched the children closely while they played in the park.* alert ▷**wary** *ant.* inattentive

water ① *v.* wet, douse, drench, sprinkle, spray, irrigate ② *v.* dilute ③ *n.* river, stream, lake, pond, ocean, sea

wave ① *v.* brandish, flourish, swing, flutter, flap, sway ② *n.* ripple, swell, breaker, billow, undulation *hom.* waive

waver *v.* falter, hesitate, vacillate, sway, swing *ant.* decide

way *n.* ① course, route, road, path, passage, track ② technique, manner, mode, procedure, method, style *hom.* weigh

weak *adj.* ① feeble, frail, puny, helpless, delicate, infirm, sickly ② foolish, soft, senseless, stupid ③ thin, watery, insipid, diluted ④ fragile, flimsy, shaky, unreliable ⑤ dim *ant.* strong *hom.* week

weaken *v.* enfeeble, relax, sag, flag, disable, cripple, paralyse, sap, tire, give way ▷**languish** *ant.* nourish

weakness *n.* defect, fault, frailty, feebleness, fragility, exhaustion *ant.* strength

wealth *n.* fortune, abundance, affluence, riches, luxury, prosperity, money, opulence *ant.* poverty

wealthy *adj.* rich, affluent, prosperous, well-off, opulent *ant.* poor

wear *v.* ① sport, carry, don ② irritate, fray, rub, scrape, waste, tire, drain ③ last, endure, remain *hom.* ware

weary ① *adj.* exhausted, tired, fatigued, sleepy, drowsy, jaded *ant.* fresh ② *v.* exhaust, tire, bore *ant.* refresh

weave *v.* ① braid, plait, integrate, spin, interlace ② lurch, sway, wind, wander

web *n.* net, tissue, webbing, network, fabric, mesh, tangle

wed *v.* marry, join, link, splice, tie the knot, combine

wedge ① *n.* block, chock, slice, chunk ② *v.* stuff, force, jam, push, thrust, squeeze

weep *v.* blubber, snivel, sob, lament, wail, mourn, drip, ooze, whimper *The lost child was found at last, whimpering in a corner.* ▷**cry** *ant.* rejoice

weigh *v.* balance, estimate, ponder, examine, consider *hom.* way

weight *n.* ① load, pressure, burden, heaviness ② importance, significance, influence, scope, gravity *hom.* wait

weighty *adj.* heavy, hefty, ponderous, onerous, important, grave, influential *ant.* trivial

weird *adj.* ① eerie, supernatural, unearthly, mysterious ▷**uncanny** ② odd, strange, unusual, curious, funny

welcome ① *adj.* pleasing, desirable, grateful ▷**agreeable** ② *v.* greet, accost, hail, salute, receive, accept, host ③ *n.* greeting, salutation, acceptance, reception

welfare *n.* well-being, comfort, happiness, benefit, advantage, good, prosperity, success, relief *ant.* harm

well ① *adj.* robust, healthy, hearty, sound *ant.* ill ② *adv.* properly, excellently, adequately, accurately, correctly, completely ③ *n.* fountain, spring, source

n. = noun
v. = verb
adj. = adjective
adv. = adverb
conj. = conjunction
prep. = preposition
ant. = antonym
hom. = homonym
▷ = cross-reference

Weather

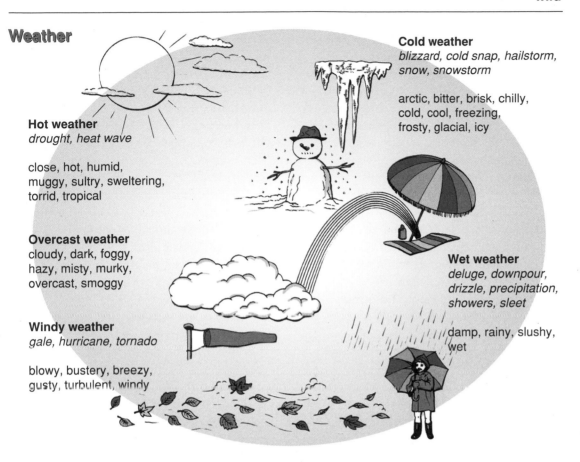

Hot weather
drought, heat wave

close, hot, humid, muggy, sultry, sweltering, torrid, tropical

Overcast weather
cloudy, dark, foggy, hazy, misty, murky, overcast, smoggy

Windy weather
gale, hurricane, tornado

blowy, bustery, breezy, gusty, turbulent, windy

Cold weather
blizzard, cold snap, hailstorm, snow, snowstorm

arctic, bitter, brisk, chilly, cold, cool, freezing, frosty, glacial, icy

Wet weather
deluge, downpour, drizzle, precipitation, showers, sleet

damp, rainy, slushy, wet

---

well-off *adj.* comfortable, well-fixed, prosperous ▷**wealthy** *ant.* poor

wet ① *adj.* moist, damp, watery, drenched, soggy, saturated *Tia sprayed the flower beds until the soil was saturated.* flooded ② *adj.* drizzling, showery, rainy ③ *v.* soak, moisten, dampen, irrigate, douse, drench

whet *v.* ① sharpen, hone, strop, grind ② excite, stimulate, arouse *ant.* satisfy

whim *n.* desire, urge, notion, impulse, fancy

whine *v.* ① howl, wail, whimper, moan, cry, snivel ② complain, grouse, grumble

whip *v.* ① beat, flog, lash, thrash, chastise, spank ② whisk, mix, stir

whirl *v.* pirouette, twirl, spin, rotate, revolve, spiral, gyrate, swirl

whisk *v.* ① mix, beat, stir ▷**whip** ② rush, hasten, hurry, spirit, sweep

whisper ① *n.* murmur, sigh, undertone, rustle ② *n.* hint, suggestion ③ *v.* breathe, murmur, mouth *ant.* shout ④ *v.* hint, confide, divulge

whistle *n. & v.* cheep, chirp, warble, call

whole *adj.* all, entire, total, full, intact, sound, complete, unbroken *hom.* hole

wholesome *adj.* clean, healthy, healthful, nutritious, beneficial, sound, good

wicked *adj.* infamous, corrupt, depraved, bad, immoral, malevolent, sinister, sinful ▷**evil** *ant.* virtuous

wickedness *n.* evil, corruption, depravity, infamy, sinfulness, villainy *ant.* goodness

wide *adj.* broad, deep, large, full, ample, extended, spacious, roomy, extensive, vast *ant.* narrow

widespread *adj.* prevalent, far-flung, general, common, prevailing, extensive, sweeping, popular *Contrary to popular belief, bats are not blind. ant.* limited

wield *v.* ① brandish, flourish, manipulate, handle ② exercise, exert, maintain

wild *adj.* ① untamed, natural ② savage, uncivilized, barbarous ③ violent, frenzied, unrestrained, ④ careless, reckless, unruly

wilderness *n.* desert, badlands, wasteland, wilds, outback, barrens, tundra

will ① *n.* option, choice, freedom ② *n.* resolution *In spite of their criticism, his resolution never wavered.* zeal, resolve, determination ③ *n.* order, wish, command, request, demand ④ *n.* legacy, testament ⑤ *v.* choose, desire, elect

willful *adj.* temperamental, headstrong, deliberate, intentional ▷**obstinate** *ant.* docile, unintentional

willing *adj.* disposed, zealous, ready, earnest, inclined, agreeable *ant.* unwilling

wilt *v.* shrivel, waste, sag, collapse, droop, flag, slouch, ebb ▷**wither**

wily *adj.* crafty, sly, tricky, deceitful, artful, clever ▷**cunning** *ant.* sincere

win *v.* succeed, triumph, get, acquire, secure, be victorious, overcome ▷**gain** *ant.* lose

wince *v.* shrink, quail, flinch, start, cringe

wind (rhymes with *pinned*) *n.* breeze, blast, gust, gale, air, draft

wind (rhymes with *mind*) *v.* coil, turn, twist, bend, snake, twine, weave *hom.* wined

wink *n. & v.* blink, flutter, flicker, glint, flash

winner *n.* champion, master ▷**victor**

wipe *v.* clean, brush, mop, remove, swab, blot, polish, rub

wire *n.* ① cord, flex ② cable, telegraph, telegram

wisdom *n.* judgment, discretion, tact, reason, sense, insight, knowledge

wise *adj.* intelligent, learned, knowing, insightful, sensible, profound, astute, subtle, discreet ▷**sage** *ant.* idiotic

wish ① *v.* desire, crave, want, hanker, long, hope, choose ② *n.* command, will, desire

wit *n.* ① fun, humour, levity, pleasantry, banter ② comic, joker ③ brains, sense, judgment, intelligence, sanity, discernment

withdraw *v.* ① retire, retreat, depart, leave ▷**flee** ② extract, take out, remove, retract, detach

withdrawn *adj.* antisocial, cool, unsociable, retiring, reclusive, aloof, solitary *ant.* friendly

wither *v.* waste, fade, pine, languish, wilt, dry up, petrify ▷**shrivel**

withhold *v.* retain, reserve, refuse, deny, hold back, keep *ant.* grant

withstand *v.* resist, oppose, endure, defy, stand up under ▷**confront** *ant.* yield

witness ① *n.* spectator, onlooker, bystander *Although the bystander wasn't involved, she reported what she had seen.* signatory ② *v.* behold, observe, see, watch, experience ③ *v.* testify, certify, sign, attest

witty *adj.* funny, amusing, comical, humorous, clever, droll *ant.* dull

wizard *n.* sorcerer, magician, conjurer

woman *n.* female, matron, dame

wonder ① *n.* marvel, miracle, rarity, curiosity ② *n.* bewilderment, surprise, admiration, astonishment ▷**awe** ③ *v.* think, question, ponder, meditate, speculate, marvel, muse

wonderful *adj.* marvellous, fabulous, spectacular, superb, incredible, excellent, great, amazing ▷**splendid** *ant.* ordinary

wood *n.* lumber, timber, planks, logs, boards, fuel, kindling *hom.* would

woods *n.* trees, forest, bush, woodland, grove, thicket

word *n.* ① expression, term, utterance, name, label ② pledge, promise, assurance, guarantee ③ report, comment, news, information, bulletin, statement

work ① *n.* toil, drudgery, labour, grind, effort ② *n.* task, job, stint, chore, duty, service, employment ③ *v.* operate, function, manipulate, run, drive, succeed ④ *v.* toil, slave, labour, slog, serve, strive ⑤ *v.* shape, form, knead

world *n.* globe, earth, sphere, planet

worry ① *v.* bother, annoy, disturb, fret, fuss, stew, brood ▷**trouble** *ant.* soothe ② *n.* vexation, anxiety, concern, distress, agitation, fear *ant.* calm

worsen *v.* aggravate, decline, deteriorate, degenerate, exacerbate *ant.* improve

worship ① *v.* revere, adore, honour, praise, idolize, venerate, serve *ant.* despise ② *n.* adoration, devotion, reverence

n. = noun
v. = verb
adj. = adjective
adv. = adverb
conj. = conjunction
prep. = preposition
ant. = antonym
hom. = homonym
▷ = cross-reference

Words Borrowed from Other Languages

French	Italian	Japanese	Afrikans	Arabic	Hindi
police	balcony	judo	aardvark	admiral	chintz
rendezvous	cameo	karate	apartheid	alcohol	cot
liaison	fiasco	sushi	trek	algebra	pyjamas
menu	influenza	origami	veldt	alkali	thug
				sherbet	veranda
Dutch	**German**	**Turkish**	**Inuit**	sofa	
boss	blitz	coffee	anorak	zero	**Native North**
brandy	delicatessen	kiosk	igloo		**American**
decoy	dollar		kayak	**Persian**	caribou
landscape	kindergarten	**Spanish**	parka	bazaar	chinook
		armada		caravan	chipmunk
Scandinavian	**Chinese**	fiesta	**Gaelic**	divan	moccasin
fiord	kowtow	macho	bog	paradise	moose
geyser	sampan	patio	brat	tulip	wigwam
ombudsman	typhoon	siesta	brogue	turban	
ski	wok	sombrero	smithereens		

worth *n.* ① value, benefit, profit, usefulness, price ② merit, excellence *Robertson Davies has left behind him books of real excellence.* quality

worthless *adj.* valueless, paltry, trifling, useless, inferior, poor, mediocre, cheap, unusable *ant.* valuable

worthwhile *adj.* valuable, helpful, useful, beneficial *ant.* useless

worthy *adj.* upright, admirable, excellent, deserving, fine, honourable, valuable, noble *ant.* vile

wound ① *v.* hurt, injure, gash, pain, distress, offend, ruffle *ant.* heal ② *n.* injury, bruise, cut, laceration

wrangle *v. & n.* squabble, fight, brawl, scrap ▷**quarrel** *ant.* accord

wrap *v.* fold, envelop, enclose, cover, clothe, conceal, surround, bundle, package *ant.* uncover *hom.* rap

wrath *n.* fury, ire, rage, passion ▷**anger** *ant.* pleasure

wreck ① *v.* demolish, smash, ruin, destroy, spoil, ravage, raze, tear down *ant.* repair ② *n.* derelict, hulk, disaster, mess, ruin

wrench *v.* twist, wring, strain, sprain, yank

wrestle *v.* struggle, battle, combat, grapple, tussle, contend ▷**fight**

wretched *adj.* ① dejected, abject, miserable ▷**despicable** ② saddening, pathetic, appalling, pitiful ▷**deplorable**

wriggle *v.* twist, writhe, squirm, worm *We were amazed that my hamster could worm his way through that narrow space.* dodge

wring *v.* choke, squeeze, throttle, strangle, twist, wrench *hom.* ring

wrinkle *n. & v.* crease, pucker, ruffle, rumple, crinkle, furrow, fold

write *v.* ① pen, scribble, jot, doodle, sign, scrawl ② compose, draft, correspond, publish ③ record, document *hom.* right, rite

writer *n.* scribe, clerk, author, essayist, narrator, playwright, poet, dramatist, columnist

writhe *v.* twist, squirm, agonize, toss, wriggle

written *adj.* recorded, set down, documented, transcribed

wrong ① *adj.* unjust, unfair, immoral, wicked, bad, corrupt, evil ② *adj.* false, mistaken, untrue, incorrect, inaccurate, erroneous ③ *v.* mistreat, offend, hurt, abuse, persecute, oppress ④ *n.* offence, injustice, evil, crime, atrocity *ant.* right

wry *adj.* ① cynical, mocking, sarcastic ② twisted, crooked, distorted *ant.* straight *hom.* rye

Y y

yank *v.* tug, pull, snatch ▷**jerk**

yap *v.* bark, yelp, cry

yard *n.* court, garden, lawn, grounds

yarn *n.* ① story, account, tale, narrative, fable, legend ② thread, wool, twine

yearly ① *adj.* annual, perennial *We still make our perennial treks to Algonquin Park.* ② *adv.* every year, annually, per annum

yearn *v.* ache, crave, long, hunger, pine

yell *v.* shout, scream, shriek, screech, call, holler, squawk, whoop ▷**bellow** *ant.* whisper

yield ① *v.* produce, bear, provide, furnish, supply, return, confer ② *v.* surrender, give in, submit, defer, relinquish, abdicate, resign, renounce ③ *n.* crop, harvest, product, output

yielding *adj.* ① compliant, submissive, unresisting, passive *ant.* stubborn ② flexible, soft, malleable *The clay was soft and malleable until it dried out in the sun.* plastic *ant.* hard

yoke ① *v.* join, couple, link, harness, team ② *n.* chain, bondage, slavery *hom.* yolk

young *adj.* youthful, inexperienced, junior, little, adolescent, boyish, girlish, immature, fresh, new, unripe *ant.* old

youngster *n.* child, youth, boy, girl, kid, teenager, adolescent

youth *n.* ① adolescence, childhood *ant.* age ② child, minor, juvenile, dependent, girl, boy ▷**youngster**

youthful *adj.* boyish, girlish, young, spry, fresh

Z z

zany *adj.* foolish, wild, crazy, droll, eccentric ▷**funny** *ant.* serious

zeal *n.* passion, eagerness, enthusiasm, fervour, ardour, devotion *ant.* indifference

zealous *adj.* enthusiastic, devoted, fervent *Dave was a fervent supporter of the school's football team.* fanatical, diligent ▷**eager** *ant.* indifferent

zenith *n.* climax, height, peak, apex

zero *n.* nothing, none, nil, zip, null, nought

zest *n.* ① relish, gusto, appetite, enthusiasm, vigour, flair ② flavour, piquancy, tang

zone *n.* area, district, region, territory, locality, tract, sector

zoom *v.* flash, fly, shoot, streak, whiz, rush, zip

n. = noun
v. = verb
adj. = adjective
adv. = adverb
conj. = conjunction
prep. = preposition
ant. = antonym
hom. = homonym
▷ = cross-reference